THE MINOR PROPHETS

VOL. VII

ZEPHANIAH AND HAGGAI

THE MINOR PROPHETS
WITH A COMMENTARY

EXPLANATORY AND PRACTICAL, AND
INTRODUCTIONS TO THE SEVERAL BOOKS

VOL. VII
ZEPHANIAH AND HAGGAI

BY

THE REV. E. B. PUSEY, D.D.

*"Open thou mine eyes, that I may behold wondrous things
out of thy law."*—Ps. cxix.

London
JAMES NISBET & CO., LIMITED
21 BERNERS STREET
1907

Printed by BALLANTYNE, HANSON & Co.
At the Ballantyne Press, Edinburgh

INTRODUCTION

TO THE

PROPHET ZEPHANIAH

ZEPHANIAH was called to his office, at all events not
long after Habakkuk. As his time was near to that
of Habakkuk, so his subject also was kindred. Both
lived when, for the sins of the reign of Manasseh,
God had pronounced upon Jerusalem an irreversible
sentence of destruction. The mission of both was
not to the whole people whose sentence was fixed,
but to the individuals who would *flee from the wrath
to come.* The form of Habakkuk's prophecy was (as
we might say) more subjective; that of Zephaniah,
more objective. Habakkuk exhibits the victory of
faith in the oppressed faithful; how it would hold to
God amid the domestic oppressions, amid the oppressions of the Chaldees by whom those oppressions
were to be punished, and, when all shall seem to
fail, should, in the certainty of its unseen life, joy
in its God. The characteristic of Zephaniah is the
declaration of the tenderness of the love of God for
that remnant of Israel, *the afflicted and poor people,*
whom God would *leave in the midst* of them.[1]

Zephaniah has, like Habakkuk, to declare the

[1] Zeph. iii. 12.

A

judgment on the world. He renews the language
of Joel as to "the day of the Lord," and points it
to nations and individuals. He opens with the
prophecy of one wide destruction of the land and
all the sinners in it, its idolaters and its oppressors,
its princes, its royal family, its merchants, its petty
plunderers, who used rapine under colour of their
masters' name, and brought guilt on themselves and
them. Nothing is either too high or too low to
escape the judgments of God. But the visitation
on Judah was part only of a more comprehensive
judgment. Zephaniah foretells the wider destruction
of enemies of God's people on all sides ; of Philistia,
Moab, Ammon, on each side of them, and the distant
nations on either side, Ethiopia (which then included
Egypt) and Assyria. All these particular judgments
contain principles of God's judgments at all times.
But in Zephaniah they seem all to converge in the
love of God for the remnant of His people. The
nation he calls *a nation not desired.*[1] Individuals he
calls to God ; *it may be ye shall be hid in the Day
of the Lord's anger.*[2] He foretells a sifting time,
wherein God would *take away the proud among her ;* [3]
yet there follows a largeness of Gospel promise and
of love,[4] the grounds of which are explained in the
Gospel, but whose tenderness of language is hardly
surpassed even by the overwhelming tenderness of
the love of Christ which passeth knowledge.[5]

The Prophet's own name, "the Lord hath hid,"
corresponds with this. The Psalmist had said, using
this same word, "He shall *hide* me in His tabernacle
in the day of evil : in the secret of His tabernacle
He shall hide me ; " [6] and, "O how great is Thy

---

[1] ii. 1.　　　　[2] ii. 3.　　　　[3] iii. 11, 12.
[4] iii. 12–17.　　[5] Eph. iii. 19.　　[6] Ps. xxvii. 5, יצפנני.

goodness, which Thou hast *laid up* [1] for them that
fear Thee. Thou shalt hide them in the secret of
Thy presence from the pride of man. Thou shalt
keep them secretly [2] in a pavilion from the strife of
tongues." "They take counsel against Thy *hidden*
ones." [3]

The date which Zephaniah prefixed to his prophecy
has not been disputed ; for no one felt any interest
in denying it. Those who disbelieve definite prophecy
invented for themselves a solution, whereby they
thought that Zephaniah's prophecy need not be
definite, even though uttered in the time of Josiah ;
so the fact remained unquestioned.

The unwonted fulness with which his descent is
given implies so much of that personal knowledge
which soon fades away, that those who speak of
other titles, as having been prefixed to the books,
or portions of books of the prophets, by later hands,
have not questioned this. The only question is,
whether he lived before or in the middle of the
reformation by Josiah. Josiah, who came to the
throne when eight years old, 641 B.C., began the
reformation in the twelfth year of his reign,[4] when
almost twenty, 630 B.C. The extirpation of idolatry
could not, it appears, be accomplished at once. The
finding of the ancient copy of the law, during the
repairs of the temple in the eighteenth year of his
reign,[5] 624 B.C., gave a fresh impulse to the king's
efforts. He then united the people with himself,
bound all the people present to the covenant [6] to
keep the law, and made a further destruction of

[1] צפנת.   [2] Ps. xxxi. 19, 20, תצפנם.
[3] Ib. lxxxiii. 3, צפוניך.   [4] 2 Chron. xxxiv. 3–7.
[5] 2 Kings xxii. ; 2 Chron. xxxiv. 8–28.
[6] 2 Kings xxiii. 3 ; 2 Chron. xxxiv. 31.

idols [1] before the solemn passover in that year.
Even after that passover some abominations had
to be removed.[2] It has been thought that the
words, *I will cut off the remnant of Baal from this
place*,[3] imply that the worship of Baal had already
in some degree been removed, and that God said
that He would complete what had been begun.
But the emphasis seems to be rather on the completeness of the destruction, as we should say, that
He would efface every remnant of Baal, than to
refer to any effort which had been made by human
authority to destroy it.

The Prophet joins together, *I will cut off the remnant of Baal, the name of the Chemarim.* The cutting
off *the name of the Chemarim*, or idolatrous priests,
is like that of Hosea, *I will take away the names of
Baalim out of her mouth, and they shall no more be
remembered by their name.*[4] As the cutting off of *the
name of the Chemarim* means their being utterly
obliterated, so, probably, does *the cutting off the
remnant of Baal.* The worship of Baal was cut off,
not through Josiah, but (as Zephaniah prophesied)
through the captivity. Jeremiah asserts its continuance during his long prophetic office.[5]

In the absence of any direct authority to the
contrary, the description of idolatry by Zephaniah
would seem to belong to the period, before the
measures to abolish it were begun. He speaks as
if everything were full of idolatry,[6] the worship of
Baal, the worship of the host of heaven upon the
housetops, swearing by Malcham, and probably the
clothing with strange apparel.

[1] 2 Kings xxiii. 4–20 ; 2 Chron. xxxiv. 33.
[2] 2 Kings xxiii. 24.   [3] Zeph. i. 4.   [4] Hosea ii. 17.
[5] Jer ii. 8 ; vii. 9 ; xi. 13 ; xix. 5 ; xxxii. 29.   [6] i. 4, 5.

The state also was as corrupt [1] as the worship.
Princes and judges, priests and prophets, were all
alike in sin ; the judges distorted the law between
man and man, as the priests profaned all which
related to God. The princes were roaring lions ;
the judges, evening wolves, ever famished, hungering
for new prey. This too would scarcely have been
when Josiah was old enough to govern in his own
person. Both idolatry and perversion of justice
were continued on from the reign of his father Amon.
Both, when old enough, he removed. God Himself
gives him the praise, that he *did judgment and
justice, then* it was *well with him ; he judged the cause
of the poor and needy, then* it was *well with him ; was
not this to know Me ? saith the Lord.*[2] His conversion
was in the eighth year of his reign. Then, *while he
was yet young,* he began to *seek after the God of David
his father.*

The mention of the *king's children,*[3] whom, God
says, He would punish in the great day of His visitation, does not involve any later date. They might
anyhow have been brothers or uncles of the king
Josiah. But, more probably, God declares that no
rank should be exempt from the judgments of that
day. He knew too that the sons of Josiah would,
for their great sins, be then punished. The sun of
the temporal rule of the house of David set in un-
mitigated wickedness and sorrow. Of all its kings
after Josiah, it is said, they *did evil in the sight of the
Lord ;* some were distinguished by guilt ; all had
miserable ends ; some of them aggravated misery !

Zephaniah, then, probably finished his course before
that twelfth year of Josiah (for this prophecy is one

---

[1] iii. 3, 4. [2] Jer. xxii. 15, 16.
[3] See below on Zeph. i. 8.

whole), and so just before Jeremiah was, in Josiah's
thirteenth year, called to his office, which he fulfilled
for half a century, perhaps for the whole age of man.

The foreground of the prophecy of Zephaniah
remarkably coincides with that of Habakkuk.
Zephaniah presupposes that prophecy and fills it up.
Habakkuk had prophesied the great wasting and
destruction through the Chaldeans, and then their
destruction. That invasion was to extend beyond
Judah (for it was said *they shall scoff at kings* [1]), but
was to include it. The instrument of God having
been named by Habakkuk, Zephaniah does not
even allude to him. Rather he brings before Judah
the other side, the agency of God Himself. God
would not have them forget Himself in His instruments. Hence all is attributed to God. *I will
utterly consume all things from off the land, saith the
Lord. I will consume man and beast; I will consume the fowls of the heaven, and the fishes of the sea,
and the stumblingblocks with the wicked, and I will
cut off man from the land, saith the Lord. I will
also stretch out Mine hand upon Judah ; and I will
cut off the remnant of Baal. In the day of the Lord's
sacrifice, I will punish the princes, &c. In the same
day also I will punish all those, &c. I will search
Jerusalem with candles. The great day of the Lord
is near, and I will bring distress upon, &c. O Canaan,
land of the Philistines, I will even destroy thee. The
Lord will be terrible unto them. Ye Ethiopians also,
ye shall be slain by My sword. And He will destroy
Nineveh.* [2] The wicked of the people had *said in
their heart, The Lord will not do good, neither will*

---

[1] Hab. i. 10.
[2] Zeph. i. 2, 3, 4, 8, 9, 12, 14, 17 ; ii. 5, 11, 12, 13.

He do evil.[1] Zephaniah inculcates, throughout his brief prophecy, that there is nothing, good or evil, of which He is not the Doer or Overruler.

But the extent of that visitation is coextensive with that prophesied by Habakkuk. Zephaniah indeed speaks rather to the effects, the desolation. But the countries, whose desolation or defeat he foretells, are the lands of those, whom the Chaldeans invaded, worsted, in part desolated. Besides Judah, Zephaniah's subjects are Philistia, Moab, Ammon, Ethiopia (which included Egypt), Nineveh. And here he makes a remarkable distinction corresponding with the events. Of the Ethiopians or Egyptians, he says only, *Ye shall be slain by My sword.*[2] Of Assyria he foretells [3] the entire and lasting desolation; the capitals of her palaces in the dust; her cedar-work bare; flocks, wild beasts, pelican and hedgehog, taking up their abode in her. Moab and Ammon and Philistia have at first sight the two-fold, apparently contradictory, lot; *the remnant of My people,* God says,[4] *shall possess them; the coast shall be for the remnant of the house of Judah;* and, that they should be a perpetual desolation. This also was to take place, after God had brought back His people out of captivity. Now all these countries were conquered by the Chaldeans, of which at the time there was no human likelihood. But they were not swept away by one torrent of conquest. Moab and Ammon were, at first, allies of Nebuchadnezzar, and rejoiced at the miseries of the people, whose prophets had foretold their destruction. But, beyond this, Nineveh was at that time more powerful than Egypt. Human knowledge could not have discerned, that Egypt should suffer defeat only, Nineveh should

---

[1] i. 12.   [2] ii. 12.   [3] ii. 13–15.   [4] ii. 9.

be utterly destroyed. It was the wont of the great
conquerors of the East, not to destroy capitals, but
to repeople them with subjects obedient to themselves. Nineveh had held Babylon by viceroys; in
part she had held it under her own immediate rule.
Why should not Babylon, if she conquered Nineveh,
use the same policy? Humanly speaking, it was
a mistake that she did not. It would have been a
strong place against the inroads of the Medo-Persian
empire. The Persians saw its value so far for
military purposes, as to build some fort there; [1]
and the Emperor Claudius, when he made it a colony,
felt the importance of the well-chosen situation.[2]
It is replaced by Mosul, a city of some " 20,000 to
40,000 " [3] inhabitants. Even after its destruction,
it was easier to rebuild it than to build a city on the
opposite bank of the Tigris. God declared that it
should be desolate. The prediction implied destruction the most absolute. It and its palaces were to
be the abode of animals which flee the presence of
man; and it perished.

Again, what less likely than that Philistia, which
had had the rule over Israel, strong in its almost
impregnable towns, three of whose five cities were
named for their strength, Gaza, *strong;* Ashdod,
mighty; Ekron, *deep-rooting;* one of which, Ashdod,
about this very time, resisted for twenty-nine years
the whole power of Egypt, and endured the longest

[1] Amm. Marcell. xxiii. 22. The Ninos taken by Meher-
dates, A.D. 59, was on the site of the old Ninos, on the other
side of the Tigris. Tac. Ann. xii. 13.
[2] The existence of the Nineve Claudiopolis is attested
by coins. See Vaux in Smith's Dict. of Greek and Roman
Geogr. v. Ninus.
[3] See Keith Johnstone, Dict. of Geography, ed. 1864, and
ed. 1867.

siege of any city of ancient or modern times—what, to human foresight, less likely, than that Philistia should come under the power of the *remnant of the house of Judah*, when returned from their captivity ? Yet it is absolutely foretold.[1] *The sea-coast shall be for the remnant of the house of Judah ; they shall feed thereupon : in the houses of Ashkelon they shall lie down in the evening. For the Lord their God shall visit them, and restore their captivity.* As unlikely was it, that Moab and Ammon, who now had entered upon the territory of the two and a half tribes beyond Jordan, should themselves become the possession of the remnant of Judah. Yet so it was.

It is then lost labour, even for their own ends, when moderns, who believe not definite prophecy, would find out some enemy [2] whom Zephaniah may have had in mind in foretelling this wide destruction. It still remains that all that Zephaniah says beforehand was fulfilled. It is allowed that he could not foretell this through any human foresight. The avowed object in looking out for some power, formidable in Zephaniah's time, is, that he could not, by any human knowledge, be speaking of the Chaldeans. But the words stand there. They were written by Zephaniah, at a time when confessedly no human knowledge could have enabled man to predict this of the Chaldeans ; nay, no human knowledge would

---

[1] ii. 7.

[2] The Père Paul Pezron (Essai d'un Comm. lit. et hist. sur les prophètes 1697) assumed three irruptions of the Scythians ; the first prophesied by Amos and Joel ; the second, in the reign of Josiah, about 631 B.C. ; the third, prophesied (he thinks) by Ezek. xxxviii., xxxix. Baseless as all this is, the characteristic of the late writers is not the selection of the Scythians as the object of the prophecy (which were a thing indifferent) but the grounds alleged for that selection.

have enabled any one to predict so absolutely
a desolation so wide and so circumstantially
delineated.

That school, however, has not been willing to
acquiesce in this, that Zephaniah does *not* speak of
the instrument, through whom this desolation was
effected. They will have it, that they know that
Zephaniah had in his mind one who was *not* the
enemy of the Jews or of Nineveh or of Moab and
Ammon, and through whom no even transient desolation of these countries was effected. The whole
argument is a simple begging of the question. " [1] The
Egyptians cannot be meant; for the Cushites, who
are threatened,[2] themselves belong to the Egyptian
army,[3] and Psammetichus only besieged Ashdod
which he also took, without emblazoning ought
greater on his shield.[4] The Chaldeans come still
less into account, because they did not found an
independent kingdom until 625 B.C., nor threaten
Judæa until after Josiah's death. On the other
hand, an unsuspicious and well-accredited account
has been preserved to us, that somewhere about this
time the Scythians overflowed Palestine too with
their hosts. Herodotus relates [5] that the Scythians,
after they had disturbed Cyaxares at the siege of
Nineveh, turned towards Egypt; and when they had
already arrived in Palestine, were persuaded by Psammetichus to return, and in their return plundered a
temple in Ascalon."

It is true that Herodotus says that " a large
Scythian army did, under their king Madyes, burst
into Asia in pursuit of the Cimmerians and entered
Media—keeping Mount Caucasus on the right," and

[1] Hitzig.   [2] ii. 12.   [3] Jer. xlvi. 9.
          [4] Herod. ii. 157.   [5] Ib. i. 105.

that " the Medes opposed and fought them and, being defeated, lost their rule." [1]

It is true also that Herodotus relates, that " They went thence towards Egypt, and when they were in Palestine-Syria, Psammetichus, king of Egypt, meeting them, turned them by gifts and entreaties from going further ; that when in their return they were in Ascalon, a city of Syria, whereas most of the Scythians passed by without harming ought, some few of them, being left behind, plundered the temple of Venus Ourania." [2] In this place, also, it is true, Herodotus uses a vague expression, that " for twenty-eight years the Scythians ruled over Asia, and that all things were turned upside down by their violence and contempt. For besides the tributes, they exacted from each what they laid upon each, and beside the tribute, they drove together and took what each had. And most of them Cyaxares and the Medes entertaining as guests, intoxicated and slew. And then the Medes recovered their empire and *became masters of what they held before.*" [3]

But, apart from the inconsistency of the period here assigned to their power, with other history, it appears from the account itself, that by " all Asia " Herodotus means " all upper Asia," as he expresses himself more accurately, when relating the expedition of Darius against them. " [4] Darius wished to take revenge on the Scythians, because they first, making an inroad into Media and defeating in battle those who went against them, began the wrong.

[1] Herod. i. 103, 104. [2] Ib. i. 105.
[3] i. 106. He uses the same wide expression as to Cyrus, after the defeat of Crœsus. " Having subdued him, he thus ruled over all Asia " (i. 130) ; whereas he had not yet conquered Babylon. [4] Ib. i. 106.

For the Scythians, as I have before said, *ruled upper Asia* for twenty-eight years. For, pursuing the Cimmerians, they made an inroad into Asia, putting down the Medes from their rule ; for these, before the Scythians came, ruled Asia." The Asia, then, which Herodotus supposes the Scythians to have ruled, is coextensive with the Asia which he supposes the Medes to have ruled previously. But this was all in the North ; for having said that "Phraortes subdued Asia, going from one nation to another," [1] he adds that, having brought Persia under his yoke, "he led an army against those Assyrians who had Nineveh, and there lost most of his army and his own life." Apart then from the fabulousness of this supposed empire established by Phraortes [2] (Cyaxares having been the real founder of the Median empire), it is plain that, according to Herodotus himself, the Asia in which the Scythians plundered and received tribute were the lands North of Assyria. The expedition against Egypt stands as an insulated predatory excursion, the object of which having been mere plunder, they were bought off by Psammetichus and returned (he tells us) doing no mischief [3] in their way, except that a few lingerers plundered a temple at Ascalon. It was to Media that they first came ; the Medes, whom they defeated ; the Median empire to which they succeeded ; Cyaxares and the Medes, who treacherously destroyed most of them ; the Medes, whose empire was restored by the destruction of some, and the return of the rest to their own land. With this agrees the more detailed account of the Scythians by Strabo, who impeaches the accuracy of the accounts of Herodotus.[4] Having

---

[1] iv. 4.   [2] i. 102.   [3] ἀσινέων. Her. l.c.
[4] " More readily might we believe Homer and Hesiod in

spoken of the migrations of leaders, and by name, of " Madyes the Scythian " [1] (under whom Herodotus states the irruption to have taken place), he says, " The Sacæ made the like inroad as the Cimmerians and the Trerians, some longer, some nigh at hand ; for they took possession of Bactriana, and acquired the best land of Armenia, which they also left, named after them Sacasene, and advanced as far as to the Cappadocians and especially those on the Euxine, whom they now call of Pontus (Pontians). But the generals of the Persians who were at the time there, attacking them by night, while they were making a feast upon the spoils, utterly extirpated them." [2] The direction which he says they took, is the same as that of the Cimmerians, whom Herodotus says that they followed. " The Cimmerians, whom they also call Trerians, or some tribe of them, often overrun the right side of the Pontus, sometimes making inroads on the Paphlagonians, at others, on the Phrygians. Often also the Cimmerians and Trerians made the like attacks, and they say that the Trerians and Cobus [their king] were at last expelled by Madyes king of the [Scythians]." [3] Strabo also explains, what is meant by the tributes, of which Herodotus speaks. He is speaking of the nomadic tribes of the Scythians generally : " Tribute was, to allow them at certain stated times, to overrun the country [for pasturage] and carry off booty. But when they roamed beyond the agreement, there arose war, and again reconciliations and renewed war. Such was the life of the nomads, always setting

their tales of heroes, and the tragic poets, than Ctesias and Herodotus and Hellanicus and others of the same sort." xi. 6, 3.
  [1] i. 3, 21.   [2] xi. 8, 4.   [3] Prol. i. 3, 21.

on their neighbours and then being reconciled
again." [1]

The Scythians, then, were no object of fear to the
Jews, whom they passed wholly unnoticed and probably unconscious of their existence in their mountain country, while they once and once only swept
unharming along the fertile tracts on the seashore,
then occupied by the old enemies and masters of
the Jews, the Philistines. But Herodotus must
also have been misinformed as to the length of time,
during which they settled in Media, or at least as
to the period during which their presence had any
sensible effects. For Cyaxares, whom he represents
as having raised the siege of Nineveh, in consequence
of the inroad of the Scythians into Media, came to
the throne, according to the numbers of Herodotus,
633 B.C. For the reign of Cyaxares having lasted
according to him forty years,[2] that of Astyages
thirty-five,[3] and that of Cyrus twenty-nine,[4] these
104 years, counted back from the known date of the
death of Cyrus, 529 or 530 B.C., bring us to 633 or
636 B.C. as the beginning of the reign of Cyaxares.
But the invasion of the Scythians could not have
taken place at the first accession of Cyaxares, since,
according to Herodotus, he had already defeated
the Assyrians, and was besieging Nineveh, when the
Scythians burst into Media. According to Herodotus, moreover, Cyaxares " first distributed Asiatics
into troops, and first ordered that each should be
apart, spearmen, and archers, and cavalry ; for
before, all were mixed pele-mele together." [5] Yet
it would not be in a very short time, that those who
had been wont to fight in a confused mass, could be

[1] xi. 8, 3.   [2] Herod. i. 106.   [3] Ib. i. 130.
          [4] Ib. i. 214.   [5] Ib. i. 103.

formed into an orderly and disciplined army. We could not then, anyhow, date the Scythian inroad earlier than the second or third year of Cyaxares. On the other hand, the date of the capture of Nineveh is fixed by the commencement of the Babylonian Empire, Babylon falling to Nabopolassar. The duration of that empire is measured by the reigns of its kings,[1] of whom, according to Ptolemy's Canon, Nabopolassar reigned twenty-one years ; Nebuchadnezzar (there called Nabocollasar), forty-three ; Evil-Merodach (Iluaroadam), two ; Neriglissar (Niricassolassar), four ; Nabunahit (Nabonadius with whom his son Belshazzar was co-regent), seventeen ; in all eighty-seven years ; and it ends in an event of known date, the capture of Babylon by Cyrus, 538 B.C. The addition of the eighty-seven years of the duration of the empire to that date carries us back to the date assigned to the capture of Nineveh by Nabopolassar in conjunction with Cyaxares, 625 B.C. The capture, then, of Nineveh was removed by eight or nine years only from that which Herodotus gives as the time of the accession of Cyaxares, and since the attack upon Nineveh can hardly have been in his first year, and the last siege probably occupied two, the twenty-eight years of Scythian dominion would dwindle down into something too inconsiderable for history. Probably they represent some period from their first incursion into Media, to the final return of the survivors, during which they marauded in Media and Upper Asia. The mode by which " the greater part " (Herodotus tells us) were

[1] Berosus, in his Chaldean history, agrees as to these dates, only adding nine months for the son of Neriglissar, Laborosoarchod, in Jos. Ant. x. 11, 1, combined with cont. Apion. i. 20, and Eus. Præp. Evang. ix. 40.

destroyed, intoxication and subsequent murder at a
banquet, implies that their numbers were no longer
considerable.

History, with the exception of that one marauding
expedition towards Egypt, is entirely silent as to
any excursions of the Scythians, except in the North.
No extant document hints at any approach of theirs
to any country mentioned by Zephaniah. There was
no reason to expect any inroad from them. With
the exception of Bactriana, which lies some 18 degrees
east of Media, and itself extended over some 7 degrees
of longitude, the countries mentioned by Strabo lie,
to what the kings of Assyria mention as the far North,
Armenia, and thence they stretched out to the west,
yet keeping mostly to the neighbourhood of the
Euxine. Considering the occasion of the mention
of the invasion of the Scythians, the relief which their
invasion of Media gave to Nineveh, it is even remarkable that there is no mention of any ravages of theirs
throughout Mesopotamia or Babylonia. Zephaniah
speaks, not of marauding, but of permanent desolation of Assyria, Philistia, Moab, Ammon, and of
destructive war also on Ethiopia. There is no reason
to think that the Scythians approached any of these
lands, except Philistia, which they passed through
unharming. The sacred writers mention even smaller
nations, by whom God chastised Judah in their times,
bands of the Syrians, of Moab, of the children of Ammon,
as well as Assyria and Babylon. Ezekiel,[1] when he
prophesies of the inroad of northern nations, Meshech
and Tubal, Gomer and Togarmah, speaks of it as
far removed in the future, prophesies not their
destroying but their own destruction.

It does not affect the argument from prophecy,

[1] Ezek. xxxviii. xxxix.

whether Zephaniah did or did not know through whom the events which he predicted should be brought to pass. But, setting aside the question whether he had, from the prophecies of Habakkuk and Isaiah, a human knowledge of the Chaldees, or whether God instructed him how what he foretold should be accomplished, or whether God spread out before his mind that which was to be, apart from time, in prophetic vision, Zephaniah *did* picture what came to pass. But it is an intense paradox, when men, 2500 years after his date, assert, not only that Zephaniah's prophecies had no relation to the Chaldees, in whom his words were fulfilled, and who are the objects of the prophecies of Habakkuk and Jeremiah, but that *they* know what *must* have been, and (as they assert) what *was* is the Prophet's mind ; and that he had in his mind, *not* those in whom his words were fulfilled, but others in whom they were *not* fulfilled, to whom he does not allude in one single trait, who left no trace behind them, and whose march along an enemy's tract on the sea-coast was of so little account, that no contemporary historian, nor Josephus, even alludes to it.[1]

It has been already observed that each prophet connects himself with one or more of those before

---

[1] The name Σκυθόπολις, which Josephus says the Greeks gave to Bethshan (Ant. 12, 8, 5), and which they alone can have given, is manifestly, as being Greek, too late to contain any tradition as to the presence of the Scythians in Palestine, three centuries before the Greeks, under Alexander, became acquainted with Palestine. S. Jerome regarded it as a corruption of *Succoth*. He says on Gen. xxxiii. 17, "In the Hebrew is read *Sucoth* (סכת). But there is to this day a city beyond Jordan into which this name enters in part, Scythopolis." Quæstt. Hebr. ad Gen. [Opp. iii. 358, ed. Vall.], quoted by Reland, p. 992.

them. They use the language of their predecessors
in some one or more sentences, apparently with this
precise object. They had overflowing fulness of
words ; yet they chose some saying of the former
prophet, as a link to those before them.   We have
seen this in Amos,[1] then in Obadiah,[2] who uses the
language of Balaam, David, Joel, Amos ; of Jeremiah, in regard to Obadiah ; [3] of Micah to his great
predecessor, Micaiah, and Amos ; [4] of Jeremiah,
Habakkuk, Zephaniah, Ezekiel to Micah ; [5] of Nuham
to Jonah ; [6] and of Isaiah (I think) to Nahum ; [7]
of Habakkuk to Isaiah and Micah.[8] It is in conformity with this, that Zephaniah, even more than
those before him, uses language of earlier prophets.
It arises, not (as people have been pleased to say)
from any declension in the originality of prophets
at his date, but from his subject. It has been said,
" If any one desire to see the utterances of the
prophets in brief space, let him read through this
brief Zephaniah." The office of Zephaniah was not
to forewarn of any instrument of God's judgments.
The destruction is prophesied, not the destroyer.
His prophecy is, more than those of most other
prophets, apart from time, to the end of time. He
prophesies of *what* shall be, not *when* it shall be, nor
by whom. He does not " expect " or " anticipate "
or " forebode " ! He absolutely declares the future
condition of certain nations ; but not the *how* of
its coming to pass. If Nineveh, Edom, and Ammon
had not been desolated, his prophecy would have
been falsified ; each fulfilment became the earnest

---

[1] See Introduction to Joel.
[2] See Introduction to Obadiah.
[3] Ib.   [4] See Introduction to Micah.   [5] Ib.
[6] See Introduction to Nahum.   [7] Ib.   [8] Ib.

of a larger fulfilment ; but all shall not be completed until *the earth and all that is therein shall be burned up.*

It belongs to this character of Zephaniah, that he gathers from other prophets before him, especially Isaiah, Joel, Amos, Habakkuk, expressions relating to, or bearing on, judgment to come, or again to that his other great subject, God's love for the remnant of His people ; yet mostly in fragments only and allusively. They were key-notes for those who knew the prophets. Thus, in calling on man to hushed submission before God, because a day of judgment was coming, he blends into one verse [1] Habakkuk's call, *Hush before the Lord,*[2] and the warning words of Isaiah, Joel, Obadiah, *Nigh is the day of the Lord ;* [3] the image of the *sacrifice,* which God had commanded, and the remarkable word, *consecrated,* of God's instruments. The allusion is contained in single words, *sacrifice, consecrated ;* the context in which they are embodied is different. The idea only is the same, that Almighty God maketh, as it were, a sacrifice to Himself of those who incorrigibly rebel against Him. Else Isaiah draws out the image at much length : *A sword of the Lord is full of bloods ; it is smeared with fat, with the blood of lambs and of goats ; with the fat of kidneys of rams : for the Lord hath a sacrifice in Bozrah, and a great slaughter in the land of Edom.*[4] Jeremiah uses the image in equal fulness of the overthrow of Pharaoh-Necho at the Euphrates : *This is a day of the Lord God of hosts, a day of*

---

[1] i. 7. [2] Hab. ii. 20.

[3] Isa. xiii. 6 ; Joel i. 15 ; iii. 14 ; Obad. 15. The words יוֹם יְיָ are used of a day of God's judgments, Isa. xiii. 9 ; Joel ii. 1, 11 ; Amos v. 18, 20 ; Ezek. xiii. 5 ; Mal. iii. 2, not with קָרוֹב. In Isa. ii. 12 it is יוֹם לַיְיָ, or in Joel ii. 1, subordinately.

[4] Isa. xxxiv. 6.

vengeance, that He may avenge Him of His adversaries : and the sword shall devour, and it shall be satiate and made drunk with blood ; for the Lord God hath a sacrifice in the North country by the river Euphrates.[1] Ezekiel expands it yet more boldly.[2] Zephaniah drops everything local, and condenses the image into the words, *The Lord hath prepared a sacrifice ; He hath consecrated His guests*, adding the new bold image, that they whom God employed were, as it were, His invited guests,[3] whom He consecrated [4] thereto.

In like way, as to the day of the Lord itself, he accumulates all words of terror from different prophets ; from Joel the words, *A day of darkness and of gloominess ; a day of clouds and of thick darkness :*[5] to these he adds *Of shouting and the sound of the trumpet*,[6] used by Amos in relation to the destruction of Moab ; the two combinations which precede occur, the one in a different sense, the other with a slightly different grammatical inflexion, in Job.[7]

From Isaiah, Zephaniah adopts that characteristic picture of self-idolising, which brings down God's judgments on its pride: (the city) *that dwelleth securely, that said in her heart, I and no I besides.*[8]

---

[1] Jer. xlvi. 10.　　　　　　[2] Ezek. xxxix. 17.

[3] Zephaniah's word, קְרָאִים occurs besides only in 1 Sam. ix. 13.

[4] Isaiah's word (xiii. 3) is מקדשי ; Zephaniah's הקדיש.

[5] יום חשך ואפלה יום ענן וערפל Joel ii. 2 ; Zeph. i. 15.

[6] שפר ותרועה Zeph. i. 16 ; Amos ii. 2.

[7] שואה ומשואה Job xxxviii. 27 ; צד ומצוקה xv. 24 ; Zeph. has צד ומצ. צרות stands parallel with מצוקות Ps. xxv. 17.

[8] Isa. xlvii. 8. ; Zeph. ii. 15, היושבת לבטח האמרה בלבבה אני ואפסי עוד.

Even where Isaiah says, *For a consumption and that decreed, the Lord God of hosts makes in the midst of all the earth*,[1] and, slightly varying it, *For a consumption and that decreed, I have heard from the Lord God of hosts upon all the earth*,[2] Zephaniah, retaining the two first words, which occur in both places, says more concisely, *For a consumption, nought but terror, will He make all the inhabitants of the earth*.[3] Yet simple as the words are, he pronounced that God would not only *bring a desolation upon the earth*, or *in the midst of the earth*, but would make its inhabitants one consumption. Nahum had said of Nineveh, *With an overflowing flood He will make the place thereof an utter consumption*.[4] The most forceful words are the simplest.

He uses the exact words of Isaiah, *From beyond the rivers of Cush*,[5] than which none can be simpler, and employs the word of festive procession, though in a different form,[6] and having thus connected his prophecy with Isaiah's, all the rest upon which the prophecy turns is varied.

In like way he adopts from Micah the three words,[7] *her-that-halteth, and-will-gather her-that-is-driven-out*. The context in which he resets them is quite different.

It has been thought that the words *I have heard the reproach of Moab*[8] may have been suggested by

---

[1] Isa. x. 23.   [2] Ib. xxviii. 22.

[3] כי כלה. He retains the simplest words, but substitutes אך נבהלה (a word formed by himself) for the ונחרצה of Isaiah.   [4] Nahum i. 8.

[5] מעבר לנהרי כוש Zeph. iii. 10; Isa. xviii. 1.

[6] יובלון Zeph. יגבל Isa. xviii. 7.

[7] והצלעה והנדחה אקבצה Micah iv. 6; Zeph. iii. 19.

[8] שמעתי חרפת מואב Zeph. ii. 8; שמענו גאון מואב Isa. xvi. 6.

those of Isaiah, who begins his lament over Moab, *We have heard of the pride of Moab ;* but the force and bearing of the words is altogether different, since it is God Who says, *I have heard,* and so He will punish.

The combination,[1] *the exulters of pride,* is common to him with Isaiah : its meaning is uncertain ; but it is manifestly different in the two places, since the one relates to God, the other to man.

The words, *They shall build houses and shall not dwell therein ; they shall plant vineyards and not drink the wine thereof,*[2] are from the original threat in Deuteronomy, from which also the two words, *They-shall-walk as-the-blind,*[3] may be a reminiscence, but with a conciseness of its own and without the characteristic expressions of Deuteronomy, adopted by other sacred writers : *They shall grope at noonday, as the blind gropeth in darkness.*[4]

Altogether these passages are evidence that Zephaniah is of later date than the prophecies in which the like language occurs ; and the fact that he does employ so much language of his predecessors furnishes a strong presumption in any single case, that he in that case also adopted from the other sacred writer the language which they have in common.

It is chiefly on this ground that a train of modern critics[5] have spoken disparagingly of the outward

---

[1] עֲלִיזֵי נַאֲוָתִי Isa. xiii. 3; עֲלִיזֵי גַּאֲוָתֵךְ Zeph. iii. 11.

[2] Zeph. i. 13 ; Deut. xxviii. 30, 39. The words are more exact than in Micah vi. 14 ; Amos v. 11.

[3] הָלְכוּ כַעִוְרִים Zeph. i. 17.   [4] Deut. xxviii. 29.

[5] Eichhorn, De Wette, Stähelin, and their followers. De Wette, however, does own, "In employing what is not his own, he is, at least, original in its expansion." Einl. 245, note *b*.

form and style of Zephaniah. It has, however, a
remarkable combination of fulness with conciseness
and force. Thus, he begins the enumeration of those
upon whom the destruction should fall, with the
words, *consuming I will consume all* [1] to an enumeration coextensive with the creation, he adds unex-
pectedly, *and the stumblingblocks with the wicked,* [2]
anticipating our Lord's words of the Day of Judgment, *They shall gather the stumblingblocks and them
that do iniquity:* [3] to the different idolatries he adds
those of a divided faith, *swearers to the Lord and
swearers by Malcham:* [4] to those who turned away
from God he adds those who were unearnest in
seeking Him. [5]

Again, after the full announcement of the destruction in the Day of the Lord, the burst in those
five words, *sift-yourselves and-sift (on) nation un-
longed for,* [6] is, in suddenness and condensation, like
Hosea ; and so again, in five words, after the picture
of the future desolation of Nineveh, the abrupt turn
to Jerusalem, *Wo rebellious and-defiled* (thou) *oppressive city,* [7] and then follow the several counts of her
indictment, in brief disjointed sentences, first nega-
tively, as a whole ; each in three or four words,
*she-listened not to-voice ; she-received not correction ;
in-the-Lord she-trusted not ; to-her-God she-approached
not ;* [8] then, in equally broken words, each class is
characterised by its sins : *her-princes in-her-midst*
are *roaring lions ; her-judges evening wolves ; not
gnawed-they-bones on-the-morrow ; her-prophets empty-
babblers, men of-deceits ; her-priests profaned holiness,
violated law.* [9] Then in sudden contrast to all this

---

[1] i. 2.   [2] i. 3.   [3] S. Matt. xiii. 41.
[4] Zeph. i. 5.   [5] i. 6.   [6] ii. 1.
[7] iii. 1.   [8] iii. 2.   [9] iii. 3, 4.

contumacy, neglect, despite of God, He Himself is exhibited as *in the midst of her;* the witness and judge of all; there, where they sinned. *The-Lord-righteous in-her-midst; He-doth not iniquity; by-morning by-morning His-judgment He-giveth to-light; He-faileth not;* [1] and then in contrast to the holiness and the judgments of God, follows in four words, the perseverance of man in his shamelessness, *and* —the fruit of all this presence and doings of the Holy and Righteous God and Judge is, *and-not knoweth* the *wrong-doer shame.* Zephaniah uses the same disjoining of the clauses in the description of God's future manifestation of His love towards them. Again it is the same thought, *The-Lord thy-God* (is) *in-thy-midst;* [2] but now in love: *Mighty, shall-save; He-shall-rejoice over-thee with-joy; He-shall-keep-silence in-His-love; He-shall-rejoice over-thee with jubilee.* The single expressions are alike condensed; *she-hearkened not to-voice,* [3] stands for what Jeremiah says at such much greater length, how God had sent all His servants *the prophets, daily rising up early and sending them, but they hearkened not unto Me nor inclined their ear, but hardened their neck.* [4] The words *shall-be-silent in-His-love,* [5] in their primary meaning, express the deepest human love, but without the wonted image of betrothal.

The whole people of Canaan [6] reminds one of Hosea; *the-men-coagulated on-their-lees* [7] is much expanded by

---

[1] iii. 5.　　　　　[2] iii. 17.　　　　　[3] iii. 2.

[4] Jer. vii. 24–28.

[5] iii. 17. Some modern commentators take umbrage at the beautiful expression. Ewald alters, with the LXX, into יחדיש which does not occur elsewhere. But the LXX renders " shall renew *thee* "; Ewald, " (God) *becomes young* (sich verjünget) in His love ! "

[6] Zeph. i. 11, comp. Hosea xii. 7.　　　　　[7] i. 12.

Jeremiah,[1] his word occurs before him in Job only and the song of Moses.[2] Single poetic expressions are, that Moab should become *the possession of briars*,[3] the word itself being framed by Zephaniah ; in the description of the desolation of Nineveh, *a voice singeth in the window ; desolation* is *on the threshold*,[4] the imagery is so bold that modern criticism has thought that the word *voice*, which occurs in the O.T. 328 times, and with pronouns 157 times more, must signify " an owl," and *desolation* must stand for " a crow." [5] Very characteristic is the word, " *He* [6] *shall famish* all the gods of the earth," expressing with wonderful irony the privation of their sacrifices, which was the occasion of the first heathen persecutions of the Christians.

When then a writer, at times so concise and poetic as Zephaniah is in these places, is, at others, so full in his descriptions, this is not prolixity, but rather vivid picturing ; at one time going through all the orders of creation ; [7] at another, different classes of the ungodly ; [8] at yet another, the different parts of the scared woe-stricken city,[9] to set before our eyes the universality of the desolation. Those who are familiar with our own great northern poet of nature, will remember how the accumulation of names adds to the vividness of his descriptions. Yet here too there is great force in the individual descriptions, as when he pictures the petty plunderers for their master, and *fill their masters' houses*—not with wealth

---

[1] Jer. xlviii. 11.
[2] Job x. 10; Exod. xv. 8.   [3] ii. 9.   [4] ii. 14.
[5] " קוֹל must answer to the Ethiopian קוֹאָע γλαύξ and our *eule* (owl); and חרב seems equal ערב." Ewald, Proph. ii. 25.
[6] See below on ii. 11.   [7] i. 3.
[8] i. 4–9.   [9] i. 10, 11.

but—*with violence and fraud*,[1] all which remains of
wealth gained by fraud and extortion being the sins
themselves, which dwell in the house of the fraudulent
to his destruction.

In the strictly prophetic part of his office, Jerusalem having been marked out by Micah and Isaiah
before him, as the place where God would make the
new revelation of Himself, Zephaniah adds, what our
Lord revealed to the Samaritan woman, [2] that Jerusalem should no longer be the abiding centre of
worship. *They shall worship Him, every man from
his place, all the isles of the nations* [3] is a prophecy
which to this day is receiving an increasing accomplishment. It is a prophecy, not of the spread of
Monotheism, but of the worship of Him to whose
worship at that time a handful of Jews could with
difficulty be brought to adhere, the desertion or
corruption or association of Whose worship with
idolatry Zephaniah had to denounce and to foretell
its punishment. The love which God should then
show to His own is expressed in words, unequalled
for tenderness ; and in conformity to that love is
the increasing growth of holiness, and the stricter
requirements of God's holy justice. Again, Zephaniah
has a prelude to our Blessed Lord's words, *to whom
much is given, of him shall much be required*,[4] or His
Apostle's, of the great awe in working out our salvation.[5] Progress is a characteristic and condition
of the Christian life : *We beseech you, that as ye have
received of us, how ye ought to walk and to please God,
ye would abound more and more*.[6] Even so Zephaniah

---

[1] i. 9. Amos has the like idea (iii. 10), but no word is the
same, except חמס.

[2] S. John iv. 21.   [3] ii. 11.   [4] S. Luke xii. 48.

[5] Phil. ii. 12.   [6] 1 Thess. iv. 1.

bids *all the meek of the earth, who have wrought His
judgments* or *law* to *seek diligently* that *meekness,*[1]
which had already characterised them, and that,
not in view of great things, but, if so be they might
be saved ; *it may be that ye may be hid in the day of
the Lord's anger,* as S. Peter saith, *If the righteous
scarcely be saved, where shall the ungodly and the
sinner appear ?* [2] It is again remarkable how he
selects meekness as the characteristic of the new
state of things which he promises. He anticipates
the contrast in the Magnificat, in which the lowest
lowliness was rewarded by the highest exaltation,
As it is said there, *He hath put down the mighty from
their seat, and hath exalted the humble and meek,*[3] so
the removal of the proud *from within thee,* and the
"leaving of an afflicted and poor people *within
thee,*" [4] is the special promise by Zephaniah.

Little is said of the captivity. It is a future
variously assumed.[5] Judah in the furthest lands,
beyond the rivers of Ethiopia, is *the daughter of My
dispersed ;* [6] the whole earth is the scene of their
shame ; [7] their praises should be commensurate with
their shame, *when I turn back your captivity before
your eyes.*[8] But this turning away of their captivity
is the only notice that their punishment should be
the going into captivity. The captivity itself is
presupposed, as certain and as known. So neither
are there any images from temporal exaltation. All
pride should be removed, as utterly unbefitting
God's holy presence : *Thou shalt no more be haughty
in My holy mountain.*[9] The words expressive of the

---

[1] ii. 3.	[2] 1 S. Peter iv. 18.	[3] S. Luke i. 52.
[4] Zeph. iii. 12.	[5] iii. 13.	[6] iii. 10.
[7] Ib. iii. 19.	[8] iii. 20, add. ii. 7.	[9] iii. 11.

abasement of those within her are proportionably
strong, *My afflicted and poor.*[1] Some are wont, in
these days, to talk of God's prophets as patriots.
They were such truly, since they loved the land of
the Lord with a Divine love. But what mere
" patriot " would limit his promises to the presence
of " a poor people in a low estate," with an unseen
presence of God ? The description belongs to *His*
kingdom, which was *not of this world :* [2] the only king
whom Zephaniah speaks of, *the king of Israel,*[3] is
Almighty God. The blessing which he promises is
the corresponding blessing of peace, *Fear thou not ;
thou shalt not see evil any more, none shall make them
afraid.*[4] But the words *Let not thy hands be slack,*[4]
imply that they shall be aggressive on the world ;
that they were not to relax from the work which
God assigned to them, the conversion of the world.

An allusion to the prophet Joel [5] makes it uncertain whether words of Zephaniah relate to the first
Coming of our Lord; or the times which should usher
in the second, or to both in one ; and so, whether, in
accordance with his general character of gathering
into one all God's judgments to His end, he is speaking of the first restoration of the one purified language
of faith and hope, when *the multitude of them that
believed were of one heart and of one soul,*[6] or whether
he had his mind fixed rather on the end, *when the
fulness of the Gentiles shall come in.*[7] The words
also (since they may be taken either way [8]) leave it
uncertain whether the Gentiles are spoken of as
bringing in the people of God (as they shall at the

[1] iii. 12.
[3] Zeph. iii. 15.
[5] iii. 2 [iv. 2, Heb.].
[7] Rom. xi. 25.

[2] S. John xviii. 36.
[4] iii. 16, 13.
[6] Acts iv. 32.
[8] See on Zeph. iii. 10.

end) or whether the first conversion of the Jews, even in the most distant countries, is his subject.

In any case, Zephaniah had a remarkable office, to declare the mercy and judgment of God, judgments both temporal and final, mercies, not of this world, promised to a temper not of this world, *The wisdom which is from above, pure, peaceable, gentle, easy to be entreated, full of mercy and good fruits, without partiality and without hypocrisy.*[1]

[1] S. James iii. 17.

ZEPHANIAH

CHAPTER I

God's severe judgment against Judah for
divers sins.

THE word of the LORD which came unto Zephaniah
the son of Cushi, the son of Gedaliah, the son of
Amariah, the son of Hizkiah, in the days of Josiah
the son of Amon, king of Judah.

CHAP. I. ver. 1.—*The word of the Lord which came unto*
Zephaniah the son of Cushi, the son of Gedaliah, the son of
Amariah, the son of Hezekiah. It seems likely that more
forefathers of the Prophet are named than is the wont of
Holy Scripture, because the last so named was some one
remarkable. Nor is it impossible that Zephaniah should have
been the great-great-grandson of the king Hezekiah ; for although Holy Scripture commonly names the one son only
who is in the sacred line, and although there is one generation more than to Josiah, yet if each had a son early,
Zephaniah might have been contemporary with Josiah. The
names seem also mentioned for the sake of their meaning ;
at least it is remarkable how the name of God appears in
most. Zephaniah, "whom the Lord hid"; Gedaliah, "whom
the Lord made great"; Amariah, "whom the Lord promised"; Hezekiah, "whom the Lord strengthened."

31

2 I * will utterly consume all *things* from off † the land, saith the LORD.

> * Heb. *By taking away I will make an end.*
> † Heb. *the face of the land.*

2. *I will utterly consume all things;* better *all.*[1] The word is not limited to "things" "animate" or "inanimate" or "men"; it is used severally of each, according to the context; here, without limitation, of "all." *God* and *all* stand over against one another ; *God* and *all* which is not of God or in God. God, he says, will *utterly consume all from off the land* [*earth*]. The Prophet sums up in few words the subject of the whole chapter, the judgments of God from his own times to the day of Judgment itself. And this Day Itself he brings the more strongly before the mind, in that, with wonderful briefness, in two words which he conforms, in sound also, the one to the other,[2] he expresses the utter final consumption of all things. He expresses at once the intensity of action and blends their separate meanings, *Taking away I will make an end of all;* and with this he

---

[1] כל is used absolutely in a title of God, "Who maketh all," עשֶׂה כל, Isa. xliv. 24; "Thou canst do all," i.e. art Almighty, Job xlii. 2 ; "Thou hast put all שַׁתָּה כל, under his feet," Ps. viii. 6; and of man, "mine eye hath seen all," Job xiii. 1 ; and personally, gathering in one all which he had said of God's doings, with לא תָחסַר "want not any thing," Deut. viii. 9 ; חֹסֶר, חָסֵר "want of every thing," Jer. xliv. 18 ; Deut. xxviii. 48, 57 ; "all were [lit. *was*] ashamed " (with sing. verb) כל חֹבָאִישׁ Isa. xxx. 5.

[2] So also Jeremiah viii. 13, in the same words, אסוֹף אֲסִיפֵם, Rashi makes them one word, supposing אָסֵף to be for אַאסֹף. A. E. mentions those who thought that א in אסוֹף was prefixed, as in אָדוֹשׁ Isa. xxviii. 28 ; but it is unnatural to assume a rare and irregular form, when the word אסוֹף is the regular form from the common word אסֵף.

unites the words used of the flood, *from off the face of the earth.*[1] Then he goes through the whole creation as it was made, pairing *man and beast,* which Moses speaks of as created on the sixth day, and the creation of the fifth day, *the fowls of the heaven and the fishes of the sea;* and before each he sets the solemn word of God, *I will end,* as the act of God Himself. The words can have no complete fulfilment, until *the earth and the works that are therein shall be burned up,*[2] as the Psalmist, too, having gone through the creation, sums up, *Thou takest away their breath, they die, and return to their dust;*[3] and then speaks of the re-creation, *Thou sendest forth Thy Spirit, they are created; and Thou renewest the face of the earth,*[4] and, *Of old Thou hast laid the foundations of the earth, and the heavens are the work of Thy hands; they shall perish, but Thou shalt endure: yea, all of them shall wax old like a garment; as a vesture shalt Thou change them, and they shall be changed.*[5] Local fulfilments there may, in their degree, be. S. Jerome speaks as if he knew this to have been. " Even the brute animals feel the wrath of the

---

[1] הָאֲדָמָה signifies " earth," almost always in the phrase עַל פְּנֵי הָאֲדָמָה, always in the phrase מֵעַל פְּנֵי הָאֲדָמָה, unless they be limited by some addition, as " which the Lord sware that He would give thee." עַל פְּנֵי הָאֲדָמָה is thus used, Gen. vi. 1; vii. 23; Exod. xxxiii. 16; Num. xii. 3; Deut. vii. 6; xiv. 2; 2 Sam. xiv. 7; Isa. xxiii. 17; Jer. xxv. 26; Ezek. xxxviii. 20, מֵעַל פְּנֵי הָאֲדָמָה " from the face of the earth" occurs, unlimited by the context. Gen. iv. 14; vi. 7; vii. 4; viii. 8; Exod. xxxii. 12; Deut. vi. 15; 1 Sam. xx. 15; 1 Kings xiii. 34; Jer. xxviii. 16; Amos ix. 8. אֲדָמָה is used of cultivable land, and so עַל פְּנֵי הָאֲדָמָה is used in connection with rain falling on the ground, 1 Kings xvii. 14; but מֵעַל פ. הא. suffers no exception, unless it be restrained by an addition.

[2] 2 S. Peter iii. 10.   [3] Ps. civ. 29.
[4] Ib. civ. 30.   [5] Ib. cii. 25.

C

3 ^a I will consume man and beast ; I will consume
the fowls of the heaven, and the fishes of the sea, and
^b the * stumblingblocks with the wicked ; and I will
cut off man from off the land, saith the LORD.

^a Hosea iv. 3.
^b Ezek. vii. 19 and xiv. 3, 4, 7; Matt. xiii. 41.   * Or, *idols*.

Lord, and when cities have been wasted and men slain,
there cometh a desolation and scarceness of beasts also and
birds and fishes; witness Illyricum, witness Thrace, witness
my native soil " [Stridon, a city on the confines of Dalmatia
and Pannonia], "where, besides sky and earth and rampant
brambles and deep thickets, all has perished." [1] But although
this fact, which he alleges, is borne out by natural history,
it is distinct from the words of the Prophet, who speaks of
the fish, not of rivers (as S. Jerome) but of the sea, which
can in no way be influenced by the absence of man, who
is only their destroyer. The use of the language of the
histories of the creation and of the deluge implies that the
Prophet has in mind a destruction commensurate with that
creation. Then he foretells the final removal of offences, in
the same words which our Lord uses of the general Judgment. *The Son of Man shall send forth His Angels, and they
shall gather out of His kingdom all things that offend, and them
that do iniquity.*[2]

3. *The stumblingblocks* [3] *with the wicked.* Not only shall
the wicked be utterly brought to an end, or, in the other
meaning of the word, *gathered into bundles to be taken away*,

[1] S. Jer.   [2] S. Matt. xiii. 41.

[3] מַכְשֵׁלוֹת i.q. מִכְשֹׁלִים Jer. vi. 21; Ezek. xxi. 24.   So
Kim., Rashi, who limits it to idolatry (as Ges.) without
reason. They are the wicked generally, not one class of
them. In Isa. iii. 6 (where alone the word occurs besides)
it is used metaphorically of the state, " this ruin."

4 I will also stretch out mine hand upon Judah,

but all causes of stumbling too ; everything, through which others can fall, which will not be until the end of all things. Then, he repeats, yet more emphatically, *I will cut off the whole race of man*[1] *from the face of the earth,* and then he closes the verse, like the foregoing, with the solemn words, *saith the Lord.* All this shall be fulfilled in the Day of Judgment, and all other fulfilments are earnests of the final Judgment.   They are witnesses of the ever-living presence of the Judge of all, that God does take account of man's deeds.   They speak to men's conscience, they attest the existence of a Divine law, and therewith of the future complete manifestation of that law, of which they are individual sentences.   Not until the Prophet has brought this circle of judgments to their close, does he pass on to the particular judgments on Judah and Jerusalem.

4. *I will also stretch out Mine Hand,* as before on Egypt.[2] Judah had gone in the ways of Egypt and learned her sins, and sinned worse than Egypt.[3] The *mighty Hand and stretched-out Arm,* with which she had been delivered, shall be again *stretched out,* yet not for her but *upon* her, *upon all the inhabitants of Jerusalem.*   In this threatened destruction of all, Judah and Jerusalem are singled out, because *judgment* shall *begin at the house of God.*[4] They who have sinned against the greater grace shall be most signally punished. Yet the punishment of those whom God had so chosen and loved is an earnest of the general judgment.   This too

---

[1] את האדם, as in the history of the creation, Gen. i. 27 ; or the flood, ib. vi. 7 ; vii. 21.

[2] Exod. vi. 6 ; Deut. iv. 34 ; v. 15 ; vii. 19 ; xi. 2 ; xxvi. 8 ; and thence Jer. xxxii. 21 ; Ps. cxxxvi. 12. Isaiah had, in the same phrase, prophesied God's judgments against Israel in the burden, v. 25 ; ix. 12, 17 ; x. 4.

[3] Jer. ii. 10, 11.   [4] 1 S. Peter iv. 17 ; Jer. xxv. 29.

and upon all the inhabitants of Jerusalem ; and ᵃ I

ᵃ Fulfilled, cir. 624 ; 2 Kings xxiii. 4, 5.

is not a partial but a general judgment "upon *all* the
inhabitants of Jerusalem."

And I will cut off the remnant of Baal, i.e. to the very
last vestige of it. Isaiah unites *name and residue,*[1] as
equivalents, together with the proverbial *posterity and descendant.*[2] Zephaniah distributes them in parallel clauses,
"the *residue*[3] of Baal and the *name* of the Chemarim."
Good and evil have each a root, which remains in the
ground when the trunk has been hewn down. There is
a remnant according to the election of grace, when *the rest*
have been *blinded;*[4] and this is a *holy seed*[5] to carry on the
line of God. Evil too has its remnant, which, unless diligently kept down, shoots up again, after the conversion
of peoples or individuals. The *mind of the flesh*[6] remains
in the regenerate also. The Prophet foretells the complete
excision of the whole *remnant of Baal,* which was fulfilled
in it after the captivity, and shall be fulfilled as to all
which it shadows forth, in the Day of Judgment. *From*

[1] Isa. xiv. 22.

[2] נין ונכד, which occur only together, Gen. xxi. 23 ; Job
xviii. 19 ; Isa. xiv. 22.

[3] שאר is not limited, like שארית, to that which remains over when a former or larger part has ceased or is
gone. It is mostly "the rest," after others who had been
named, yet still it may be the larger number ; as, "the rest
of those chosen," 1 Chron. xvi. 41 ; "the rest of their
brethren, the priests and the Levites," Ezra iii. 9 (8, Eng.) ;
"the rest of the chief of the fathers," ib. iv. 3 ; "the rest
of their companions," ib. 7 ; "the rest of the people,"
Neh. x. 28 ; xi. 1 ; "the rest of Israel," Ib. 20 ; "the rest
of the Jews," Esther ix. 16. So in Isaiah, "the rest of Syria"
besides Damascus, Isa. xvii. 3, and "the rest of the Spirit,"
Mal. ii. 15 (see ib.).

[4] Rom. xi. 5, 7.   [5] Isa. vi. 13.   [6] φρόνημα σαρκός.

this place; for in their frenzy, they dared to bring the worship of Baal into the very temple of the Lord.[1] "Who would ever believe that in Jerusalem, the holy city, and in the very temple idols should be consecrated? Whoso seeth the ways of our times will readily believe it. For among Christians and in the very temple of God, the abominations of the heathen are worshipped. Riches, pleasures, honours, are they not idols which Christians prefer to God Himself?"[2]

And the name of the Chemarim with the priests. Of the *idolatrous priests*[3] the very name shall be cut off, as God promises by Hosea, that He will *take away the names of Baalim,*[4] and by Zechariah, that He *will cut off the names of the idols out of the land.*[5] Yet this is more. Not the *name* only *of the Chemarim,* but themselves with their name, their posterity, shall be blotted out ; still more, it is God Who cuts off all memory of them, blotting them out of the book of the living and out of His own. They had but *a name* before, *that they were living, but were dead.*[6] "The Lord shall take away names of vainglory, wrongly admired, out of the Church ; yea, the very names of the priests with the priests who vainly flatter themselves with the name of Bishops and the dignity of Presbyters without their deeds. Whence he markedly says, not, *and the deeds of priests with*

---

[1] 2 Kings xxiii. 4, 6.   [2] Rib.

[3] The *chemarim* is the name of idolatrous priests generally (it occurs also 2 Kings xxiii. 5 ; Hosea x. 5). In 2 Kings, where is the account of the first fulfilment of this prophecy, they appear as priests of the idolatrous high-places, distinct from the priests of Baal and of the *host of heaven.* The name is probably the Syriac name of "priest," used in Holy Scripture of idolatrous priests, because the Syrians were idolaters. See Gesenius, Gesch. d. Hebr. Sprache, p. 58. In Chald. כּוֹמְרָא is limited to idolatrous priests. See Buxt. and Levy.

[4] Hosea ii. 17.   [5] Zech. xiii. 2.   [6] Rev. iii. 1.

will cut off the remnant of Baal from this place, *and*
the name of ^a the Chemarims with the priests ;

^a Hosea x. 5.

---

the priests, but the *names ;* who only bear the false name of
dignities, and with evil works destroy their own names." [1]
The *priests* are *priests of the Lord,* who live not like priests,
corrupt in life and doctrine, and corrupters of God's people.[2]
The judgment is pronounced alike on what was intrinsically
evil, and on good which had corrupted itself into evil.   The
title of priest is nowhere given to the priest of a false God,
without some mention in the context, implying that they
were idolatrous priests; as the priests of Dagon,[3] of the
high-places as ordained by Jeroboam,[4] of Baal,[5] of Bethel,[6]
of Ahab,[7] of those who were not gods,[8] of On, where the
sun was worshipped.[9]   *The priests,* then, were God's priests,
who in the evil days of Manasseh had manifoldly corrupted
their life or their faith, and who were still evil.   The *priests*
of Judah, with its kings, its princes, and the people of the
land, were in Jeremiah's inaugural vision enumerated as
those who *shall,* God says, *fight against thee, but shall not
prevail against thee.*[10]   *The priests said not, Where is the Lord ?
and they that handle the law knew Me not.*[11]   In the general
corruption, [12] *A wonderful and horrible thing is committed in the
land, the prophets prophesy falsely, and the priests bear rule at
their hands ;* [13] *the children of Israel and the children of Judah,
their kings, their princes, their priests, and their prophets, and*

[1] S. Jer.   [2] See Jer. ii. 8 ; v. 31.   [3] 1 Sam. v. 5.
[4] 1 Kings xiii. 2, 33 ; 2 Kings xxiii. 20 ; 2 Chron. xi. 15.
[5] 2 Kings x. 19 ; xi. 18 ; 2 Chron. xxiii. 17.
[6] Amos vii. 10.   [7] 2 Kings x. 11.   [8] 2 Chron. xiii. 9.
[9] Gen. xli. 45–50, &c.   The name " Potipherah," probably
belonging to " Phre," implies this.
[10] Jer. i. 18, 19.   [11] Ib. ii. 7, 8.
[12] Ib. v. 30, 31.   [13] עַל יְדֵיהֶם.

5 And them ^a that worship the host of heaven

a 2 Kings xxiii. 12 ; Jer. xix. 13.

the men of Judah, and the inhabitants of Jerusalem, have turned unto Me the back, and not the face.[1] Jeremiah speaks specifically of heavy moral sins. *From the prophet even unto the priest every one dealeth falsely ;* [2] *both prophet and priest are profane ;* [3] *for the sins of her prophets, the iniquities of her priests, that have shed the blood of the just in the midst of her.*[4] And Isaiah says of their sensuality : *The priests and the prophets have erred through strong drink ; they are swallowed up of wine, they are out of the way through strong drink.*[5]

5. *And them that worship the host of heaven upon the* [flat] *housetops.* This was fulfilled by Josiah, who destroyed *the altars that were on the top of the upper chamber of Ahaz.*[6] Jeremiah speaks as if this worship was almost universal, as though well-nigh every roof had been profaned by this idolatry. *The houses of Jerusalem, and the houses of Judah, shall be defiled as the place of Tophet, because of all the houses upon whose roofs they have burned incense unto all the host of heaven, and have poured out drink offerings unto other gods.*[7] *The Chaldeans that fight against this city, shall come and set fire on this city, and burn it with the houses, upon whose roofs they have offered incense unto Baal, and poured out drink offerings to other gods, to provoke Me to anger.*[8] They worshipped *on the housetops,* probably to have a clearer view of that magnificent expanse of sky, *the moon and stars which* God had *ordained ;* [9] the *queen of heaven,* which they worshipped instead of Himself. There is something so mysterious in that calm face of the moon, as it *walketh in beauty ;* [10] God seems to have invested it with such delegated

[1] Jer. xxxii. 32, 33.   [2] Ib. vi. 13 ; viii. 10.
[3] Ib. xxiii. 11.   [4] Lam. iv. 13.   [5] Isa. xxviii. 7.
[6] 2 Kings xxiii. 12.   [7] Jer. xix. 13.   [8] Ib. xxxii. 29.
[9] Ps. viii. 3.   [10] Job xxxi. 26.

upon the housetops; ᵃ and them that worship *and*

ᵃ 1 Kings xviii. 21 ; 2 Kings xvii. 33, 41.

influence over the seasons and the produce of the earth,
that they stopped short in it, and worshipped the creature
rather than the Creator.   Much as men now talk of
"Nature," admire " Nature," speak of its "laws," not as
laws imposed upon it, but inherent in it, laws affecting us
and our well-being ; only not in their ever-varying vicissitudes, *doing whatsoever God commandeth them upon the*
face of the world in the earth, whether for correction, or for His
land, or for mercy ! ¹ The idolaters *worshipped and served*
the creature more than the Creator, Who is blessed for ever; ²
moderns equally make this world their object, only they
idolise themselves and their discoveries, and worship their
own intellect.

This worship *on the housetops* individualised the public
idolatry; it was a rebellion against God, family by family ; a
sort of family-prayer of idolatry.   *Did we,* say the mingled
multitude to Jeremiah, *make our cakes to worship her, and*
pour out our drink offerings unto her, without our men ? ³ Its
family character is described in Jeremiah.   *The children*
gather wood, and the fathers kindle the fire, and the women
knead the dough, to make cakes to the queen of heaven, and to
*pour out drink offerings unto other gods.*⁴ The idolatry spread
to other cities.   *We will certainly do,* they say, *as we have*
done, we and our fathers, our kings and our princes, in the
*cities of Judah, and in the streets of Jerusalem.*⁵ The incense
went up continually *as a memorial to God* from the Altar of
incense in the temple : the *roofs of the houses* were so many
altars, from which, street by street and house by house, the
incense went up to her, for whom they dethroned God, *the*

¹ Job xxxvii. 12, 13.   ² Rom. i. 25.   ³ Jer. xliv. 19.
⁴ Ib. vii. 18.   ⁵ Ib. xliv. 17.

queen of heaven. It was an idolatry with which Judah was especially besotted, believing that they received all goods of this world from her and not from God. When punished for their sin, they repented of their partial repentance and maintained to Jeremiah that they were punished for *leaving off to burn incense to the queen of heaven.*[1]

And them that worship the Lord, but with a divided heart and service ; *that swear by* [rather *to* [2]] *the Lord,* swear fealty and loyal allegiance to Him, while they do acts which deny it, in that *they swear by Malcham,* better [it is no appellative although allied to one] *their king,*[3] most probably, I think, " Moloch."

This idolatry had been their enduring idolatry in the wilderness, after the calves had been annihilated ; it is *the* worship, against which Israel is warned by name in the law ;[4] then, throughout the history of the Judges, we hear of the kindred idolatry of Baal,[5] *the* Lord (who was called also " eternal king "[6] and from whom individuals named themselves " son of [the] king," " servant of [the] king "[7]) or the manifold Baals[8] and Ashtaroth or Astarte. But after these had been removed on the preaching of Samuel,[9] this idolatry does not reappear in Judah until the inter-

---

[1] Jer. xliv. 3, 15, 18.

[2] As in the E. M., comp. 2 Chron. xv. 14 ; Isa. xix. 18 ; xlv. 23. It can only mean this.

[3] מַלְכָּם as מַלְכְּכֶם Amos v. 26, and מַלְכָּם Jer. xlix. 1, 3, where the E. V. too renders *their king.*

[4] Lev. xviii. 21 ; xx. 2–4.

[5] Always used with the article expressed or understood, בַּבַּעַל, לַבַּעַל, הַבַּעַל, unless the specific name (Bael-berith, Bael-zebub, Bael-peor) is mentioned.

[6] Numid, 1, 2, 3 in Ges. Thes. p. 795.

[7] עֲבַרְמֶלֶךְ, בַּרְמֶלֶךְ ap. Ges. l.c.

[8] הַבְּעָלִים in Judges, 1 Sam., 2 Kings, 2 Chron., Jeremiah, Hosea.

[9] 1 Sam. vii. 6 ; xii. 10.

^a that swear * by the LORD, and that swear ^b by
Malcham ;

  ^a Isa. xlviii. 1 ; Hosea iv. 15.   * Or, *to the Lord.*
        ^b Joshua xxiii. 7 ; 1 Kings xi. 33.

---

marriage of Jehoram with the house of Ahab.[1] The kindred
and equally horrible worship of *Molech, the abomination of
the children of Ammon,*[2] was brought in by Solomon in his
decay, and endured until his high-place was defiled by
Josiah.[3] It is probable, then, that this was *their king,*[4]
of whom Zephaniah speaks, whom Amos[5] and after him
Jeremiah, called *their king ;* but speaking of Ammon. Him,
the king of Ammon, Judah adopted as *their king.* They
owned God as their king in words ; Molech they owned by
their deeds ; *they worshipped and sware fealty to the Lord* and
they *sware by their king;* his name was familiarly in their
mouths ; to him they appealed as the Judge and witness of
the truth of their words, his displeasure they invoked on
themselves, if they sware falsely. " Those in error were
wont to swear by heaven, and, as matter of reverence to
call out, 'By the king and lord Sun.' Those who do so
must of set purpose and wilfully depart from the love
of God, since the law expressly says, ⁶ *Thou shalt worship
the Lord thy God, and serve Him* alone, *and swear by His
Name.*"[7]

  ¹ 2 Kings viii. 16–18, 26, 27 ; 2 Chron. xxi. 6, 12, 13 ;
xxii. 2–4.
  ² 1 Kings xi. 7.   ³ 2 Kings xxiii. 13, 14.
  ⁴ Molech is always an appellative, except 1 Kings xi. 7.
Else (by a pronunciation belonging probably to Ammon) it
is הַמֹּלֶךְ Lev. xx. 5, or לַמֹּלֶךְ Lev. xviii. 21; xx. 2, 4;
2 Kings xxiii. 10; Jer. xxxii. 35. As a proper name, it is
Milcom, 1 Kings xi. 5, 33 ; 2 Kings xxiii. 13.
  ⁵ See on Amos i. 15.
  ⁶ Deut. vi. 13.   ⁷ S. Cyr.

The former class who *worshipped on the roofs* were mere idolaters. These *worshipped*, as they thought, *the Lord*, bound themselves solemnly by oath to Him, but with a reserve, joining a hateful idol to Him, in that they, by a religious act, owned it too as god. The act which they did was in direct words, or by implication, forbidden by God. The command to *swear by the Lord* implied that they were to swear by none else. It was followed by the prohibition to go after other gods.[1] Contrariwise to swear by other gods was forbidden as a part of their service. *Be very courageous to keep and to do all that is written in the book of the Law of Moses, neither make mention of the name of their gods, nor cause to swear by them, neither serve them, but cleave unto the Lord your God.*[2] *How shall I pardon thee for this? Thy children have forsaken Me, and have sworn by those who are no gods.*[3] *They taught My people to swear by Baal.*[4] They thought perhaps that in that they professed to serve God, did the greater homage to Him, professed and bound themselves to be His (such is the meaning of *swear to the Lord*); they might, without renouncing His service, do certain things, *swear by their king,* although in effect they thereby owned him also as god. To such Elijah said, *How long halt ye between two opinions? If the Lord be God, follow Him; but if Baal, then follow him;*[5] and God by Jeremiah rejects with abhorrence such divided service. *Ye trust in lying words, which will not profit. Will ye steal, murder, commit adultery, swear falsely, and burn incense unto Baal, and walk after other gods, and come and stand before Me in this house, which is called by My name, saying, We are delivered to do all these abominations.*[6] And Hoesa, *Neither go ye to Beth-aven, and swear there, The Lord liveth.*[7]

[1] Deut. vi. 13, 14; x. 30, comp. Isa. lxv. 16; Jer. iv. 2.
[2] Joshua xxiii. 6–8, comp. Amos viii. 14.
[3] Jer. v. 7.   [4] Ib. xii. 16.
[5] 1 Kings xviii. 21.   [6] Jer. vii. 8–10.   [7] Hosea iv. 15

6 And ^a them that are turned back from the
LORD ; and *those* that ^b have not sought the LORD,
nor enquired for him.

^a Isa. i. 4 ; Jer. ii. 13, 17 and xv. 6.　　　^b Hosea vii. 7.

Such are Christians, "who think that they can serve together the world and the Lord, and please two masters,
God and Mammon; who, *being soldiers of Jesus Christ* and
having sworn fealty to Him, *entangle themselves with the
affairs of this life*[1] and offer the same image to God and to
Cæsar."[2] To such, God, Whom with their lips they own,
is not their God; their idol is, as the very name says, *their
king*, whom alone they please, displeasing and dishonouring
God. We must not only fear, love, honour God, but love,
fear, honour all besides for Him Alone.

6. *And them that are turned back from* [lit. *have turned
themselves back from following after*[3]] *the Lord*. From this
half-service, the Prophet goes on to the avowed neglect of
God, by such as wholly fall away from Him, not setting
His Will or law before them, but *turning away from* Him.
It is their misery that they were set in the right way once,
but themselves *turned themselves back*, now no longer *following* God, but *their own lusts, drawn away and enticed* by
them.[4] How much more Christians, before whose eyes
Christ Jesus is set forth, not as a Redeemer only, but as
an Example that they should *follow His steps!*[5]

*And those that have not sought the Lord, nor enquired for
Him*. This is marked to be a distinct class. *And those
who*. These did not openly break with God, or turn away

[1] 2 Tim. ii. 3, 4.　　　　　　　　　　[2] S. Jer.
[3] Such is the uniform use of נָסוֹג. Its common construction is with אָחוֹר; with מֵאַחַר, as here, Isa. lix. 13 ;
Kal, with מִן of pers., Ps. lxxx. 19 ; Nif. with מִן of thing,
2 Sam. i. 22.
[4] S. James i. 14.　　　　　[5] S. Peter ii. 21.

7 [a] Hold thy peace at the presence of the LORD

[a] Hab. ii. 20; Zech. ii. 13.

overtly from Him; they kept (as men think) on good terms with Him, but, like *the slothful servant*, rendered Him a listless, heartless service. Both words express diligent search.[1] God is not found then in a careless way. They who *seek* Him not *diligently*,[2] do not find Him. *Strive*, our Lord says, *to enter in at the strait gate; for many, I say unto you, shall seek to enter in, and shall not be able.*[3] She who had lost the one piece of silver, *sought diligently*,[4] till she had found it.

Thus he has gone through the whole cycle. First, that most horrible and cruel worship of Baal, the *idolatrous priests* and those who had the name of *priests* only, mingled with them, yet not openly apostatising; then the milder form of idolatry, the star-worshippers; then those who would unite the worship of God with idols, who held themselves to be worshippers of God, but whose real king was their idol; then those who openly abandoned God; and lastly, those who held with Him just to satisfy their conscience-qualms, but with no heart-service. And so, in words of Habakkuk and in reminiscence of his awful summons of the whole world before God, he sums up:

7. *Hold thy peace at the presence of the Lord God* [lit. *Hush*, in awe *from the Face of God*]. In the Presence of God, even the righteous say from their inmost heart, *I am vile, what shall I answer Thee? I will lay mine hand upon my mouth.*[5] *Now mine eye seeth Thee, wherefore I abhor myself, and repent in dust and ashes.*[6] *Enter not into judgment with Thy servant, O Lord; for in Thy sight shall no man living be justified.*[7] How much more must the *man without*

[1] בָּקַשׁ, intensive; דָּרַשׁ of search below the surface.
[2] S. Matt. ii. 8.   [3] S. Luke xiii. 24.   [4] Ib. xv. 8.
[5] Job xl. 4.   [6] Ib. xlii. 5, 6.   [7] Ps. cxliii. 2.

GOD : [a] for the day of the LORD *is* at hand : for

[a] Isa. xiii. 6.

---

the wedding garment be *speechless*,[1] and every false plea, with
which he deceived himself, melt away before the Face of
God ! The voice of God's Judgment echoes in every heart,
we indeed justly.[2]

For the Day of the Lord is at hand. Zephaniah, as is his
wont, grounds this summons, which he had renewed from
Habakkuk, to hushed silence before God, on Joel's prophetic warning,[3] to show that it was not yet exhausted. *A*
day of the Lord, of which Joel warned, had come and was
gone; but it was only the herald of many such days ;
judgments in time, heralds and earnests, and, in their
degree, pictures of the last which shall end time.

"All time is God's, since He Alone is the Lord of time ;
yet that is specially said to be His time when He doth
anything special. Whence He saith, *My time is not yet
come ;* [4] whereas all time is His." [5] The Day of the Lord
is, in the first instance, "the day of captivity and vengeance on the sinful people," [6] as a forerunner of the Day
of Judgment, or the day of death to each, for this too
is near, since, compared to eternity, all the time of this
world is brief.

For the Lord hath prepared a sacrifice. God had rejected
sacrifices, offered amid unrepented sin ; they were *an
abomination to Him.*[7] When man will not repent and offer
himself as *a living sacrifice, holy and acceptable to God,*[8] God,
at last, rejects all other outward oblations, and the sinner
himself is the sacrifice and victim of his own sins. The
image was probably suggested by Isaiah's words, *The Lord
hath a sacrifice in Bozrah, and a great slaughter in the land of*

[1] S. Matt. xxii. 11, 12.   [2] S. Luke xxiii. 41.
[3] Joel i. 15 ; ii. 1.   [4] S. John vii. 6.   [5] Dion.
[6] S. Jer.   [7] Isa. i. 11–15.   [8] Rom. xii. 1.

^a the LORD hath prepared a sacrifice, he hath * bid his guests.

^a Isa. xxxiv. 6; Jer. xlvi. 10; Ezek. xxxix. 17; Rev. xix. 17.

* Heb. *sanctified*, or *prepared*.

Idumea ; [1] and Jeremiah subsequently uses it of the over-throw of Pharaoh at the Euphrates, *This is the day of the Lord of Hosts ; that He may avenge Him of His adversaries ; for the Lord God hath a sacrifice in the north country by the river Euphrates.* [2] *The Lord hath made all things for Himself, yea even the wicked for the day of evil.* [3] All must honour God, either fulfilling the will of God and the end of their own being and of His love for them, by obeying that loving Will with their own free-will, or, if they repudiate it to the end, by suffering It.

He hath bid [lit. *sanctified* [4]] *His guests.* God had before, by Isaiah, called the heathen whom He employed to punish Babylon, *My sanctified ones.* [5] Zephaniah, by giving the title to God's instruments against Judah, declares that themselves, having become in deeds like the heathen, were as heathen to Him. The instruments of His displeasure, not they, were so far His chosen, His called. [6] Jeremiah repeats the saying, *Thus saith the Lord against the house of the king of Judah ;—I have sanctified against thee destroyers, a man and his weapons.* [7] That is, so far, a holy war in the purpose of God, which fulfils His will ; whence Nebuchad-nezzar was *His servant,* [8] avenging His wrongs. [9] " To be sanctified, here denotes not the laying aside of iniquity

[1] Isa. xxxiv. 6.   [2] Jer. xlvi. 10.
[3] Prov. xvi. 4.   [4] See E.M.
[5] Isa. xiii. 3.   [6] קְרָאָי.
[7] Jer. xxii. 6, 7.   [8] Ib. xxv. 9.
[9] See on Joel iii. 9 ; Micah iii. 5.

8 And it shall come to pass in the day of the

---

nor the participation of the Holy Ghost, but, as it were, to
be fore-ordained and chosen to the fulfilment of this end." [1]
That is in a manner hallowed, which is employed by God
for a holy end, though the instrument, its purposes, its
aims, its passions, be in themselves unholy. There is an
awe about "the scourges of God." As with the lightning
and the tornado, there is a certain presence of God with
them, in that through them His Righteousness is seen;
although they themselves have as little of God as the *wind
and storm* which *fulfil His word*. Those who were once
admitted to make offerings to God make themselves sacrifices to His wrath; these, still heathen and ungodly, and
in all besides reprobate, are His Priests, because in this,
although without their will, they do His Will.

8. *I will punish* [lit. *visit upon*]. God seems oftentimes
to be away from His own world. Men plot, design, say,
in word or in deed, *who is Lord over us?* God is, as it were,
a stranger in it, or as a man, who hath *taken a journey into
a far country*. God uses our own language to us. *I will
visit*, inspecting (so to say), examining, sifting, reviewing,
and when man's sins require it, allowing the weight of His
displeasure to fall upon them.

The princes. The Prophet again, in vivid detail (as his
characteristic is), sets forth together sin and punishment.
Amid the general chastisement of all, when all should
become one *sacrifice*, they who sinned most should be
punished most. The evil priests had received their doom.
Here he begins anew with the mighty of the people and so
goes down, first to special spots of the city, then to the
whole, man by man. Josiah being a godly king, no mention
is made of him. Thirteen years before his death,[2] he received the promise of God, *because thine heart was tender,*

---

[1] S. Cyr.   [2] 2 Kings xxii. 19, 20.

Lord's sacrifice, that I will * punish ^a the princes,

* Heb. *visit upon.*   ^a Jer. xxxix. 6.

---

and thou hast humbled thyself before the Lord—I will gather thee unto thy fathers, and thou shalt be gathered unto thy grave in peace, and thou shalt not see all the evil which I will bring upon this place. In remarkable contrast to Jeremiah, who had to be, in detail and continual pleading with his people, a prophet of judgment to come, until those judgments broke upon them, and so was the reprover of the evil sovereigns who succeeded Josiah, Zephaniah has to pronounce God's judgments only on the *princes* and *the king's children.* Jeremiah, in his inaugural vision, was forewarned, that *the kings of Judah, its princes, priests, and the people of the land* [1] should war against him, because he should speak unto them all which God should command him. And thenceforth Jeremiah impleads or threatens kings and the princes together.[2] Zephaniah contrariwise, his office lying wholly within the reign of Josiah, describes the princes again as *roaring lions,*[3] but says nothing of the king, as neither does Micah,[4] in the reign, it may be, of Jotham or Hezekiah. Isaiah speaks of *princes,* as *rebellious and companions of thieves.*[5] Jeremiah speaks of them as idolaters.[6] They appear to have had considerable influence, which on one occasion they employed in defence of Jeremiah,[7] but mostly for evil.[8] Zedekiah inquired of Jeremiah secretly for fear of them.[9] They brought destruction upon themselves by what men praise, their resistance to Nebuchadnezzar, but against the declared mind of God.

[1] Jer. i. 18.
[2] Ib. ii. 26 ; iv. 9 ; viii. 1 ; xxiv. 8 ; xxxii. 37 ; xxxiv. 21.
[3] Zeph. iii. 3.   [4] Micah iii. 1, 9.
[5] Isa. i. 23.   [6] Jer. xxxii. 32–34 ; xliv. 21.
[7] Ib. xxvi. 16.   [8] Ib. xxxvii. 15 ; xxxviii. 4, 16.
[9] Ib. xxxvii. 17 ; xxxviii. 14–27.

D

and the king's children, and all such as are clothed
with strange apparel.

Nebuchadnezzar unwittingly fulfilled the Prophet's word,
when he *slew all the nobles of Judah, the eunuch who was
over the war, and seven men of them that were near the king's
person, and the principal scribe of the host.*[1]

And the king's children. Holy Scripture mentions chief
persons only by name. Isaiah had prophesied the isolated,
lonely, loveless lot of descendants of Hezekiah, who should
be *eunuchs in the palace of the king of Babylon,*[2] associated
only with those intriguing pests of Eastern courts,[3] a lot
in itself worse than the sword (although to Daniel God
overruled it to good), and Zedekiah's sons were slain before
his eyes and his race extinct. Jehoiakim died a disgraced
death, and Jehoiachin was imprisoned more than half the
life of man.

And all such as are clothed with strange apparel. Israel
was reminded by its dress that it belonged to God. It
was no great thing in itself; *a band of dark blue*[4] *upon the
fringes at the four corners* of *their garments.* But *the band of
dark blue* was upon the high-priest's mitre, with the plate
engraved, *Holiness to the Lord,*[5] fastened upon it; *with a
band of dark blue* also was the breastplate bound to the
ephod of the high-priest.[6] So then, simple as it was, it
seems to have designated the whole nation, as *a kingdom of
priests, an holy nation.*[7] It was appointed to them, *that ye
may look upon it, and remember all the commandments of
the Lord and do them, and that ye seek not after your own
heart and your own eyes, after which ye use to go a whoring;*

[1] Jer. xxxix. 6; lii. 25–27.
[2] Isa. xxxix. 7. See Daniel the Prophet, p. 16.
[3] See ib. pp. 21, 22.
[4] Num. xv. 38; Deut. xxii. 12.
[5] Exod. xxviii. 36.　　[6] Ib. xxxix. 21.　　[7] Ib. xix. 6.

that ye may remember and do all My commandments, and be holy unto your God.[1] They might say, "it is but *a band of blue;*" but the *band of blue* was the soldier's badge, which marked them as devoted to the service of their God; indifference to or shame of it involved indifference to or shame of the charge given them therewith, and to their calling as a peculiar people. The choice of the *strange apparel* involved the choice to be as the nations of the world; *we will be as the heathen, as the families of the countries.*[2]

All luxurious times copy foreign dress, and with it, foreign manners and luxuries; whence even the heathen Romans were zealous against its use. It is very probable that with the foreign dress foreign idolatry was imported.[3] The Babylonian dress was very gorgeous, such as was the admiration of the simpler Jews. *Her captains and rulers clothed in perfection, girded with girdles upon their loins, with flowing dyed attire upon their heads.*[4] Ezekiel had to frame words to express the Hebrew idea of their beauty. Jehoiakim is reproved among other things for his luxury.[5] Outward dress always betokens the inward mind, and in its turn acts upon it. An estranged dress betokened an estranged heart, whence it is used as an image of the whole spiritual mind.[6] "The garment of the sons of the king and the apparel of princes which we receive in Baptism, is Christ, according to that, *Put ye on the Lord Jesus Christ,* and *Put ye on bowels of mercy, goodness, humility, patience,* and the rest. Wherein we are commanded to be clothed with the new man from heaven according to our Creator, and to *lay aside* the clothing of *the old man with his deeds.*[7]

---

[1] Num. xv. 39, 40. [2] Ezek. xx. 32.
[3] Jon., Rashi, and S. Jer. connect it with idolatry.
[4] Ezek. xxiii. 12, 15. [5] Jer. xxii. 14, 15.
[6] Rom. xiii. 14; Col. iii. 12; Eph. iv. 24.
[7] Eph. iv. 22.

9 In the same day also will I punish all those that leap on the threshold, which fill their masters' houses with violence and deceit.

Whereas, then, we ought to be clothed in such raiment, for mercy we put on cruelty, for patience, impatience, for righteousness, iniquity ; in a word, for virtues, vices; for Christ, Antichrist. Whence it is said of such a one, *He is clothed with cursing as with a garment.*[1] These the Lord will visit most manifestly at His Coming."[2] "Thinkest thou that hypocrisy is *strange apparel?* Of a truth. For what stranger apparel than sheeps' clothing to ravening wolves ? What stranger than for him who [3] *within is full of iniquity,* to appear outwardly *righteous before men?*"[4]

9. *I will punish all those that leap on the threshold.* Neither language nor history nor context allow this to be understood of the idolatrous custom of Ashdod, not to tread on the threshold [5] of the temple of Dagon. It had indeed been a strange infatuation of idolatry, that God's people should adopt an act of superstitious reverence for an idol in the very instance in which its nothingness and the power of the true God had been shown. Nothing is indeed too brutish for one who chooses an idol for the true God, preferring Satan to the good God. Yet the superstition belonged apparently to Ashdod alone; the worship of Dagon, although another form of untrue worship, does not appear, like that of Baal, to have fascinated the Jews ; nor would Zephaniah,

---

[1] Ps. cix. 16.
[2] S. Jer.
[3] S. Matt. xxiii. 28.
[4] Rup.
[5] מִפְתָּן is used, 1 Sam. v. 4, 5; Ezek. ix. 3; x. 4, 18; xlvi. 2; xlvii. 1; elsewhere סַף. There is a trace of this explanation in the Chald., "who walk in the laws of the Philistines," and in S. Jerome, doubtless from his Jewish teachers. Isaiah's reproof that they *have soothsayers like the Philistines* (ii. 6) is altogether different.

to express a rare superstition, have chosen an idiom, which might more readily express the contrary, that they "leapt *on* the threshold," not over it.[1] They are also the same persons, who *leap on the threshold*, and who *fill their masters' houses with violence and deceit*. Yet this relates, not to superstition, but to plunder and goods unjustly gotten. As then, before, he had declared God's judgments upon idolatry, so does he here upon sins against the second table, whether by open violence, or secret fraud, as do also Habakkuk,[2] and Jeremiah.[3] All, whether open or hidden from man, every wrongful dealing (for every sin as to a neighbour's goods falls under these two, violence or fraud), shall be avenged in that day. Here again all which remains is the sin. They enriched, as they thought, their masters, by art or by force; they schemed, plotted, robbed; they succeeded to their heart's wish; but, "ill-gotten, ill-spent!" They *filled their masters' houses* quite full; but wherewith? with violence and deceit, which witnessed against them, and brought down the judgments of God upon them.

10. *A cry from the fish-gate.* The *fish-gate* was probably in the north of the wall of *the second city.* For in Nehemiah's rebuilding, the restoration began at the sheep-gate [4] (so called, doubtless, because the sheep for the sacrifices were brought in by it), which, as being near the temple, was repaired by the priests; then it ascended northward by two towers, *the towers of Meah* and *Hananeel;* then two companies repaired some undescribed part of the wall,[5] and

---

[1] דָּלַג עַל is, in the only other place, Cant. ii. 8, " bounding *on* the mountains " ; " bounding over " (like our " leapt a wall ") happens to be expressed by an acc., 2 Sam. xviii. 30 ; Ps. xviii. 29 ; " passing over " had been expressed more clearly by פָּסַח עַל, as in Exod. xii. 23, 27.

[2] Hab. i. 2, 3.   [3] Jer. v. 27.   [4] Neh. iii. 1.   [5] Ib. iii. 2.

the LORD, *that there shall be* the noise of a cry from

---

then another company *built the fish-gate.*[1] Four companies
are then mentioned, who repaired, in order, to the *old gate,*
which was repaired by another company.[2] Three more
companies repaired beyond these; *and they left Jerusalem
unto the broad wall.*[3] After three more sections repaired by
individuals, two others repaired a *second measured portion,
and the tower of the furnaces.*[4] This order is reversed in the
account of the dedication of the walls. The people being
divided *into two great companies of them that give thanks,*[5]
some place near *the tower of the furnaces* was the central
point from which both parted to encompass the city in
opposite directions. In this account we have two addi-
tional gates mentioned, *the gate of Ephraim,*[6] between *the
broad wall* and the *old gate,* and *the prison-gate,* beyond *the
sheep-gate,* from which the repairs had begun. *The gate of
Ephraim* had obviously not been repaired, because, for some
reason, it had not been destroyed. Else Nehemiah, who
describes the rebuilding of the wall so minutely, must have
mentioned its rebuilding. It was obviously to the north,
as leading to Ephraim. But the tower of Hananeel must
have been a very marked tower. In Zechariah Jerusalem
is measured from north to south, *from the tower of Hananeel
unto the king's winepresses.*[7] It was then itself at the
north-east corner of Jerusalem, where towers were of the
most importance to strengthen the wall, and to command
the approach to the wall either way. *The fish-gate,* then,
lying between it and *the gate of Ephraim,* must have been on
the north side of the city, and so on the side where the
Chaldean invasions came; yet it must have been much
inside the present city, because the city itself was enlarged

---

[1] Neh. iii. 3.   [2] Ib. iii. 4–6.   [3] Ib. iii. 7, 8.
[4] Ib. iii. 9–11.   [5] Ib. xii. 31–38.   [6] Ib. xii. 39.
[7] Zech. xiv. 10.

by Herod Agrippa on the north, as it was unaccountably
contracted on the south.   The then limits of Jerusalem
are defined.   For Josephus thus describes *the second wall*.
"It took its beginning from that gate which they called
Gennath, which belonged to the first wall; it only encom-
passed the northern quarter of the city, and reached as far
as the tower of Antonia."[1]   The tower of Antonia was
situated at the north-west angle of the corner of the
temple.   The other end of the wall, the Gennath or *garden*
gate, must have opened on cultivated land; and Josephus
speaks of the gardens on the north and north-west of the
city which were destroyed by Titus in levelling the ground.[2]
But near the tower of Hippicus, the north-western extremity of the first wall, no ancient remains have been
discovered by excavation;[3] but they *have* been traced north,
from "an ancient Jewish semicircular arch, resting on
piers 18 feet high, now buried in rubbish."   These old
foundations have been traced at three places[4] in a line on

---

[1] B. J. v. 4, 2.   [2] Ib. v. 3, 2.

[3] Pierotti, "Jerusalem Explored," p. 32, from whom this
account is taken.   Signor Pierotti's work is "the fruit of
eight years of continual labour devoted to a study of the
topography of Jerusalem upon the spot, in which I have been
constantly occupied in excavating and removing the rubbish
accumulated over the place during so many centuries, in
retracing the walls, in examining the monuments and ancient
remains, and in penetrating and traversing the conduits and
vaults."—"I have," he says, "made excavations and watched
those made by others, have formed intimacies with the inhabitants of the country, have sought for information on the
spot, regardless of personal risk, have worked with my own
hands underground, and so have obtained much knowledge of
that which lies below the surface of the soil in Jerusalem."—
Jerusalem Explored, Pref., p. viii.

[4] (1) At the meat-bazaar near the convent of S. Mary the
Great.   "In digging down to the rock to lay the new foundations, 10 feet below the surface, I came upon large stones,

^a the fish gate, and an howling from the second, and
a great crashing from the hills.

^a 2 Chron. xxxiii. 14.

---

the east of the Holy Sepulchre (which lay consequently
outside the city) up to the judgment gate, but not north
of it.[1] The line from west to east, i.e. to the tower of
Antonia, is marked generally by "very large stones, evi-
dently of Jewish work, in the walls of houses, especially
in the lower parts."[2] They are chiefly in the line of the
Via Dolorosa.

The fish-gate had its name probably from a fish-market
(markets being in the open places near the gates [3]), the fish

boldly rusticated and arranged in a manner that reminded
me of the Phœnician work of the time of Solomon." (2) On
the east of the Church of the Resurrection. (3) "Close to
the west of the present *judgment gate.*" "In digging down
for the rock, I found, 18 feet below the surface, a fragment
of a wall, resembling, in all respects, that first described."
Ib. p. 33.

[1] This appeared from excavations made in repairing the
then Russian consulate, and from "inquiries of all who in
former years had built in this neighbourhood." Ib.

[2] "These were found when the Effendi Kadduti repaired
and partly rebuilt the house in the Via Dolorosa at the
Station of Veronica. A similar discovery was made by the
Mufti in strengthening his house at the *Station of Simon of
Cyrene,* and by the Effendi Soliman Giari, opposite to the
Mufti's house on the north. The Armenian Catholic monks
requested me to examine and level a piece of land, at the
Station of the first fall of Christ; which, as representative of
his nation, he had just bought. In the lower part of the wall
enclosing it on the north, very large stones and an ancient
gate were found. In the foundations of the Austrian hospice,
laid in 1857, to the north of the Armenian property, large
stones were discovered, and also further to the east, in the
new convent of the Daughters of Sion."—Pierotti, pp. 33, 34.

[3] See 2 Kings vii. 1 ; Neh. xiii. 16, 19.

being brought either from the Lake of Tiberias or from Joppa. Near it the wall ended which Manasseh, after his restoration from Babylon,[1] *built without the city of David, on the west side of Gihon, in the valley.* This, being unprotected by its situation, was the weakest part of the city. " The most ancient of the three walls could be considered as impregnable, as much on account of its extreme thickness as of the height of the mountain on which it was built, and the depths of the valleys at its base, and David, Solomon, and the other kings neglected nothing to place it in this stage." [2] Where they had made themselves strong, there God's judgment should find them.

And a howling from the second city, as it is supplied in Nehemiah, who mentions the perfect set over it.[3] It was here that Huldah the prophetess lived,[4] who prophesied the evils to come upon Jerusalem, after Josiah should be *gathered to* his *grave in peace.* It was probably the lower city, which was enclosed by the second wall. It was a second or new city, as compared to the original city of David, on Mount Moriah. On this the enemy who had penetrated by the fish-gate would first enter ; then take the strongest part of the city itself. Gareb[5] and Bezetha were outside of the then town ; they would then be already occupied by the enemy before entering the city.

A great crashing from the hills. These are probably Zion and Mount Moriah, on which the temple stood, and so the capture is described as complete. Here should be not a

---

[1] 2 Chron. xxxiii. 14.   [2] Jos. de B. J. v. 4, 2.

[3] Neh. xi. 9, E.V. " was second over the city " on account of the absence of the article, עַל הָעִיר מִשְׁנֶה. I prefer taking it as in a sort of apposition, as Ewald does, Lehrb. n. 287, l. p. 734, ed. 8.

[4] 2 Kings xxii. 14 ; 2 Chron. xxxiv. 22. It is called by Josephus ἄλλη, " another " city. Ant. xv. 11, 5.

[5] Jer. xxxi. 39.

a mortar

11 ^a Howl, ye inhabitants of ~~Maktesh~~, for all the

^a James v. 1.

cry or howling only, but an utter destruction.[1] Mount
Moriah was the seat of the worship of God; on Mount
Zion was the state, and the abode of the wealthy. In human
sight they were impregnable. The Jebusites mocked at
David's siege, as thinking their city impregnable;[2] but
God was with David and he took it. He and his successors
fortified it yet more, but its true defence was that *the Lord
was round about His people*,[3] and when He withdrew His
protection, then this natural strength was but their destruction, tempting them to resist first the Chaldeans then the
Romans. Human strength is but a great *crash*, falling by
its own weight and burying its owner. "This threefold
cry,[4] from three parts of the city, had a fulfilment before
the destruction by the Romans. In the lower part of the
city Simon tyrannised, and in the middle John raged, and
there was a great crashing from the hills, i.e. from the temple
and citadel where was Eleazar, who stained the very altar
of the temple with blood, and in the courts of the Lord
made a pool of blood of divers corpses." "In the assaults
of an enemy the inhabitants are ever wont to flee to the
tops of the hills, thinking that the difficulty of access will
be a hindrance to him, and will cut off the assaults of the
pursuers. But when God smiteth, and requireth of the
despisers the penalties of their sin, not the most towered
city nor impregnable circuits of walls, not height of hills,
or rough rocks, or pathless difficulty of ground, will avail to
the sufferers. Repentance alone saves, softening the Judge

[1] Not, as some, "a cry of destruction," as in Isa. xv. 5.
Isaiah has indeed the words זעקת שבר "cry of destruction," but here שבר, יללה, צעקה are plainly parallel to one
another.
[2] 2 Sam. v. 6.   [3] Ps. cxxv. 2.   [4] From Rup.

and allaying His wrath, and readily inviting the Creator
in His inherent goodness to His appropriate gentleness.
Better is it, with all our might to implore that we may not
offend Him.   But since human nature is prone to evil, and
in many things we all offend,[1] let us at least by repentance
invite to His wonted clemency the Lord of all, Who is by
nature kind." [2]

11. *Howl, ye inhabitants of Maktesh*, lit. *Mortar*,[3] "in
which," S. Jerome says, " corn is pounded ; a hollow vessel,
and fit for the use of medical men, in which properly ptisans
are wont to be beaten (or made).   Striking is it, that
Scripture saith not, ' who dwell in the valley or in the alley,'
but who *dwell in the mortar*, because as corn, when the pestle
striketh, is bruised, so the army of the enemy shall rush
down upon you." [4]   The place intended is probably so much
of the valley of the Tyropœon which intersected Jerusalem
from north to south, as was enclosed by the second wall,
on the north, and the first wall on the south.   The valley
" extended as far as the fountain of Siloam," [5] and united
with the valley of Jehoshaphat a little below Ophel.   It was
" full of houses," [6] and from its name as well as from its
situation it was probably the scene of petty merchandise,
where the occasions in which men could and did break the
law and offend God, were the more continual, because they
entered into their daily life, and were a part of it.   The
sound of the pestle was continually heard there ; another
sound should thereafter be heard, when they should not
bruise, but be themselves bruised.   The name *Maktesh* was
probably chosen to express how their false hopes, grounded

---

[1] S. James iii. 2.   [2] S. Cyr.
[3] Prov. xxvii. 22.   It is also a proper name in Judges xv. 19,
since Lehi, in which it was situate (אשר בלחי), was a proper
name.   Ib. and 9, and 14.
[4] S. Jer.   [5] See Signor Pierotti's map.
[6] Jos. B. J. v. 4, 1.

merchant people are cut down ; all they that bear
silver are cut off.

---

on the presence of God's temple among them while by their
sins they profaned it, should be turned into true fears.
They had been and thought themselves *Mikdash*, " a holy
place, sanctuary " ; they should be *Maktesh*,[1] wherein all
should be utterly bruised in pieces.

" Whoso considereth the calamities of that siege, and
how the city was pressed and hemmed in, will feel how
aptly he calls them *the inhabitants of a mortar ;* for, as grains
of corn are brought together into a mortar, to the end that,
when the pestle descendeth, being unable to fly off, they
may be bruised, so the people flowing together, out of all
the countries of Judæa, was narrowed in by a sudden siege,
and through the savage cruelty of the above leaders of the
sedition, was unutterably tortured from within, more than
by the enemy without." [2]

For all the merchant people [lit. *the people of Canaan*] *are
cut down ;* i.e. " they who in deeds are like the people of
Canaan," [3] according to that, *Thou art of Canaan and not
of Judah*,[4] and *Thy father is an Amorite and thy mother a
Hittite*.[5] So our Lord says to the reprobate Jews, *Ye are
of your father the devil.*[6]

All they that bear [lit. *all laden with*[7]] *silver are cut off.*
The silver, wherewith they *lade* themselves, being gotten
amiss, is a load upon them, weighing them down until they
are destroyed.

[1] The two words do so occur in an epistle of the Samaritans
(Cellar. Epist. Sichemit. p. 25), Ges.

[2] S. Jer.   [3] Ch.   [4] Hist. of Susannah, 56.

[5] Ezek. xvi. 3. See also on Hosea xii. 7.

[6] S. John viii. 44.

[7] A passive adj. (קְטִיל from קָטוּל). As an act. adj. (קְטִיל
from קָטֵל) it would rather imply that they cast it on others.

12 And it shall come to pass at that time, *that* I
will search Jerusalem with candles, and punish the

---

12. *I will search* [lit. *diligently*]. The word is always
used of a minute diligent search, whereby places, persons,
things, are searched and sifted one by one in every corner,
until it be found whether a thing be there or no.[1] Hence
also of the searching out of every thought of the heart,
either by God,[2] or in repentance by the light of God.[3]

Jerusalem with candles : so that there should be no corner,
no lurking-place so dark, but that the guilty should be
brought to light. The same diligence, which Eternal
Wisdom used, to *seek and to save that which was lost,* [4] *light-
ing a candle and searching diligently,* till It find each lost
piece of silver, the same shall Almighty God use that no
hardened sinner shall escape. "What the enemy would
do, using unmingled frenzy against the conquered, that
God fitteth to His own Person, not as being Himself the
Doer of things so foreign, but rather permitting that what
comes from anger should proceed in judgment against the
ungodly." [5] It was an image of this, when, at the taking of
Jerusalem by the Romans, they " dragged out of common
sewers and holes and caves and tombs, princes and great
men and priests, who for fear of death had hid themselves." [6] How much more in that day when *the secrets of
all hearts shall be revealed* by Him Who [7] *searcheth the hearts*

[1] Nif., of Esau by enemies Obad. 6, Pih., for Laban's idols,
Gen. xxxi. 35 ; for Joseph's cup, ib. xliv. 12 ; for David in
hiding places, 1 Sam. xxiii. 23 ; Ahab's house, 1 Kings xx. 6 ;
for worshippers of God in Baal's temple, 2 Kings x. 23 ; in
caves of Carmel, Amos ix. 3 ; Divine wisdom, Prov. ii. 4 ;
God's ways, Ps. lxxvii. 2. The form is intensive here.

[2] Prov. xx. 27.   [3] Lam. iii. 40.   [4] S. Luke xv. 8.

[5] S. Cyr.   [6] S. Jer.   See Jos. de B. J. vi. 9, 4 ; vii. 2 fin.

[7] Ps. vii. 9 ; xxvi. 2 ; Jer. xi. 20 ; xvii. 10 ; xx. 12 ;
Rev. ii. 23.

become as refuse of wine

men that are * ᵃ settled on their lees : ᵇ that say in

* Heb. *curded*, or, *thickened*.

ᵃ Jer. xlviii. 11 ; Amos vi. 1.   ᵇ Ps. xciv. 7.

---

and reins, and to Whose Eyes,[1] *which are like flaming Fire,
all things are naked and open!*   The *candles* wherewith
God searcheth the heart, are men's own consciences,[2] His
Own revealed word,[3] the lives of true Christians.[4] These,
through the Holy Ghost in each, may enlighten the heart of
man, or, if he takes not heed, will rise in judgment against
him, and show the falsehood of all vain excuses. "One
way of escape only there is. If we judge ourselves, we
shall not be judged. I will *search out my* own *ways* and
my desires, that He Who *shall search out Jerusalem with
candles,* may find nothing in me, unsought and unsifted.
For He will not twice judge the same thing. Would that
I might so follow and track out all my offences, that in
none I need fear His piercing Eyes, in none be ashamed at
the light of His candles! Now I am seen, but I see not.
At hand is that Eye to Whom all things are open, although
Itself is not open. Once *I shall know, even as I am known.*[5]
Now *I know in part,* but I am not known in part, but
wholly."[6]

The men that are settled on their lees, stiffened and contracted.[7] The image is from wine which becomes harsh,

[1] Rev. i. 14.   [2] Prov. xx. 27.
[3] Ps. cxix. 105; Prov. vi. 23 ; 2 Peter i. 19.
[4] Phil. ii. 15.
[5] 1 Cor. xiii. 12.
[6] S. Bern. Serm. 55 in Cant.
[7] קפא is used in two cases of the (as it were) congealing
of the waves when they *stood on an heap,* Exod. xv. 8 ; of
the curdling into cheese, Job x. 10.   Jon. paraphrases "who
are tranquil in their possessions."   The Arabic authorities,
Abulw. Tanch. David B. Abr. agree in the sense "congealed,"

if allowed to remain upon the lees, unremoved. It is drawn out by Jeremiah,[1] *Moab hath been at ease [2]from his youth, and he hath settled on his lees, and hath not been emptied from vessel to vessel, neither hath he gone into captivity; therefore his taste remained in him, and his scent is not changed.* So they upon whom *no changes come, fear not God.*[3] The lees are the refuse of the wine, yet stored up (so the word[4] means) with it, and the wine rests, as it were, upon them. So do men of ease rest in things defiled and defiling, their riches or their pleasure, which they hoard up, on which they are bent, so that they "lift not their mind to things above, but, darkened with foulest desires, are hardened and stiffened in sin."[5]

That say in their heart, not openly scoffing, perhaps thinking that they believe; but people *do* believe as they love. Their most inward belief, the belief of their heart and affections, what they wish, and the hidden spring of their actions, is, *The Lord will not do good, neither will He do evil.* They act as believing so, and by acting inure themselves to believe it. They think of God as far away, *Is not God in the height of heaven? And behold the height of the stars, how high they are! And thou sayest, How doth God know? Can He judge through the dark cloud? Thick clouds are a covering to Him, that He seeth not; and He walketh in the circuit of heaven.*[6] *The ungodly in the pride of his heart* (thinketh): *He will not inquire; all his devices* (speak), *There is no God. Strong are his ways at all times; on high are Thy judgments out of his sight.*[7] *They slay the widow and the*

---

and do not call in the Arab. פַק which is primarily " dried," then is used of the wrinkling of a cloth in drying, or of the face of the old, not " contracted," as Ges. On Zech. xiv. 6, see ibid.

[1] Jer. xlviii. 11.   [2] שָׁקַט.
[3] See Ps. lv. 19.   [4] שְׁמָרִים.
[5] Dion.   [6] Job xxii. 12–14.   [7] Ps. x. 4, 5.

their heart, The LORD will not do good, neither will
he do evil.

---

*stranger, and murder the fatherless, and they say, The Lord
shall not see, neither shall the God of Jacob regard it.*[1] *Such
things they did imagine and were deceived; for their own
wickedness blinded them. As for the mysteries of God, they
knew them not.*[2] *Faith without works is dead.*[3] Faith which
acts not dies out, and there comes in its stead this other
persuasion, that God will not repay. There are more
Atheists than believe themselves to be such. These act
as if there were no Judge of their deeds, and at last come
themselves to believe that God will not punish.[4] What
else is the thought of all worldlings, of all who make idols
to themselves of any pleasure or gain or ambition, but,
"God will not punish"? "God cannot punish the
[wrongful, selfish] indulgence of the nature which He has
made." "God will not be so precise." "God will not
punish with everlasting severance from Him, the sins of
this short life." And they see not that they ascribe to
God, what He attributes to idols, i.e. not-gods. *Do good or
do evil that we may be dismayed and behold it together.*[5] *Be not
afraid of them; for they cannot do evil, neither also is it in
them to do good.*[6] These think not that God does good; for
they ascribe their success to their own diligence, wisdom,
strength, and thank not God for it. They think not that
He sends them evil. For they defy Him and His laws,
and think that they shall go unpunished. What remains
but that He should be as dumb an idol as those of the
heathen?

[1] Ps. xciv. 5, 6.　　　　　[2] Wisd. ii. 21–22.
[3] S. James ii. 20.　　　　　[4] Isa. v. 19; Mal. ii. 17.
[5] Isa. xli. 23. Perhaps Zeph. meant to suggest this by
using words which God by Isaiah had used of idols.
[6] Jer. x. 5.

13 Therefore their goods shall become a booty,
and their houses a desolation : they shall also build

---

13. *Therefore their goods,* lit. *And their strength.* It is the
simple sequel in God's Providence. It is a continued
narrative. God will visit those who say, that God does
not interfere in man's affairs, *and,* it shall be seen *whose
words shall stand,*[1] God's *or their's.* All which God had
threatened in the law shall be fulfilled. God, in the fulfilment of the punishment, which He had foretold in the
law,[2] would vindicate not only His present Providence, but
His continual government of His own world. All which is
strength to man, shall the rather fail, because it is strength,
and they presume on it and it deceives them. Its one end
is to *become a prey* of devils. Riches, learning, rule, influence, power, bodily strength, genius, eloquence, popular
favour, shall all fail a man, and he, when stripped of them,
shall be the more bared because he gathered them around
him. " Wealth is ever a runaway and has no stability, but
rather intoxicates and inclines to revolt and has unsteady
feet. Exceeding folly is it to think much of it. For it
will not rescue those lying under the Divine displeasure,
nor will it free any from guilt, when God decreeth punishment, and bringeth the judgment befitting on the trans-
gressors. How utterly useless this eagerness after wealth
is to the ungodly, he teacheth, saying, that *their strength
shall be a prey* to the Chaldean." [3]

And their houses a desolation. " For they are, of whom
it may be said very truly, *This is the man that took not God
for his strength, but trusted unto the multitude of his riches, and
strengthened himself in his wickedness.*[4] But if indeed their
houses are adorned costily, they shall not be theirs, for

---

[1] Jer. xliv. 28.   [2] Lev. xxvi. 32, 33; Deut. xxviii. 15 to end.
[3] S. Cyr.   [4] Ps. lii. 7.

E

houses, ^a but not inhabit *them ;* and they shall plant
vineyards, but ^b not drink the wine thereof.

a Deut. xxviii. 30, 39 ; Amos v. 11.　　b Micah vi. 15.

they shall be burned, and themselves go into captivity,
leaving all in their house, and deprived of all which would
gladden.　And this God said clearly to the king of Judah
by Jeremiah,[1] *Thou hast builded thyself a large house and wide
chambers, ceiled with cedar, and painted with vermilion.　Shalt
thou reign because thou closest thyself in cedar ?"* [2]　"As
the house of the body is the bodily dwelling, so to each
mind its house is that, wherein through desire it is wont to
dwell,"[3] and *desolate* shall they be, being severed for ever
from the things they desired, and for ever deserted by
God.　*They shall also build houses but not inhabit them,* as the
rich man said to his soul, *Soul, thou hast much goods laid up
for many years.—Thou fool, this night thy soul shall be required of thee ; then whose shall those things be, which thou hast
provided ?* [4]　Before the siege by the Romans, Jerusalem
and the temple had been greatly beautified, only to be
destroyed.　*And they shall plant vineyards, but not drink the
wine thereof.*　This is the woe, first pronounced in the law,[5]
often repeated and ever found true.　Wickedness makes
joy its end, yet never finds it, seeking it where it is not,
out of God.

14. *The great Day of the Lord is near.*　The Prophet again
expands the words of Joel, accumulating words expressive
of the terrors of that Day, showing that though [6]*the great
and very terrible Day of the Lord, a day* (Joel had said[7]) *of
darkness and gloominess, of clouds and of thick darkness,* which
was then *coming* and *nigh at hand,*[8] had come and was gone,

1 Jer. xxii. 14, 15.　　　　2 S. Cyr.
3 S. Greg. Mor. viii. 14.　　4 S. Luke xii. 19, 20.
5 Deut. xxviii. 39.　　　　6 Joel ii. 31.
7 Ib. ii. 2.　　　　　　　8 Ib. ii. 1.

14 ^a The great day of the LORD *is* near, *it is*

it was only a forerunner of others; none of them final; but each, because it *was* a judgment and an instance of the justice of God, an earnest and forerunner of other judgments to the end. Again, *a great Day of the Lord* was *near*. This *Day* had itself, so to speak, many hours and divisions of the day. But each hour tolleth the same knell of approaching doom. Each calamity in the miserable reigns of the sons of Josiah was one stroke in the passing-bell, until the destruction of Jerusalem by the Chaldeans for the time closed it. The judgment was complete. The completeness of that excision made it the more an image of every other like day until the final destruction of all which, although around or near to Christ, shall in the Great Day be found not to be His, but to have rejected Him. "Truly was vengeance required, *from the blood of righteous Abel to the blood of Zechariah, whom they slew between the temple and the Altar*,[1] and at last when they said of the Son of God, *His blood be upon us and upon our children*,[2] they experienced a bitter day, because they had provoked the Lord to bitterness; a Day, appointed by the Lord, in which not the weak only but the mighty shall be bowed down, and wrath shall come upon them to the end. For often before they endured the wrath of the Lord, but that wrath was not to the uttermost. What need now to describe how great calamities they endured in both captivities, and how they who rejected the light of the Lord, walked in darkness and thick darkness, and they who would not hear the trumpet of the solemn feast-days, heard the shout of the enemy. But of the *fenced cities* and *lofty corner-towers* of Judæa, which are till now destroyed even to the ground, the eyes, I deem, can judge better than the ears. We

[1] S. Matt. xxiii. 35.   [2] Ib. xxvii. 25.

near, and hasteth greatly, *even* the voice of the

---

especially, now living in that province, can see, can prove
what is written. We scarcely discern slight traces of ruins
of what once were great cities. At Shiloh, where was the
tabernacle and ark of the testament of the Lord, scarcely
the foundations of the altar are shown. Rama and Bethoron
and the other noble cities built by Solomon, are shown to
be little villages. Let us read Josephus and the prophecy
of Zephaniah ; we shall see his history before our eyes.
And this must be said not only of the captivity, but even
to the present day. The treacherous husbandmen, having
slain the servants, and, at last, the Son of God, are prevented from entering Jerusalem, except to wail, and they
purchase at a price leave to weep the ruin of their city, so
that they who once bought the Blood of Christ, buy their
tears ; not even their tears are costless. You may see on
the day that Jerusalem was taken and destroyed by the
Romans, a people in mourning come, decrepit old women
and old men, in aged and ragged wretchedness, showing in
their bodies and in their guise the wrath of the Lord. The
hapless crowd is gathered, and amid the gleaming of the
Cross of Christ, and the radiant glory of His Resurrection,
the standard also of the Cross shining from Mount Olivet,
you may see the people, piteous but unpitied, bewail the
ruins of their temple, tears still on their cheeks, their arms
livid and their hair dishevelled, and the soldier asketh a
guerdon, that they may be allowed to weep longer. And
doth any, when he seeth this, doubt of the *day of trouble*
and distress, the day of darkness and gloominess, the day of
clouds and thick darkness, the day of the trumpet and alarm?
For they have also trumpets in their sorrow, and, according
to the prophecy, the voice of *the solemn feast-day is turned*
into mourning. They wail over the ashes of the Sanctuary
and the altar destroyed, and over cities once fenced, and

day of the LORD : the mighty man shall cry there
bitterly.

---

over the high towers of the temple, from which they once
cast headlong James the brother of the Lord." [1]

But referring the Day of the Lord to the end of the
world or the close of the life of each, it too is *near; near,*
the Prophet adds to impress the more its nearness ; for it
is at hand to each ; and when eternity shall come, all time
shall seem like a moment, *A thousand years, when past, are
like a watch in the night;* [2] one fourth part of one night.

And hasteth greatly. For time whirls on more rapidly to
each, year by year, and when God's judgments draw near,
the tokens of them thicken, and troubles sweep one over
the other, events jostle against each other. *The voice of the
day of the Lord.* That Day, when it cometh, shall leave no
one in doubt what it meaneth ; it shall give no *uncertain
sound,* but shall, trumpet-tongued, proclaim the holiness
and justice of Almighty God; its voice shall be the Voice
of Christ, which *all that are in the graves shall hear and
come forth; they that have done good, unto the resurrection of
life; and they that have done evil unto the resurrection of
damnation.* [3]

The mighty men shall cry there bitterly; for *bitter is the
remembrance of death to a man that liveth at rest in his possessions, unto the man that hath nothing to vex him, and that hath
prosperity in all things;* [4] and, *There is no mighty man that
hath power over the spirit to retain the spirit; neither hath he
power in the day of death; and there is no discharge in that
war; neither shall wickedness deliver those that are given to it.* [5]
Rather, wrath shall come upon *the kings* of the earth, *and the
great men and the rich men and the mighty men, and* they shall

---

[1] S. Jer.   [2] Ps. xc. 4.   [3] S. John v. 28, 29.
        [4] Ecclus. xli. 1.   [5] Eccl. viii. 8.

15 *b* That day *is* a day of wrath, a day of trouble
and distress, a day of wasteness and desolation, a
day of darkness and gloominess, a day of clouds and
thick darkness,

ª Isa. xxii. 5 ; Jer. xxx. 7 ; Joel ii. 2, 11 ; Amos v. 18 ;
ver. 18.

---

will to *hide* themselves *from the Face of Him that sitteth on
the Throne and from the wrath of the Lamb ; for the great Day
of His wrath is come : and who shall be able to stand ?* [1]

The mighty man shall cry there bitterly. The Prophet has
spoken of time, *the day of the Lord.* He points out the more
vividly the unseen sight and place, *there ;* so David says,
There they feared a fear. [2] He sees the place ; he hears the
bitter cry. So nigh is it in fact ; so close the connection of
cause and effect, of sin and punishment. There shall be a
great and *bitter cry,* when there shall be no place for repentance. It shall be a [3] mighty cry, but mighty in the
bitterness of its distress. *Mighty men shall be mightily
tormented,* [4] i.e. those who have been mighty against God,
weak against Satan, and shall have used their might in
his service.

15. *A day of wrath,* in which all the wrath of Almighty
God, which evil angels and evil men have treasured to them
for that day, shall be poured out : *the* day of wrath, because
then they shall be brought face to face before the Presence
of God, but thenceforth they shall be cast out of it for
ever.

A day of trouble and distress. Both words express, how
anguish shall narrow and hem them in ; so that there shall

[1] Rev. vi. 15–17.　　　　　　[2] Ps. xiv. 5.
[3] The Arab. word, צרח, is used of " a loud shrill cry."
It occurs only here and (Hif.) in Isa. xlii. 13.
[4] Wisd. vi. 6.

16 A day of [a] the trumpet and alarm against the fenced cities, and against the high towers.

[a] Jer. iv. 19.

---

be no escape ; above them, God displeased ; below, the flames of Hell ; around, devils to drag them away, and Angels casting them forth *in bundles to burn them;* without, *the books* which *shall be opened;* and within, conscience leaving them no escape.

A day of wasteness and desolation, in which all things shall return to their primeval void, before *the Spirit of God brooded upon the face of the waters,* His Presence being altogether withdrawn.

A day of darkness and gloominess; for sun and moon shall lose their brightness, and no brightness from the Lamb shall shine upon the wicked, but they shall be driven into *outer darkness.*

A day of clouds and thick darkness, hiding from them the Face of the Sun of Righteousness, and covering Him, so that their *prayers* should *not pass through.*[1]

16. *A day of the trumpet and alarm,*[2] i.e. of the loud blast of the trumpet, which sounds alarm and causes it. The word[3] is especially the shrill loud noise of the trumpet (for sacred purposes in Israel itself, as ruling all the movements of the tabernacle and accompanying their feast); then also of the "battle-cry." They had not listened to the voice of the trumpet, as it called them to holy service ; now they shall hear *the voice of the Archangel and the trump of God.*[4]

Against the high towers, lit. *corners,*[5] and so *corner-towers.*

---

[1] Lam. iii. 44.

[2] " Alarm " seems to be used in the sense of " sounding alarm," alarum.

[3] תרועה.   [4] 1 Thess. iv. 16.

[5] See E.M. on iii. 6. It is the *corner* of a house, of a street, of a court, a city. Hence " the gate of the corner," 2 Kings

17 And I will bring distress upon men, that they shall ^a walk like blind men, because they have sinned against the Lord : and ^b their blood shall be poured out as dust, and their flesh ^c as the dung.

^a Deut. xxviii. 29 ; Isa. lix. 10.   ^b Ps. lxxix. 3.
^c Ps. lxxxiii. 10 ; Jer. ix. 22 and xvi. 4.

This peculiarity describes Jerusalem, whose walls "were made artificially standing in a line curved inwards, so that the flanks of assailants might be exposed."[1] By this same name[2] are called the mighty men and chiefs of the people, who, humanly speaking, hold it together and support it; on these chiefs in rebellion against God, whether devils or evil men, shall punishment greatly fall.

17. *I will bring distress upon men.* I will hem them in, in anguish on all sides. God Himself shall meet them with His terrors, wherever they turn. *I will hem them in, that they may find it so.*[3]

That they shall walk like blind men, utterly bereft of counsel, seeing no more than the blind which way to turn, grasping blindly and frantically at anything, and *going on* headlong to their own destruction. So God forewarned them in the law: *Thou shalt grope at noon day, as the blind gropeth in darkness;*[4] and Job, of the wicked generally, *They meet with the darkness in the day-time, and grope in the noon-day as in the night;*[5] and, *They grope in the dark without light,*

xiv. 13 ; 2 Chron. xxvi. 9 ; Jer. xxxi. 38. In 2 Chron. xxvi. 15, פנות cannot be "battlements" (as Ges., &c)., since the engines were erected upon them. Neither then here is there any ground to invent a new meaning for the word.

[1] Tac. Hist. v. 11 ; Jos. de B. J. v. 5, 3.

[2] Judges xx. 2 ; 1 Sam. xiv. 38 ; Isa. xix. 13 ; Zech. x. 4.

[3] Jer. x. 18. Moses had said this of His instruments, *And He shall hem thee in, in all thy gates.* Deut. xxviii. 52.

[4] Deut. xxviii. 29.   [5] Job v. 14.

18 [a] Neither their silver nor their gold shall be able to deliver them in the day of the LORD's wrath ;

[a] Prov. xi. 4 ; Ezek. vii. 19.

---

and He maketh them to stagger like a drunken man ; [1] and Isaiah foretelling of those times, *We grope for the wall, as the blind ; and we grope, as if we had no eyes ; we stumble in the noon-day as in the night.* [2] *Because they have sinned against the Lord,* and so He hath turned their wisdom into foolishness, and since they have despised Him, He hath made them objects of contempt. [3] *Their blood shall be poured out like dust,* as abundant and as valueless ; utterly disregarded by Him, as Asaph complains, *their blood have they shed like water ;* [4] contemptible and disgusting as what is vilest ; *their flesh* [5] *as the dung,* refuse, decayed, putrefied, offensive, enriching by its decay the land, which had been the scene of their luxuries and oppressions. Yet the most offensive, disgusting, physical corruption is but a faint image of the defilement of sin. This punishment, in which the carrion-remains should be entombed only in the bowels of vultures and dogs, was especially threatened to Jehoiakim : *He shall be buried with the burial of an ass, dragged and cast forth beyond the gates of Jerusalem.* [6]

18. *Neither their silver nor their gold shall be able to deliver them in the day of the Lord's wrath.* Gain unjustly gotten was the cause of their destruction. For, as Ezekiel closes

---

[1] Job xii. 25.   [2] Isa. lix. 10.   [3] 1 Sam. ii. 30.

[4] Ps. lxxix. 3. שָׁפַךְ is used of the pouring out both liquids and solids.

[5] Insulated as the use is, לְחוּם must have had the meaning of the Arab. לָחְמَ "flesh." So LXX Ch. Vulg. Syr. David B. Abr. Abulw. Tanch., Anon-Arab. Tr., retain the word in Arabic ; Abulw. notices that "the Heb. is akin to the Arabic word." Tanch. cites Job vi. 7.

[6] Jer. xxii. 19.

but the whole land shall be [a] devoured by the fire
of his jealousy : for [b] he shall make even a speedy
riddance of all them that dwell in the land.

[a] Zeph. iii. 8.　　　　　　　　[b] Ver. 2, 3.

the like description : "They shall cast their silver into the
streets, and their gold shall be removed ; their silver and
their gold shall not be able to deliver them in the day of
the wrath of the Lord ; they shall not satisfy their souls
nor fill their bowels : *because it is the stumbling block of their
iniquity*." [1]　Much less shall any possession, outward or inward, be of avail in the Great Day ; since in death the rich
man's *pomp shall not follow him,* [2] and every gift which he
has misused, whether of mind or spirit, even the knowledge
of God without doing His Will, shall but increase damnation.　"Sinners will then have nothing but their sins."

Here the Prophet uses images belonging more to the immediate destruction ; at the close the words again widen,
and belong, in their fullest literal sense, to the Day of
Judgment.　*The whole land,* rather, as at the beginning, *the
whole earth shall be devoured by the fire of His jealousy ; for He
shall make even a speedy riddance of all them that dwell in the
land :* rather, *He shall make an utter, yea altogether* [3] *a terrific
destruction* [4] *of all the dwellers of the earth.*　What Nahum had
foretold of Nineveh, [5] *He shall make the place thereof an utter
consumption,* that Zephaniah foretells of all the inhabitants of the world.　For what is this, *the whole earth shall be*

[1] Ezek. vii. 19.　　　　　　　　[2] Ps. xlix. 17.

[3] אַךְ "nothing but."

[4] נְבְהָלָה unites here the senses of terror and destruction,
as in Ps. civ. 29, *Thou hidest Thy face, they are troubled,*
יִבָּהֵלוּן *and perish* ; Isa. lxv. 23, *they shall not bear* לַבֶּהָלָה for
destruction, ‖ לֹא יִגְעוּ לְרִיק.

[5] See on Nahum i. 8.

CHAPTER II

1 *An exhortation to repentance.* 4 *The judgment of the Philistines,* 8 *of Moab and Ammon,* 12 *of Ethiopia and Assyria.*

[a] GATHER yourselves together, yea, gather together, O nation * not desired ;

[a] Joel ii. 16.   * Or, not desirous.

---

devoured by the fire of His jealousy, but what S. Peter says, *The earth also and the works that are therein shall be burned up ?* [1] And what is that he says, *He shall make all the dwellers of the earth an utter, yea altogether a hasty destruction,* but a general judgment of all, who belong to the world, whose home, citizenship, whose whole mind is in the world, not as true Christians, who are strangers and pilgrims here, and their *citizenship is in Heaven ?* [2] These God shall make an utter, terrific, speedy destruction, a living death, so that they shall at once both be and not be ; be, as continued in being ; not be, as having no life of God, but only a continued death in misery. And this shall be through the jealousy of Almighty God, that Divine quality in Him, whereby He loves and wills to be loved, and endures not those who give to others the love for which He gave so much and which is so wholly due to Himself Alone. "Thou demandest my love, and if I give it not, art wroth with me, and threatenest me with grievous woes. Is it then a slight woe to love Thee not ? " [3] What will be that anger, which is Infinite Love, but which becomes, through man's sin, Hate ?

CHAP. II.—Having set forth the terrors of the Judgment Day, the Prophet adds an earnest call to repent-

[1] 2 Peter iii. 10.   [2] Heb. xi. 13 ; Phil. iii. 20.
[3] S. Aug. Conf. i. 5, p. 3, Oxf. Tr.

ance ; and then declares how judgments, forerunners of that Day, shall fall, one by one, on those nations around, who know not God, and shall rest upon Nineveh, the great beautiful ancient city of the world. " See the mercy of God. It had been enough to have set before the wise the vehemence of the coming evil. But because He willeth not to punish, but to alarm only, Himself calleth to repentance, that He may not do what He threatened." [1]   " Having set forth clearly the savageness of the war and the greatness of the suffering to come, he suitably turns his discourse to the duty of calling to repentance, when it was easy to persuade them, being terrified. For sometimes when the mind has been numbed, and exceedingly bent to evil, we do not readily admit even the will to repent, but fear often drives us to it, even against our will. He calls us then to friendship with Himself. For as they revolted, became aliens, serving idols and giving up their mind to their passions, so they would, as it were, retrace their steps, and lay hold of the friendship of God, choosing to serve Him, nay and Him Alone, and obey His commandments. Wherefore while we have time, while the Lord, in His forbearance as God, gives way, let us enact repentance, supplicate, say weeping, *Remember not the sins and offences of my youth ;* [2] let us unite ourselves with Him by sanctification and sobriety. So shall we be sheltered in the day of wrath, and wash away the stain of our falls, before the Day of the Lord come upon us. For the Judge will come, He will come from heaven at the due season, and will reward each according to his work." [3]

1. *Gather yourselves together, yea, gather together,* [4] rather,

---

[1] S. Jer.   [2] Ps. xxv. 7.   [3] S. Cyr.

[4] The Eng. Vers. follows the LXX Ch. Syr., S. Jer., which render " Gather yourselves together," as if, from the first meaning, " gather dry sticks or stubble," it came to signify " gather " generally, and thence, in the reflective form, " gather yourselves together."

Sift yourselves, yea sift.[1] The exact image is from gathering
stubble or dry sticks, which are picked up one by one,
with search and care. So must men deal with the dry and
withered leaves of a past evil life. The English rendering,
however, comes to the same meaning. We use "collect
one's self," for bringing one's self, all one's thoughts, together, and so, having full possession of one's self. Or
gathering ourselves might stand in contrast with being
"abroad," as it were, out of ourselves amid the manifoldness of things seen. "Thou who, taken up with the
business of the world, hurriest to and fro amid divers
things, return to the Church of the saints, and join thyself
to their life and assembly, whom thou seest to please God,
and bring together the dislocated members of thy soul,
which now are not knit together, into one frame of wisdom,
and cleave to its embrace." [2] *Gather yourselves* into one,
wherein ye have been scattered; to the One God, from
Whom they had wandered, seeking pleasure from His many
creatures; to His one fold and Church, from which they
had severed themselves outwardly by joining the worship
of Baal, inwardly, by serving him and his abominable rites ;
joining and joined to the assembly of the faithful, by
oneness of faith and life.

In order to repent, a man must know himself thoroughly ;
and this can only be done by taking act by act, word by
word, thought by thought, as far as he can, not in a con-

[1] The word is first used of gathering dry stubble together
(Exod. v. 7, 12), then of "dry sticks" one by one (Num.
xv. 32, 33 ; 1 Kings xvii. 10, 12). A heathen speaks of
"gathering out thorns" (ἐξακανθίζειν), i.e. minutely examining and bringing out to light every fault. (Cic. ad Att.
vi. 6, 2.) And another writes to his steward, "Shalt thou
with stronger hand pull out thorns from my field, or I from
my mind ? " Hor. Ep. i. 14, 4.

[2] S. Jer.

fused heap or mass, as they lie in any man's conscience, but
one by one, each picked up apart, and examined, and added
to the sear unfruitful heap, plucking them as it were, and
gathering them out of himself, that so they may, by the
Spirit of burning, the fire of God's Spirit kindling repentance, be burned up, and not the sinner himself be fuel for
fire with them. The word too is intensive, "Gather together all which is in you, thoroughly, piece by piece" (for
the sinner's whole self becomes chaff, dry and empty). To
use another image, "Sift yourselves thoroughly, so that
nothing escape, as far as your diligence can reach, and then
—*And gather on*, i.e. "glean on"; examine yourselves, "not
lightly and after the manner of dissemblers before God,"
but repeatedly, gleaning again and again, to see if by any
means anything have escaped : continuing on the search
and ceasing not. The first earnest search into the soul
must be the beginning, not the end. Our search must be
continued, until there be no more to be discovered, i.e.
when sin is no more, and we see ourselves in the full light
of the Presence of our Judge. For a first search, however
diligent, never thoroughly reaches the whole deep disease
of the whole man ; the most grievous sins hide other
grievous sins, though lighter. Some sins flash on the conscience at one time, some at another ; so that few, even
upon a diligent search, come at once to the knowledge of
all their heaviest sins. When the mist is less thick, we
see more clearly what was before one dark dull mass of
imperfection and misery. "Spiritual sins are also with
difficulty sifted (as they are) by one who is carnal.
Whence it happens, that things in themselves heavier he
perceives less or very little, and conscience is not grieved
so much by the memory of pride or envy, as of impurities
and crimes." [1] So having said, "Sift yourselves through

[1] S. Bern. de Cons. c. 5.

and through," he says, "sift on." A diligent sifting and
search into himself must be the beginning of all true repentance and pardon. "What remains, but that we give
ourselves wholly to this work, so holy, and needful? *Let
us search and try our ways and our doings*,[1] and let each
think that he has made progress, not if he find not what
to blame, but if he blame what he finds. Thou hast not
sifted thyself in vain, if thou hast discovered that thou
needest a fresh sifting; and so often has thy search not
failed thee, as thou judgest that it must be renewed. But
if thou ever dost this, when there is need, thou dost it
ever. But ever remember that thou needest help from
above and the mercy of Jesus Christ our Lord Who is over
all, God blessed for ever."[2] The whole course of self-
examination then lies in two words of Divine Scripture.
And withal he warns them, instead of gathering together
riches which shall *not be able to deliver them in the day of
trouble*, to gather themselves into themselves, and so *judge
themselves thoroughly*,[3] *that they be not judged of the Lord*.[4]

O nation not desired,[5] i.e. having nothing in itself to be

---

[1] Lam. iii. 40. The two words, *search* and *try*, חפר, חקר
are both used of a deep search of a thing which lies deep
and hidden. Both originally mean "dig." Both are used
of a Divine knowledge of the inmost soul; the former of
the mind as enlightened by God (Prov. xx. 27), the latter of
God's searching it out Himself (Jer. xvii. 10; Ps. xliv. 21;
cxxxix. 1; Job xiii. 9), and of the Divine Wisdom (Job
xxviii. 27).

[2] Id. Serm. 58, in Cant. fin.

[3] διακρίνατε, which answers to the intensive form here,
"judge yourselves through and through."

[4] 1 Cor. xi. 31, 32.

[5] The E.M. has "or not desirous," the word נכסף
signifying to long, Gen. xxxi. 30; Ps. lxxxiv. 2. But in both
places the object of desire is mentioned, "thy father's house,"
in Gen., "the courts of the Lord" in the Ps. Israel had

2 Before the decree bring forth, *before* the day
pass ᵃ as the chaff, before ᵇ the fierce anger of the
LORD come upon you, before the day of the LORD's
anger come upon you.

ᵃ Job xxi. 18 ; Ps. i. 4 ; Isa. xvii. 13 ; Hosea xiii. 3.
ᵇ 2 Kings xxiii. 26.

---

desired or loved, but rather, for its sin, hateful to God.
God yearneth with pity and compassion over His creatures ;
He *hath a desire to the work of His Hands.*[1] Here Israel is
spoken to, as what he had made himself, hateful to God
by his sins, although still an object of His tender care, in
what yet remained to him of nature or grace which was
from Himself.

2. *Before the decree bring forth.* God's word is full (as it
were) of the event which it foretelleth ; it contains its own
fulfilment in itself, and *travaileth* until it come to pass,
giving signs of its coming, yet delaying until the full time.
Time is said to bring forth what is wrought in it. *Thou
knowest not what a day shall bring forth.*

Before the day pass as the chaff, or, parenthetically, *like
chaff the day passeth by.* God's counsels lie wrapt up, as it
were, in the womb of time, wherein He hides them, until
the moment which He has appointed, and they break forth

strong but bad longings. "Not desirous" would not by
itself convey, "having no desire to return to God," or as Ch.,
"who willeth not to return to the law." The same objection
lies, over and above, to the rendering "unashamed," coll.
Chald. כסף "turned pale" from shame, disgrace, horror.
Buxt. For there is nothing to limit the "turning pale" to
"shame." The root כסף in Heb. only means "longed,"
Ps. xvii. 12 ; Job xiv. 15, of which נכסף is here the
passive. People turn pale from fear or horror, not from
shame.

[1] Job xiv. 15. The word is the same.

3 ^a Seek ye the LORD, ^b all ye meek of the earth,

       ^a Ps. cv. 4 ; Amos v. 6.   ^b Ps. lxxvi. 9.

---

suddenly to those who look not for them. The mean
season is given for repentance, i.e. the day of grace, the
span of repentance still allowed, which is continually whirl-
ing more swiftly by; and woe if it be fruitless as chaff!
Those who profit not by it shall also be as chaff, carried
away pitilessly by the whirlwind to destruction. Time, on
which eternity hangs, is a slight, uncertain thing, as little
to be counted upon, as the light dry particles which are the
sport of the wind, driven uncertainly hither and thither.
But when it is *passed,* then *cometh,* not *to* them, but *upon*
them, from Heaven, overwhelming them, [1] *abiding upon*
them, not to pass away, *the heat of the anger of Almighty
God.* This warning he twice repeats, to impress the certainty and speed of its coming.[2] It is the warning of our
Lord, *Take heed, lest that day come upon you unawares.*[3]

   3. *Seek ye the Lord.* He had exhorted sinners to penitence ; he now calls the righteous to persevere and increase
more and more. He bids them *seek diligently,*[4] and that
with a threefold call, to seek Him from Whom they received daily the threefold blessing,[5] Father, Son, and
Holy Ghost, as he had just before threatened God's im-
pending judgment with the same use of the mysterious
number, three. They, whom he calls, were already, by the
grace of God, *meek,* and *had wrought His judgment.* "Sub-
mitting themselves to the word of God, they had done and
were doing the judgment of God, *judging themselves that
they be not judged ;* the beginning of which judgment is, as
sinners and guilty of death, to give themselves to the Cross
of the Lord, i.e. to be *baptized* in *His Death and be buried*

---

   [1] S. John iii. 36.   [2] Gen. xli. 32.
   [3] S. Luke xxi. 34.
   [4] The Hebrew form is intensive.   [5] Num. vi. 23–26.

                                              F

which have wrought his judgment ; seek righteous-

with Him by Baptism into death ; [1] but the perfection of
that judgment or righteousness is, to *walk in newness of life,
as He rose from the dead through the glory of the Father."* [2]

"Since the meek already have God through grace as the
Possessor and Dweller in their heart, how shall they seek
Him but that they may have Him more fully and more
perfectly, knowing Him more clearly, loving Him more
ardently, cleaving to Him more inseparably, that so they
may be heard by Him, not for themselves only, but for
others ? " [3] It is then the same Voice as at the close of the
Revelation, *the righteous, let him be still more righteous ; the
holy, let him be still more holy.* [4] They are the *meek,* who are
exhorted *diligently* to *seek meekness,* and they who had
wrought His judgment, who are *diligently* to *seek Righteousness.* And since our Lord saith, *Learn of Me, for I am meek
and lowly of heart,* [5] He bids "those who imitated His meekness and did His judgment, to seek the Lord in their
meekness." [6] Meekness and Righteousness may be His
Attributes, Who is All-gentleness and All-Righteousness,
the Fountain of all, wheresoever it is, in gentleness receiving penitents, and, *as the Righteous Judge, giving the
crown of righteousness* to those who *love Him and keep His
commandments,* yea He joineth righteousness with meekness, since without His mercy no man living could be
justified in His Sight. "God is sought by us, when, of
our choice, laying aside all listlessness, we thirst after
doing what pleases Him ; and we shall do judgment too,
when we fulfil His Divine law, working out what is good
unshrinkingly ; and we shall gain the prize of righteousness, when crowned with glory for well-doing and running

[1] Rom. vi. 3, 4.   [2] Rup.
[3] Dion.   [4] Rev. xxii. 11.
[5] S. Matt. xi. 29.   [6] S. Jer.

ness, seek meekness : ª it may be ye shall be hid in
the day of the LORD's anger,

ª Joel ii. 14 ; Amos v. 15 ; Jonah iii. 9.

the well-reported and blameless way of true piety to God
and of love to the brethren; for ¹ *love is the fulfilling of
the law.*" ²

It may be ye shall be hid in the day of the Lord's anger.
"Shall these too then scarcely be *hid in the day of the
Lord's anger?* Doth not the Apostle Peter say the very
same? *If it first begin at us, what shall be the end of them
that obey not the Gospel of God? And if the righteous scarcely
be saved, where shall the ungodly and the sinner appear?* ³ So
then, although any be *meek,* although he *have wrought the
judgment* of the Lord, let him ever suspect himself, nor
think that he has *already attained,* since neither can any
righteous be saved, if he be judged *without mercy.*" ⁴ "He
saith, *it may be;* not that there is any doubt that the meek
and they who perseveringly seek God, shall then be saved,
but to convey how difficult it is to be saved, and how fear-
ful and rigorous is the judgment of God." ⁵ To be hid is
to be sheltered from wrath under the protection of God ;
as David says, *In the time of trouble He shall hide me;* ⁶ and,
*Thou shalt hide them [that trust in Thee] in the secret of Thy
presence from the pride of man; Thou shalt keep them secretly
in a pavilion from the strife of tongues.*⁷ And in Isaiah, *A
man shall be as an hiding-place from the wind, and a covert
from the tempest;* ⁸ and, *There shall be a tabernacle for a
shadow in the daytime from the heat, and for a place of refuge,
and for a covert from storm and from rain.*⁹

¹ Rom. xiii. 10.   ² S. Cyr.
³ 1 S. Peter iv. 17, 18.   ⁴ Rup.
⁵ Dion.   ⁶ Ps. xxvii. 5.
⁷ Ib. xxxi. 20.   ⁸ Isa. xxxii. 2.   ⁹ Ib. iv. 6.

4 cities of Phillist

4 ¶ For ª Gaza shall be forsaken, and Ashkelon a

ª Jer. xlvii. 4, 5 ; Ezek. xxv. 15 ; Amos i. 6, 7, 8 ;
Zech. ix. 5, 6.

---

4. *For.* As a ground for repentance and perseverance,
he goes through heathen nations, upon whom God's wrath
should come. " As Isaiah, Jeremiah, Ezekiel, after visions
concerning Judah, turn to other nations round about, and
according to the character of each, announce what shall
come upon them, and dwell at length upon it, so doth this
prophet, though more briefly." [1] And thus under five
nations, who lay west, east, south and north, he includes
all mankind on all sides, and, again, according to their
respective characters towards Israel, as they are alien from,
or hostile to the Church ; the Philistines,[2] as a near, mali-
cious, infesting enemy ; Moab and Ammon,[3] people akin to
her (as heretics) yet ever rejoicing at her troubles and
sufferings ; Ethiopians,[4] distant nations at peace with her,
and which are, for the most part, spoken of as to be
brought unto her ; Assyria,[5] as the great oppressive power
of the world, and so upon it the full desolation rests.
In the first fulfilment, because Moab and Ammon aiding
Nebuchadnezzar (and all, in divers ways, wronging God's
people [6]), trampled on His sanctuary, overthrew His temple
and blasphemed the Lord, the prophecy is turned against
them. So then, before the captivity came, while Josiah
was yet king, and Jerusalem and the temple were, as yet,
not overthrown, the prophecy is directed against those who
mocked at them. *Gaza shall be forsaken.* Out of the five
cities of the Philistines, the Prophet pronounces woe upon

[1] S. Jer.   [2] ii. 4–7.   [3] ii. 8–10.
[4] v. 12.   [5] v. 13–15.
[6] Isa. xvi. 4 ; Amos i. 13–15 ; ii. 1–3 ; Jer. xlviii. 27–30,
42 ; xlix. 1 ; Ezek. xx. 3, 6, 8.

the same four as Amos [1] before, Jeremiah [2] soon after, and Zechariah [3] later. Gath, then, the fifth, had probably remained with Judah since Uzziah [4] and Hezekiah. [5] In the sentence of the rest, regard is had (as is so frequent in the Old Testament) to the names of the places themselves, that, henceforth, the name of the place might suggest the thought of the doom pronounced upon it. The names expressed boastfulness, and so, in the Divine judgment, carried their own sentence with them, and this sentence is pronounced by a slight change in the word. Thus *'Azzah* (Gaza), *strong*, shall be *'Azoobah, desolated; Ekron, deep-rooting*, [6] shall become *Teaker, be uprooted;* the *Cherethites* (*cutters off*) shall become (*Cheroth*) *diggings; Chebel, the band* of the sea-coast, shall be in another sense *Chebel*, an *inheritance*, [7] divided by line to the remnant of Judah; and *Ashdod* (*the waster* [8]) shall be taken in their might, not by craft, nor in the way of robbers, but *driven forth* violently and openly in the *noon-day*.

For Gaza shall be forsaken. Some vicissitudes of these towns have been noted already. [9] The fulfilment of the

---

[1] Amos i. 6–8.   [2] Jer. xxv. 20.

[3] Zech. ix. 5, 6.   [4] 2 Chron. xxvi. 6.

[5] 2 Kings xviii. 8.

[6] It seems to me most probable that the origin of the meanings is preserved in the Ch. עֲקַר "root" (which itself is the source of other metaphoric meanings, as "the root of a thing"; "the root," i.e. the foundation "of faith," its fundamental doctrines; "the root," in Lexicography, see Buxtorf), and that the Chald. עֲקַר "pluck up, remove," and עֲקַר, here and Eccl. iii. 2, is a denominative. The proper name is older probably than even Moses.

[7] ii. 5, 7.

[8] The root שׁדד has throughout the meaning of "wasting," not of "strength." שַׁדַּי "the Almighty," is probably from a kindred root, שׁדה.

[9] See on Amos i. 6–8.

39 yr. siege

desolation : they shall drive out Ashdod ᵃ at the noon
day, and Ekron shall be rooted up.

ᵃ Jer vi. 4 and xv. 8.

---

prophecy is not tied down to time ; the one marked contrast
is, that the old heathen enemies of Judah should be destroyed, the house of Judah should be restored, and should
re-enter upon the possession of the land, promised to them
of old.   The Philistine towns had, it seems, nothing to fear
from Babylon or Persia, to whom they remained faithful
subjects.   The Ashdodites (who probably, as the most
important, stand for the whole [1]) combined with Sanballat,
the Ammonites and the Arabians,[2] to hinder the rebuilding of
the walls of Jerusalem.   Even an army was gathered, headed
by Samaria.[3] They gave themselves out as loyal, Jerusalem as rebellious.[4]   The old sin remaining, Zechariah renewed the sentence by Zephaniah against the four cities ; [5]
a prophecy which an unbeliever also has recognised as picturing the march of Alexander.[6] "All the other cities of
Palestine having submitted," [7] Gaza alone resisted the conqueror for two or five months.   It had come into the hands of
the Persians in the expedition of Cambyses against Egypt.[8]
The Gazeans having all perished fighting at their posts,
Alexander sold the women and children, and repeopled the
city from the neighbourhood.[9] Palestine lay between the
two rival successors of Alexander, the Ptolemies and Seleu-

---

[1] Their language alone is mentioned, Neh. ix. 24, אשדודית,
in contrast with Jewish יהודית ; but neither is it mentioned that the Jews married any other Philistine women.
If Gath was destroyed, Ashdod lay nearest to them.

[2] Neh. iv. 7.   [3] Ib. iv. 2.

[4] Ib. ii. 19 ; vi. 6.   [5] Zech. ix.

[6] Eichhorn, Einl. iv. 605. See Daniel the Prophet, p. 280
sqq.

[7] Polyb. Reliq. xvi. 40.   [8] Mela, i. 11.   [9] Arrian, ii. 27.

cidæ, and felt their wars.[1] Gaza fell through mischance
into the hands of Ptolemy,[2] eleven years after the death
of Alexander,[3] and soon after, was destroyed by Antiochus [4]
(198 B.C.), "preserving its faith to Ptolemy" as before to
the Persians, in a way admired by a heathen historian. In
the Maccabee wars, Judas Maccabæus chiefly destroyed the
idols of Ashdod, but also *spoiled their cities* ; [5] Jonathan set
it on fire, with its idol-temple, which was a sort of citadel
to it ; [6] Ascalon submitted to him ; [7] Ekron with its borders
were given to him by Alexander Balas ; [8] he burnt the
suburbs of Gaza ; [9] Simon took it, expelled its inhabitants,
filled it with believing Jews and fortified it more strongly
than before ; [10] but, after a year's siege, it was betrayed to
Alexander Jannæus, who slew its senate of 500 and razed
the city to the ground.[11] Gabinius restored it and Ashdod.[12]
After Herod's death, Ashdod was given to Salome ; [13] Gaza,
as being a Greek city,[14] was detached from the realm of
Archelaus and annexed to Syria. It was destroyed by the
Jews in their revolt when Florus was "procurator," A.D. 55.[15]
Ascalon and Gaza must still have been strong, and were
probably a distinct population in the early times of Anti-
pater, father of Herod, when Alexander and Alexandra set
him over all Idumæa, since "he is said" then "to have made
friendship with the Arabs, Gazites, and Ascalonites, like-
minded with himself, and to have attached them by many
and large presents." [16]

Yet though the inhabitants were changed, the hereditary

[1] Polyb. v. 68.   [2] Diod. Sic. xix. 84.
[3] Hecat. in Jos. c. Ap. i. 22 ; Opp. ii. 455.
[4] Polyb. Reliq. xvi. 40.   [5] 1 Macc. v. 68.   [6] Ib. x. 84.
[7] Ib. 86.   [8] Ib. 89.   [9] Ib. xi. 61.
[10] Ib. xiii. 43–48.   [11] Jos. Ant. xiii. 13, 3.
[12] Ib. xiv. 5, 3.   [13] Ib. xvii. 8, 1.
[14] B. J. ii. 6, 3.   [15] κατέσκαπτον, Jos. B. J. ii. 18, 1.
[16] Ant. xiv. 1, 3.

hatred remained. Philo in his Embassy to Caius, A.D. 40,
used the strong language, "The Ascalonites have an im-
placable and irreconcilable enmity to the Jews, their
neighbours, who inhabit the holy land."[1] This continued
toward Christians. Some horrible atrocities, of almost
inconceivable savagery, by those of Gaza and Ascalon,
A.D. 361, are related by Theodoret[2] and Sozomen.[3] "Who is
ignorant of the madness of the Gazeans?"[4] asks S. Gregory
of Nazianzus, of the times of Julian. This was previous to
the conversion of the great Gazite temple of Marna into a
Christian Church by Eudoxia.[5] On occasion of Constantine's
exemption of the Maiumas Gazæ from their control, it is
alleged that they were "extreme Heathen."[6] In the time
of the Crusades the Ascalonites are described by Christians
as their "most savage enemies."[7]

It may be that a likeness of sin may have continued on a
likeness of punishment. But the primary prediction was
against the people, not against the walls. The sentence,
Gaza shall be forsaken, would have been fulfilled by the
removal or captivity of its inhabitants, even if they had not
been replaced by others. A prediction against any ancient

[1] Philo. Leg. ad. Caium, T. ii. p. 576, Mang. The words
are ἀσυμβατός τις καὶ ἀκατάλλακτος δυσμένεια.

[2] Theod. H. E. iii. 7.   [3] Soz. H. E. v. 10.

[4] Orat. 4, in Julian. c. 36.

[5] "This too we see to be fulfilled *in our times*. The temple
of Serapis at Alexandria, and of Marna at Gaza, rose to be
temples of the Lord." S. Jerome on Isa. xvii.

[6] ἐς ἄγαν Ἑλληνίζουσιν. Soz. v. 3.

[7] William of Tyre (pp. 917, 840, 865) calls them "hydra
immanissima," "hostes immanissimi"—"like restless gnats
persevering in the purpose of injuring," comp. pp. 781, 787,
797. "Ascalona was ever an adversary of Jerusalem."
Robertus Monachus, p. 77, in v. Raumer Palæst. p. 173,
ed. 4. It was called "the spouse of Syria," as an impregnable fortress.

British town would have been fulfilled, if the Britons in it had been replaced or exterminated by Danes, and these by Saxons, and these subdued by the Normans, though their displacers became wealthy and powerful in their place. Even on the same site it would not be the same Gaza, when the Philistine Gaza became Edomite, and the Edomite Greek, and the Greek Arabian.[1] Ashdod (as well as Gaza) is spoken of as a city of the Greeks;[2] New Gaza is spoken of as a mixture of Turks, Arabians, Fellahs, Bedouins out of Egypt, Syria, Petræa.[3] Felix Faber says, "There is a wonderful commixture of divers nations in it, Ethiopians, Arabs, Egyptians, Syrians, Indians, and eastern Christians; no Latins."[4] Its Jewish inhabitants fled from it in the time of Napoleon : now, with few exceptions, it is inhabited by Arabs.[5]

But these, Ghŭzzeh, Eskalon, Akir, Sedud, are at most successors of the Philistine cities, of which there is no trace above the surface of the earth. It is common to speak of "remnants of antiquity," as being or not being to be found in any of them ; but this means that, where these exist, there are remains of a Greek or Roman, not of a Philistine city.

Of the four cities, *Akkaron*, Ekron ("the firm-rooting"), has not left a vestige. It is mentioned by name only, after the times of the Bible, by some who passed by it.[6] There was "a large village of Jews" so called in the time of Eusebius and S. Jerome,[7] "between Azotus and Jamnia."

[1] See on Amos i. 6.
[2] Ps. Epiphanius de vitis Proph. p. 246.
[3] Ritter, xvi. 49.
[4] Fabri Evagatorium, T. ii. p. 379.
[5] Schwartz, d. Heil. Land, p. 91, 1853.
[6] "Passing through Azotus, between which and Jamnia, which is situate on the sea [i.e. the maritime Jamnia], we left Accaron on one side." Fulcher. Carnot. A.D. 1100, Gesta Peregr. Franc. c. 23, p. 464, quoted Raumer s. verb.
[7] De locis Hebr. T. iii. p. 146. Vall.

Now a village of "about fifty mud-houses without a single remnant of antiquity except two large finely built wells"[1] bears the name of Akir. S. Jerome adds, "Some think that Accaron is the tower of Strato, afterwards called Cæsarea." This was perhaps derived from misunderstanding his Jewish instructor.[2] But it shows how entirely all knowledge of Ekron was then lost.

Ashdod or *Azotus* which, at the time when Zephaniah prophesied, held out a twenty-nine years' siege against Psammetichus, is replaced by "[3] a moderate sized village of mud-houses, situated on the eastern declivity of a little flattish hill," "entirely modern, not containing a vestige of antiquity." "A beautiful sculptured sarcophagus with some fragments of small marble shafts," "near the Khan on the south-west," belong of course to later times. "The whole south side of the hill appears also as if it had been once covered with buildings, the stones of which are now thrown together in the rude fences." Its Bishops are mentioned from the Council of Nice to A.D. 536,[4] and so probably continued till the Mohammedan devastation. It is not mentioned in the Talmud.[5] Benjamin of Tudela calls it Palmis, and says, "It is desolate, and there are no Jews in

[1] Porter, Handb. p. 275.

[2] "The verse, *Ekron shall be uprooted*, the Talmud says, relates to Cæsarea, the daughter of Edom, which is situate among the sands. It does not mean that Ekron is Cæsarea, which would be absurd, but only shows its hatred against that city, and foretells its destruction, resting on a Biblical text, as is the habit of the Talmudists." Neubauer, Geogr. du Talmud, p. 92. See also ib. p. 12. Estori in his Kaftor uperach gives קסרי as another name of עקר, but Zunz quotes the Succah f. 276, as distinguishing קיסרי from קיסריון, Cæsarea (on the geogr. of Pal. App. to Benj. Tud. ii. 441).

[3] Porter, Handb. pp. 272, 273.

[4] Reland, p. 609.

[5] It does not appear in Neubauer, Geographie du Talmud.

it." [1] "Neither Ibn Haukal [Yacut], Edrisi, Abulfeda, nor
William of Tyre mention it." [2]

Ascalon and Gaza had each a port, Maiuma Gazæ, Maiuma
Ascalon, lit. "a place on the sea" (an Egyptian name [3]),
belonging to Ascalon or Gaza. The name involves that
Ascalon and Gaza themselves, the old Philistine towns,
were not on the sea. They were, like Athens, built inland,
perhaps (as has been conjectured) from fear of the raids of
pirates, or of inroads from those who (like the Philistines
themselves, probably, or some tribe of them) might come
from the sea. The port probably of both was built in much
later times; the Egyptian name implies that they were
built by Egyptians, after the time when its kings Necos
and Apries (Pharaoh-Necho and Pharaoh-Hophra, who
took Gaza [4]) made Egypt a naval power.[5] This became a
characteristic of these Philistine cities. They themselves
lay more or less inland, and had a city connected with them
of the same name on the shore. Thus there was an
"Azotus by the sea," [6] and an "Azotus Ispinus." There
were "two Iamniæ, one inland." [7] But Ashdod lay further
from the sea than Gaza; Yamnia (the Yabneel of Joshua,[8]

---

[1] "Palmis, which is Ashdod of the Philistines." מג ed.
Asher.

[2] Asher, note ib. T. ii. p. 99.

[3] "The name Maiuma seems to belong to the Egyptian
language, and to offer the two words MA IOM, "place by the
sea." Quatremère, les sultans Mamlouks de Makrizi, T. i. 2,
App. p. 229.

[4] Jer. xlvii. 1.

[5] See Herod. ii. 159, 161, and Rawlinson on ii. 182; Herod.
T. ii. p. 277.

[6] Ἄζωτος πάραλος. Excerpta in Græca notitia Patriarch.
in Reland, p. 215. Schwartz (d. Heil. Land, p. 91) places
Ashdod at an hour from the "Mediterranean."

[7] Plin. N. H. v. 12.

[8] Joshua xv. 11.

in Uzziah's time, Yabneh[1]), further than Ashdod.   The port of Yamnia was burnt by Judas.[2]

The *name* Maiumas does not appear till Christian times, though "the port of Gaza" is mentioned by Strabo:[3] to it, Alexander brought from Tyre the machines with which he took Gaza itself.[4]   That port, then, must have been at some distance from Gaza.   Each port became a town, large enough to have, in Christian times, a bishop of its own. The Epistle of John of Jerusalem, inserted in the Acts of the Council of Constantinople, A.D. 536, written in the name of Palestine i., ii., and iii., is signed by a Bishop of Maiumen of Ascalon, as well as by a Bishop of Ascalon, as it is by a Bishop of Maiumas of Gaza as well as by a Bishop of Gaza.[5] Yabne, or Yamnia, was on a small eminence,[6] six and a half hours from the sea.[7]   The Maiumas Gazæ became the more known.   To it, as being Christian, Constantine gave the right of citizenship, and called it Constantia from his son, making it a city independent of Gaza.   Julian the Apostate gave to Gaza (which, though it had bishops and martyrs, had a heathen temple at the beginning of the fifth century) its former jurisdiction over it, and though about twenty furlongs off, it was called " the maritime portion of Gaza."[8] It had thenceforth the same municipal officers ; but, " as regards the Church alone," Sozomen adds, " They still appear to be two cities; each has its own bishop and clergy, and festivals and martyrs, and commemorations of those who had been their bishops, and *boundaries of the fields around*

---

[1] 2 Chron. xxvi. 6.   [2] 2 Macc. xii. 9.

[3] Strabo, xvi. 2, 30, p. 759.

[4] " The engines, with which he took Tyre, being sent for by him, arrive from the sea."   Arr. ii. 27.

[5] Conc. T. v. 1164.   Col.

[6] Irby and Mangles, p. 57.

[7] Michaud et Poujoulat, Corresp. d'Orient, v. pp. 373, 374.

[8] Soz. v. 3.

whereby the altars which belong to each Episcopate are
parted." The provincial Synod decided against the desire
of a Bishop of Gaza, in Sozomen's time, who wished to
bring the clergy of the Maiumites under himself, ruling
that "although deprived of their civil privileges by a
heathen king, they should not be deprived of those of the
Church."

In A.D. 400, then, the two cities were distinct, not joined
or running into one another.

S. Jerome mentions it as "Maiumas, the emporium of
Gaza, seven miles from the desert on the way to Egypt by
the sea;"[1] Sozomen speaks of "Gaza by the sea, which
they also call Maiumas;"[2] Evagrius, "that which they also
call Maiumas, which is over against the city Gaza,"[3] "a little
city."[4] Mark the deacon, A.D. 421, says, "We sailed to the
maritime portion of Gaza, which they call Maiumas,"[5] and
Antoninus Martyr, about the close of the sixth century,
"We came from Ascalon to Mazomates, and came thence,
after a mile, to Gaza,—that magnificent and lovely city."[6]
This perhaps explains how an anonymous geographer,
enumerating the places from Egypt to Tyre, says so distinctly, "After Rinocorura lies the new Gaza, being itself
also a city; then the desert Gaza"[7] (writing, we must
suppose, after some of the destructions of Gaza); and
S. Jerome could say equally positively: "The site of the
ancient city scarce yields the traces of foundations; but
the city now seen was built in another place in lieu of that
which fell."[8]

[1] Vita S. Hilarion, n. 3; Opp. ii. 15. Vall.
[2] Soz. vii. 21.   [3] Ev. ii. 5.   [4] Ib. 8.
[5] Marcus Diac. A.D. 421, in Vita S. Porphyrii, c. 8, ap.
Bolland. Feb. 26.
[6] Itin. B. Antonini, pp. 24, 25.
[7] Hudson, Geograph. Minores, T. iv. p. 39.
[8] T. iii. p. 218.

Keith, who in 1844 explored the spot, found widespread traces of some extinct city.

"[1] At seven furlongs from the sea the manifold but minute remains of an ancient city are yet in many places to be found.—Innumerable fragments of broken pottery, pieces of glass (some beautifully stained), and of polished marble, lie thickly spread in every level and hollow, at a considerable elevation and various distances, on a space of several square miles. In fifty different places they profusely lie, in a level space far firmer than the surrounding sands," "from small patches to more open spaces of twelve or twenty thousand square yards." "The oblong sandhill, greatly varied in its elevation and of an undulated surface, throughout which they recur, extends to the west and west-south-west from the sea nearly to the environs of the modern Gaza." "In attempts to cultivate the sand (in 1832) hewn stones were found, near the old port. Remains of an old wall reached to the sea.—Ten large fragments of wall were embedded in the sand. About two miles off are fragments of another wall. Four intermediate fountains still exist, nearly entire in a line along the coast, doubtless pertaining to the ancient port of Gaza. For a short distance inland, the débris is less frequent, as if marking the space between it and the ancient city, but it again becomes plentiful in every hollow. About half a mile from the sea we saw three pedestals of beautiful marble. Holes are still to be seen from which hewn stones had been taken."

On the other hand, since the old Ashkelon had, like Gaza, Jamnia, Ashdod, a seaport town belonging to it but distinct from itself (the city itself lying distinct and inland), and since there is no space for two towns distinct from one another, within the circuit of the Ashkelon of the Crusades, which is limited by the nature of the ground, there seems

[1] Keith on Prophecy, from Personal Examination, pp. 378, 379.

to be no choice but that the city of the Crusades, and the present skeleton, should have been the Maiumas Ascalon, the seaport. The change might the more readily take place, since the title "port" was often omitted. The new town obliterated the memory of the old, as Neapolis, Naples, on the shore, has taken place of the inland city (whatever its name was), or Utrecht, it is said, has displaced the old Roman town, the remains of which are three miles off at Vechten,[1] or Sichem is called Neapolis, Nablous, which yet was three miles off.[2] Er-riha is, probably, at least the second representative of the ancient Jericho; the Jericho of the New Testament, built by Herod, not being the Jericho of the prophets. The Corcyra of Greek history gave its name to the island; it is replaced by a Corfu in a different but near locality, which equally gives its name to the island now. The name of Venetia migrated with the inhabitants of the province, who fled from Attila, some twenty-three miles, to a few of the islands on the coast, to become again the name of a great republic.[3] In our own country, "old Windsor" is said to have been the residence of the Saxon monarchs; the present Windsor was originally "new Windsor": old Sarum was the Cathedral city, until the reign of Henry III.; but, as the old towns decayed, the new towns came to be called Windsor, Sarum, though not the towns which first had the name. What is now called Shoreham, not many years ago was called "new Shoreham," in distinction from the neighbouring village.[4]

---

[1] Reland, who lived at Utrecht, says that Roman antiquities were daily dug up at Vechten, where were the remains of a Roman fort. Pal. p. 105.

[2] S. Jerome.   [3] Gibbon, c. 35.

[4] In like way Alresford, Basford, Brentford, Goole, Isleworth, must have been at one time, New Alr., New Basford, &c., but, as the more considerable, have appropriated the name which belonged to both the old and new places.

William of Tyre describes Ashkelon as "situated on the
seashore, in the form of a semicircle, whose chord or dia-
meter lies on the seashore ; but its circumference or arc
on the land, looking east. The whole city lies as in a
trench, all declining towards the sea, surrounded on all
sides by raised mounds, on which are walls with numerous
towers of solid masonry, the cement being harder than the
stone, with walls of due thickness and of height propor-
tionate ; it is surmounted also with outer walls of the
same solidity."[1] He then describes its four gates, east,
north, south towards Jerusalem, Gaza, Joppa, and the west,
called the sea-gate, because "by it the inhabitants have an
egress to the sea."

A modern traveller, whose description of the ruins exactly
agrees with this, says, "The walls are built on a ridge of
rocks that winds round the town in a semicircular direction
and terminates at each end in the sea : the ground falls
within the walls in the same manner as it does without,
so that no part of it could be seen from the outside of the
walls. There is no bay nor shelter for shipping, but a small
harbour advancing a little way into the town towards its
eastern extremity seems to have been formed for the
accommodation of such small craft as were used in the
better days of the city."[2] The harbour, moreover, was
larger during the Crusades, and enabled Ascalon to receive
supplies of corn from Egypt and thereby to protract its
siege. Sultan Bibars filled up the port and cast stones
into the sea, A.D. 1270, and destroyed the remains of the
fortifications, for fear that the Franks, after their treaty

---

[1] Willermus Tyr. Hist. xvii. 22, in Gesta Dei per Francos,
p. 924. The solidity of the walls and of the cement are described in the same way, in the latter part of the seventeenth
century, by d'Arvieux and Padre Malone da Maleo Terra
Santa, p. 471.

[2] Dr. Richardson, Travels along the Mediterr. ii. p. 201.

with the king of Tunis, should bring back their forces against Islamism and establish themselves there.[1] Yet Abulfeda, who wrote a few years later, calls it "one of the Syrian ports of Islam."[2]

This city, so placed on the sea, and in which too the sea enters, cannot be the Ashkelon, which had a port, which was a town distinct from it. The Ascalon of the Philistines, which existed down into Christian times, must have been inland.

Benjamin of Tudela in the twelfth century, who had been on the spot, and who is an accurate eyewitness,[3] says, "From Ashdod are two parasangs to Ashkelonah;[4] this is new Ashkelon which Ezra the priest built on the seashore, and they at first called it Benibra,[5] and it is distant from

---

[1] According to Ibn Férat in Reinaud Chroniques Arabes n. xcvi. Michaud, Biblioth. des Croisades, iv. 525.

[2] Ab. Tab. Syriæ, p. 78. Köhler. תַּעַר, a gap, opening, access, or an enemy's frontier (Freytag), "is in ordinary Arabic used for a port, as תַּעַר בִּירוּת 'the port of Beyrout,' and תַּעַר דמיטה 'the port of Damietta.'" Prof. Chenery.

[3] p. מג 2, ed. Asher. The enumeration of "about 200 Rabbanite Jews," with the names of the chief, "about 40 karaites, and about 300 Cuthæans," shows personal acquaintance. The former name of the "new Ascalon" and the supposed distance of the ruins of the old, he must have learned on the spot.

[4] Benj. Tud. pronounces the new city Ashkelona, as the Latins did. When speaking himself, he says Ashkelon.

[5] "Benibra" looks like a corruption of בֵית נמרה, "a place of pure water," like "Bebaten, Bedora, Beestera, Begabar," &c., in Reland, 617 sqq. The Gadite town of that name becomes in Eus. βηθναβρίς. S. Jerome has another Benamerium, north of Zoar, now N'mairah. Tristram, Land of Moab, p. 57. A well in Ascalon is mentioned by Eusebius. "There are many wells (named) in Scripture and are yet shown in the country of Gerar, and at Ascalon." v. φρέαρ. William of Tyre says: "It has no fountains, either

G

the old Ashkelon, which is desolate, four parasangs." When the old Ashkelon perished, is unknown. If, as seems probable from some of the antiquities dug up, the Ashkelon, at which Herod was born and which he beautified, was the seaport town, commerce probably attracted to it gradually the inhabitants of the neighbouring town of Ascalon, as the population of the Piræus now exceeds that of Athens.

The present Ashkelon is a ghastly skeleton; all the framework of a city, but none there. "The soil is good," but the "peasants who cultivate it" prefer living outside in a small village of mud-huts, exposed to winds and sand-storms, because they think that God has abandoned it, and that evil spirits (the Jân and the Ghûl) dwell there.[1]

Even the remains of antiquity, where they exist, belong to later times. A hundred men excavated in Ashkelon for fourteen days in hopes of finding treasure there. They dug eighteen feet below the surface, and found marble shafts, a Corinthian capital, a colossal statue with a Medusa's head on its chest, a marble pavement and white-marble pedestal.[2] The excavation reached no Philistine Ashkelon.

"Broken pottery," "pieces of glass," "fragments of polished marble," "of ancient columns, cornices, &c."[3] were the relics of a Greek Gaza.

within the compass of the walls, or near it; but it abounds in wells, both within and without, which supply palatable water, fit for drinking. For greater caution the inhabitants had built some cisterns within, to receive rain-water." Benj. of T. also says, "There in the midst of the city is a well which they call Beer Ibrahim-al-khalil [the well of Abraham the friend (of God)] which he dug in the days of the Philistines." Keith mentions "twenty fountains of excellent water opened up anew by Ibrahim Pasha," p. 274.

[1] Mr. Cyril Graham in Keith, p. 376.
[2] Travels of Lady H. Stanhope, iii. 159–169.
[3] Keith, p. 378.

Though then it is a superfluity of fulfilment, and what can be found belongs to a later city, still what can be seen has an impressive correspondence with the words *Gaza is forsaken;* for there are miles of fragments of some city connected with Gaza. The present Gaza occupies the southern half of a hill built with stone for the Moslem conquerors of Palestine. "Even the traces of its former existence, its vestiges of antiquity, are very rare; occasional columns of marble or gray granite, scattered in the streets and gardens, or used as thresholds at the gates and doors of houses, or laid upon the front of watering-troughs. One fine Corinthian capital of white marble lies inverted in the middle of the street." [1] These belong then to times later than Alexander, since whose days the very site of Gaza must have changed its aspect.

Ashkelon shall be a desolation. The site of the port of Ascalon was well chosen, strong, overhanging the sea, fenced from the land, stretching forth its arms towards the Mediterranean, as if to receive in its bosom the wealth of the sea, yet shunned by the poor hinds around it. It lies in such a living death, that it is "[2] one of the most mournful scenes of utter desolation" which a traveller "even in this land of ruins ever beheld." But this too cannot be the Philistine city. The sands which are pressing hard upon the solid walls of the city, held back by them for the time, yet threatening to overwhelm "the spouse of Syria," and which accumulated in the plain below, must have buried the old Ashkelon, since in this land, where the old names so cling to the spot, there is no trace of it.

Ekron shall be uprooted; and at Akîr and Esdûd "celebrated at present for its scorpions," [3] the few stones which remain, even of a later town, are but as gravestones to mark the burial-place of departed greatness.

---

[1] Robinson, Travels, ii. 38.   [2] Smith, ib. p. 66, *note*.
[3] Volney, Voyage en Syrie, c. 31, p. 311; Keith, p. 370.

Phillistine

5 Woe unto the inhabitants of [a] the sea coast, the
nation of the Cherethites! the word of the LORD *is*
against you ; O [b] Canaan, the land of the Philistines,

[a] Ezek. xxv. 16.   [b] Joshua xiii. 3.

"In like way, all who glory in bodily strength and
worldly power and say, *By the strength of my hand I have
done it,* shall be left desolate and brought to nothing in the
day of the Lord's anger."[1]   And "the waster," they who by
evil words and deeds injure or destroy others and are an
offence unto them, these *shall be cast out* shamefully, *into outer
darkness* "when the saints shall receive the fullest brightness "[2] in the *mid-day* of the Sun of Righteousness.   The
judgment shall not be in darkness, save to them, but in
mid-day, so that the justice of God shall be clearly seen,
and darkness itself shall be turned into light, as was said
to David, *Thou didst this thing secretly, but I will do it before
all Israel and before the sun;*[3] and our Lord, *Whatsoever ye
have spoken in darkness shall be heard in the light ; and that
which ye have spoken in the ear in closets shall be proclaimed
upon the housetops ;*[4] and S. Paul, *The Lord shall come, Who
both will bring to light the hidden things of darkness, and will
make manifest the counsels of the heart.*[5]   And "they who by
seducing words in life or in doctrine uprooted others, shall
be themselves rooted up."[6]

5. The *woe* having been pronounced on the five cities
apart, now falls upon the whole nation of the Cherethites
or Philistines.   The Cherethites are only named as equivalent to the Philistines, probably as originally a distinct
immigration of the same people.[7]   The name is used by

[1] S. Jer.

[3] 2 Sam. xii. 12.

[5] 1 Cor. iv. 5.

[7] See on Amos ix. 7.

[2] Rup.

[4] S. Luke xii. 3.

[6] S. Matt. xv. 13.

I will even destroy thee, that there shall be no inhabitant.

---

the Egyptian slave of the Amalekite [1] for those whom the author of the first book of Samuel calls Philistines.[2] Ezekiel uses the name parallel with that of *Philistines*, with reference to the destruction which God would bring upon them.[3]

The word of the Lord comes not to them, but *upon* them, overwhelming them. To them He speaketh not in good, but in evil; not in grace, but in anger; not in mercy, but in vengeance. Philistia was the first enemy of the Church. It showed its enmity to Abraham and Isaac and would fain that they should not sojourn among them.[4] They were the hindrance that Israel should not go straight to the promised land.[5] When Israel passed the Red Sea, *sorrow took hold of them.*[6] They were close to salvation in body, but far in mind. They are called *Canaan,* as being a chief nation of it,[7] and in that name lay the original source of their destruction. They inherited the sins of Canaan and with them his curse, preferring the restless beating of the barren, bitter sea on which they dwelt, "the waves of this troublesome world," to being a part of the true Canaan. They

---

[1] 1 Sam. xxx. 14.   [2] Ib. xxx. 16.

[3] הכרתי את כרתים Ezek. xxv. 16. It may be that they were so called as coming from Crete as the LXX supposed, rendering "Cretans" in Ezek., and here (as also the Syr.) "sojourners of the Cretans." Hence perhaps also Tacitus' statement (Hist. v. 2) that the Jews had been expelled from Crete. The other versions render the word as an appellative, "destroying" or "destroyed." Aq. and ἐ, ἔθνος ὀλέθριον, Theod. ἔθνος ὀλεθρίας Symm. ἔθνος ὀλεθρευόμενον. S. Jer, gives perditorem.

[4] Gen. xxi. 34; xxvi. 14, 15, 18.

[5] Exod. xiii. 17.   [6] Ib. xv. 14.

[7] Gen. xv. 21.

6 And the sea coast shall be dwellings *and* cottages for shepherds, [a] and folds for flocks.

[a] See Isa. xvii. 2 ; ver. 14.

---

would absorb the Church into the world, and master it, subduing it to the heathen Canaan, not subdue themselves to it, and become part of the heavenly Canaan.

6. *The sea-coast* [1] *shall be dwellings and cottages,* lit. cuttings or diggings.[2] This is the central meaning of the word ; the place of the Cherethites (the *cutters off*) shall be *cheroth* of shepherds, places which they dug up that their flocks might be enclosed therein. The tracts once full of fighting men, the scourge of Judah, should be so desolate of its former people as to become a sheep-walk. Men of peace should take the place of its warriors.

So the shepherds of the Gospel with their flocks have entered into possession of warlike nations, turning them to the Gospel. They are shepherds, the chief of whom is

[1] The words " band of the sea " are repeated with emphasis, vers. 5, 6, and the first words v. 7.

[2] So Kim. Ibn. Denan has "caves which shepherds inhabit "; Arab. transl. "domiciles which shepherds dig." Abulw. and Tanchum derive it from בָּרה 2 Kings vi. 23, " a feast." Abulw. thinks this not improbable, as an irregular plural. Tanchum, "stations of shepherds where they turn their flocks to feed and sit down to eat, or places in which they dig for watering the flocks." The climate of Judæa, however, does not admit of underground habitations, like Nineveh, and in the country of the Philistines flocks would be supplied by wells with trenches. No Arabic authority suggests a derivation from וְכֵר "nest" (as Ewald). The allusion to Cherethim would be lost by this invented root. Rashi has " a place where the shepherds eat." A. E. explains כְּרֹת, as if it were from בָּרַת, " which the shepherds כרתו for themselves." The Moabite stone has מכרתת l. 25, apparently of " a ditch " " or moat."

7 And the coast shall be for ^a the remnant of the
house of Judah; they shall feed thereupon; in the

^a Isa. xi. 11; Micah iv. 7 and v. 7, 8; Hag. i. 12 and
ii. 2; ver. 9.

---

that Good Shepherd, Who laid down His Life for the
sheep.   And these are the sheep of whom He speaks,
*Other sheep I have, which are not of this fold; them also I must
bring, and they shall hear My Voice; and there shall be one
fold and One Shepherd.*[1]

7. *And the coast shall be.* Or probably,[2] *It shall be a
portion for the remnant of the house of Judah.* He uses the
word, employed in the first assignment of the land to
Israel;[3] and of the whole people as belonging to God,
" Jacob is the *lot* of His inheritance."[4] The *tract of the sea,*
which, with the rest, was assigned to Israel, which, for its
unfaithfulness, was seldom, even in part, possessed, and
at this time was wholly forfeited, should be a portion for
the mere *remnant* which should be brought back. David
used the word in his psalm of thanksgiving, when he had
brought the ark to the city of David, how God had "confirmed the covenant to Israel, saying, Unto thee will I give

[1] S. John x. 16.
[2] Grammatically, חבל may be either the subject or
predicate. For even in prose (Joshua xix. 29) it is used without
the article, of the sea-coast, the mention of the sea having
preceded, " the goings forth thereof were to the sea, מחבל to
Mizpeh." Yet there is no emphasis in the repetition of
the word from the preceding verse. The LXX renders
חבל as the subject, the Ch. Vulg. as the predicate.
[3] " The ten *portions* of Manasseh," Joshua xvii. 5; " Why
hast thou given me one lot and one *portion* ? " ib. xvii. 14;
" out of the *portion* of the children of Judah was the inheritance of the children of Simeon," ib. xix. 9.
[4] Deut. xxxii. 9.

houses of Ashkelon shall they lie down in the evening : * for the LORD their God shall ª visit them,
and ᵇ turn away their captivity.

> * Or, *when, &c.*   ª Exod. iv. 31 ; Luke i. 68.
>   ᵇ Ps. cxxvi. 1 ; Jer. xxix. 14 ; ch. iii. 20.

the land of Canaan, the *lot* of your inheritance;"[1] and
Asaph,[2] *He cast out the heathen before them and divided to
them an inheritance by line.* It is the reversal of the doom
threatened by Micah, *Thou shalt have none that shall cast
a cord by lot in the congregation of the Lord.*[3] The word is
revived by Ezekiel in his ideal division of the land to the
restored people.[4] *The gifts and calling of God are without
repentance.*[5] The promise, which had slumbered during
Israel's faithlessness, should be renewed to its old extent.
"There is no prescription against the Church."[6] The boat
threatens to sink; it is tossed, half-submerged, by the
waves ; but its Lord *rebukes the wind and the sea ; wind and
sea obey Him, and there is a great calm.*[7]

For the remnant of the house of Judah. Yet, who save He
in Whose hand are human wills, could now foresee that
Judah should, like the ten tribes, rebel, be carried captive,
and yet, though like and worse than Israel in its sin,[8]
should, unlike Israel, be restored? The rebuilding of
Jerusalem was, their enemies pleaded, contrary to sound
policy:[9] the plea was for the time accepted; for the rebellions of Jerusalem were recorded in the chronicles of
Babylon.[10] Yet the falling short of the complete restoration

---

[1] 1 Chron. xvi. 18 ; Ps. cv. 11.
[2] Ps. lxxviii. 55.   [3] Micah ii. 5.
[4] Ezek. xlvii. 13.   [5] Rom. xi. 29.
[6] "Nullum tempus ecclesiæ," though said of its property.
[7] S. Matt. viii. 26, 27.
[8] Jer. iii. 8–11 ; Ezek. xvi. 46–52 ; xxiii. 11.
[9] Ezra iv. 12–16.   [10] Ib. iv. 19–22.

8 ¶ ^a I have heard the reproach of Moab, and ^b the

^a Jer. xlviii. 27 ; Ezek. xxv. 8.   ^b Ezek. xxv. 3, 6.

depended on their own wills. God turned again their captivity ; but *they* only, *whose spirit God stirred*, willed to return. The temporal restoration was the picture of the spiritual. They who returned had to give up lands and possessions in Babylonia, and a remnant only chose the land of promise at such cost. Babylonia was as attractive as Egypt formerly.

In the houses of Ashkelon shall they lie down in the evening. One city is named for all. *They shall lie down*, he says, continuing the image from their flocks, as Isaiah, in a like passage,[1] *The first-born of the poor shall feed, and the needy shall lie down in safety.*

The true Judah shall overspread the world; but it too shall only be a *remnant ;* these shall, in safety, *go in and out and find pasture.*[2] *In the evening* of the world they shall find their rest ; for then also in the time of Anti-Christ, the Church shall be but a remnant still. *For the Lord their God shall visit them,* for He is the Good Shepherd, Who came to seek the one sheep which was lost and Who says of Himself, *I will seek that which was lost, and bring again that which was driven away, and will bind up that which was broken, and will strengthen that which was sick ;*[3] and Who in the end will more completely *turn away their captivity*, bring His banished to their everlasting home, the Paradise from which they have been exiled, and separate for ever the sheep from the goats who now oppress and scatter them abroad.[4]

8. *I,* "God, Who know all things, *I heard,* i.e. have known within Me, in My mind, not anew but from eternity, and now I show in effect that I know it ; where-

¹ Isa. xiv. 30.   ² S. John x. 9.

³ Ezek. xxxiv. 16.   ⁴ Ib. xxxiv. 17–19.

revilings of the children of Ammon, whereby they

fore I say that I hear, because I act after the manner of
one who perceiveth something anew."[1] I, the just Judge,
heard.[2] He was present and *heard*, even when, because He
avenged not, He seemed not to hear, but laid it up in store
with Him to avenge in the due time.[3]

*The reproach of Moab and the reviling of the children of
Ammon, whereby they have reproached My people.* Both
words, *reproached, reviled,* mean, primarily, cutting speeches ;
both are intensive, and are used of blaspheming God as
unable to help His people, or reviling His people as forsaken by Him. If directed against man, they are directed
against God through man. So David interpreted the
taunt of Goliath, *reviled the armies of the living God,*[4] and the
Philistine cursed David *by his gods.*[5] In a Psalm David
complains, *the reproaches of them that reproached Thee are
fallen upon me ;*[6] and a Psalm which cannot be later than
David, since it declares the national innocency from
idolatry, connects with their defeats, the voice of him *that
reproacheth and blasphemeth*[7] (joining the two words used
here). The sons of Corah say, *With a sword in my bones,
mine enemies reproach me, while they say daily unto me, Where
is thy God ?*[8] So Asaph, *The enemy hath reproached, the
foolish people hath blasphemed Thy Name ;*[9] and, *we are become a reproach to our neighbours. Wherefore should the
heathen say, Where is their God ? render unto our neighbours—
the reproach wherewith they have reproached Thee, O Lord.*[10]

[1] Dion.
[2] See Isa. xvi. 6 ; Jer. xlviii. 29 ; Ezek. xxxv. 12, 13.
[3] Deut. xxxii. 34, 35.
[4] 1 Sam. xvii. 26, 36, 45, coll. 10, 25.
[5] 1 Sam. xvii. 43.   [6] Ps. lxix. 9.
[7] Ib. xliv. 16.   [8] Ib. xlii. 10.
[9] Ib. lxxiv. 10, 18.   [10] Ib. lxxix. 4, 10, 12.

And Ethan, *Remember, Lord, the reproach of Thy servants—wherewith Thine enemies have reproached, O Lord, wherewith they have reproached the footsteps of Thine Anointed.*[1]

In history the repeated blasphemies of Sennacherib and his messengers are expressed by the same words. In earlier times the remarkable concession of Jephthah, *Wilt not thou possess what Chemosh thy god giveth thee to possess? so whomsoever the Lord our God shall drive out before us, them will we possess,*[2] implies that the Ammonites claimed their land as the gift of their god Chemosh, and that that war was, as that later by Sennacherib, waged in the name of the false god against the True.

The relations of Israel to Moab and Ammon have been so habitually misrepresented, that a review of those relations throughout their whole history may correct some wrong impressions. The first relations of Israel towards them were even tender. God reminded His people of their common relationship and forbade him even to take the straight road to his own future possessions, across their land against their will. *Distress them not, nor contend with them,* it is said of each, *for I will not give thee of their land for a possession ; for I have given it unto the children of Lot for a possession.*[3] Idolaters and hostile as they were, yet, for their father's sake, their title to their land had the same sacred sanction, as Israel's to his. *I,* God says, *have given it to them as a possession.* Israel, to their own manifest inconvenience, *went along through the wilderness, and compassed the land of Edom, and the land of Moab, but came not within the border of Moab.*[4] By destroying Sihon king of the Amorites and Og king of Bashan, Israel removed formidable enemies, who had driven Moab and Ammon out of a portion of the land which they had conquered from

---

[1] Ps. lxxxix. 50, 51.   [2] Judges xi. 24.
[3] Deut. ii. 9, 19.   [4] Judges xi. 18.

have reproached my people, and ^a magnified *them-selves* against their border.

^a Jer. xlix. 1.

---

the Zamzummim and Anakim,[1] and who threatened the remainder. *Israel dwelt in all the cities of the Amorites.*[2]

Heshbon, Dibon, Jahaz, Medeba, Nophah were *cities in the land of the Amorites, in* which *Israel dwelt.* The exclusion of Moab and Ammon from the congregation of the Lord to the tenth generation[3] was not, of course, from any national antipathy, but intended to prevent a debasing intercourse; a necessary precaution against the sensuous-ness of their idolatries. Moab was the first[4] in adopting the satanic policy of Balaam, to seduce Israel by sensuality to their idolatries; but the punishment was appointed to the partners of their guilt, the Midianites,[5] not to Moab. Yet Moab was the second nation, whose ambition God overruled to chasten His people's idolatries. Eglon, king of Moab, united with himself Ammon and Amalek against Israel. The object of the invasion was, not the recovery of the country which Moab had lost to the Amorites, but Palestine proper. The strength of Moab was apparently not sufficient to occupy the territory of Reuben. They took possession only of *the city of palm trees;*[6] either the ruins of Jericho or a spot close by it; with the view appa-rently of receiving reinforcements or of securing their own retreat by the ford. This garrison enabled them to carry their forays over Israel, and to hold it enslaved for eighteen

[1] Deut. ii. 10, 20, 21.   [2] Num. xxi. 25, 31.
[3] Deut. xxiii. 3.
[4] Num. xxv. 1, 3. The rank of the Midianitish lady who gave herself as a partner of the sin of the Simeonite chief (ib. 6, 14, 15, 18) shows how much store the Midianites set on that seduction.
[5] Num. xxv. 17 and xxxi.   [6] Judges iii. 13.

years.   The oppressiveness of this slavery is implied by the
cry and conversion of Israel to the Lord, which was always
in great distress.   The memory of Eglon, as one of the
oppressors of Israel, lived in the minds of the people in the
days of Samuel.[1]   In the end, this precaution of Moab
turned to its own destruction ; for, after Eglon was slain,
Ephraim, under Ehud, took the fords, and the whole
garrison, 10,000 of Moab's warriors, *every strong man and
every man of might*,[2] were intercepted in their retreat and
perished.   For a long time after this, we hear of no fresh
invasion by Moab.   The trans-Jordanic tribes remained in
unquestioned possession of their land for 300 years,[3] when
Ammon, not Moab, raised the claim, *Israel took away my
land*,[4] although claiming the land down to the Arnon, and
already being in possession of the southernmost portion of
that land, Aroer, since Israel smote him *from Aroer unto
Minnith*.[5]   The land, then, according to a law recognised by
nations, belonged by a twofold right to Israel : (1) that it
had been won, not from Moab, but from the conquerors of
Moab, the right of Moab having passed to its conquerors ;[6]
(2) that undisputed and unbroken possession "for time
immemorial" as we say, 300 years, ought not to be disputed.[7]   The defeat by Jephthah stilled them for near fifty
years till the beginning of Saul's reign, when they refused
the offer of the *men of Jabesh-Gilead* to serve them, and,
with a mixture of insolence and savagery, annexed as a
condition of accepting that entire submission, *that I may
thrust out all your right eyes, to lay it as a reproach to Israel*.[8]
The signal victory of Saul[9] still did not prevent Ammon,
as well as Moab, from being among the enemies whom Saul

[1] 1 Sam. xii. 9.   [2] Judges iii. 29.
[3] Ib. xi. 26.   [4] Ib. xi. 13.   [5] Ib. xi. 33.
[6] Grotius de jure belli et pacis, iii. c. vi. n. vii. and notes.
[7] Id. ib. ii. c. iv. n. ii. and ix. and notes.
[8] 1 Sam. xi. 1, 2.   [9] Ib. xi. 11.

worsted.[1] The term *enemies* implies that *they* were the
assailants. The history of Naomi shows their prosperous
condition, that the famine, which desolated Judah,[2] did
not reach them, and that they were a prosperous land, at
peace, at that time, with Israel. If all the links of the
genealogy are preserved,[3] Jesse, David's father, was grandson of a Moabitess, Ruth, and perhaps on this ground
David entrusted his parents to the care of the king of
Moab.[4] Sacred history gives no hint what was the cause
of his terrible execution upon Moab. But a Psalm of
David speaks to God of some blow, under which Israel had
reeled. *O God, Thou hast abhorred us, and broken us in
pieces; Thou hast been wroth: Thou hast made the land to
tremble and cloven it asunder; heal its breaches, for it shaketh;
Thou hast shewed Thy people a hard thing, Thou hast made
it drink wine of reeling;*[5] and thereon David expresses his
confidence that God would humble Moab, Edom, Philistia.
While David then was engaged in the war with the Syrians
of Mesopotamia and Zobah,[6] Moab must have combined
with Edom in an aggressive war against Israel. *The valley
of salt,*[7] where Joab returned and defeated them, was
probably within Judah, since *the city of salt*[8] was one of
the six cities of the wilderness. Since they had defeated

---

[1] הרשיע, not " vexed," ib. xiv. 47.

[2] Ruth i. 1.   [3] Ib. iv. 21, 22.

[4] 1 Sam. xxii. 3, 4.   [5] Ps. lx. 1–3.

[6] Ib. tit.

[7] It was probably the narrow valley some three miles long
between the northern end of that remarkable salt mountain,
the Jebel or Khasm Usdum and the Dead Sea. See the
description in Tristram's Land of Isr., p. 326 sqq. At its
north extremity at the mouth of Wady Zuweirah there are
considerable traces of (perhaps Roman) buildings. A tower
placed here would command the entrance of the valley of
salt, and this may well have been the site of the *city of salt.*

[8] Joshua xv. 62.

Judah, they must have been overtaken there on their return.[1]

Yet this too was a religious war. "*Thou*," David says,[2] " hast given a *banner to them that fear Thee*, to be raised aloft because of the truth."

There is no tradition that the kindred Psalm of the sons of Corah, Psalm xliv., belongs to the same time. Yet the protestations to God of the entire absence of idolatry could not have been made at any time later than the early years of Solomon. Even were there Maccabee Psalms, the Maccabees were but a handful among apostates. They could not have pleaded the national freedom from unfaithfulness to God, nor, except in two subordinate and self-

---

[1] Seetzen guessed (Reisen, ii. 356), and Robinson considered it certain (ii. 109) that " the valley of salt " was the lower part of the 'Arabah, close to the Dead Sea, between Edom and Judæa. But (i.) This is spoken of as a " great plain " (Seetzen, p. 355), and although the word נְיא is twice used of as large valley : (1) the valley over against Baal Peor, where all Israel was encamped, Deut. iii. 29 ; iv. 46 ; (2) that of Zephathah, where Asa, with an army of 580,000 men, defeated Zerah the Ethiopian with 1,000,000 (2 Chron. xiv. 10), this is the exception. In eleven other places it is used of a narrow valley. (ii.) The depression, south of the Dead Sea down to the Red Sea, had in the time of Moses the same title as now, the " Arabah," Deut. i. 1 ; ii. 8. (iii.) The space near the Dead Sea, which is salt, " the Sebkha, or desolate sand-swamp " (Tristram, Moab, p. 41), is impracticable for men ; much more for an army. " The Sebkha or salt-flat is a large flat, of at least six by ten miles from north to south. Taught by the experience of M. de Saulcy, we made no attempt to cross it to the northwards, as the mud would have been far too deep and treacherous for us to pass in safety " (id., Land of Israel, p. 336). " The land south of the Sebkha is not salt, but rich and fertile " (id. p. 338). See de Saulcy, Voyage en Syrie, &c., pp. 248–256.

[2] Ps. lx. 4.

willed expeditions,[1] were they defeated. Under the Persian
rule, there were no armies nor wars ; no immunity from
idolatry in the later history of Judah. Judah did not in
Hezekiah's time go out against Assyria ; the one battle, in
which Josiah was slain, ended the resistance to Egypt.
Defeat was, at the date of this Psalm, new and surprising,
in contrast with God's deliverances of old ;[2] yet the inroad,
by which they had suffered, was one of spoiling,[3] not of
subdual. Yet this too was a religious war, from their
neighbours. They were slain for the sake of God,[4] they
were covered with shame on account of the reproaches and
blasphemies[5] of those who triumphed over God, as powerless
to help ; they were a scorn and derision to the petty nations
around them. It is a Psalm of unshaken faith amid great
prostration : it describes in detail what the 60th Psalm
sums up in single heavy words of imagery ; but both alike
complain to God of what His people had to suffer for
His sake.

The insolence of Ammon in answer to David's message of
kindness to their new king, like that |to the men of Jabesh
Gilead, seems like a deliberate purpose to create hostilities.
The relations of the previous king of Ammon to David had
been kind,[6] perhaps, because David being a fugitive from
Israel, they supposed him to be Saul's enemy. The enmity
originated, not with the new king, but with *the princes of
the children of Ammon.*[7] David's treatment of these nations[8]
is so unlike his treatment of any others whom he defeated,
that it implies an internecine warfare, in which the safety
of Israel could only be secured by the destruction of its
assailants.

Mesha, king of Moab, records one war, and alludes to

---

[1] 1 Macc. v. 56–60, 67.   [2] Ps. xliv. 1–3.
[3] Ib. xliv. 10, 12.   [4] Ib. xliv. 22.
[5] Ib. xliv. 13, 14.   [6] 2 Sam. x. 2, 3.
[7] Ib. x. 3.   [8] Ib. viii. 2 ; xii. 31.

others, not mentioned in Holy Scripture. He says, that
before his own time, "Omri, king of Israel, afflicted Moab
many days ; " that "his son [Ahab] succeeded him, and he
too said, 'I will afflict Moab.'" This affliction he explains to
be that "[1] Omri possessed himself of the land of Medeba"
[expelling,[2] it is implied, its former occupiers] "and that"
(apparently, Israel[3]) "dwelt therein," "[in his days and in]
the days of his son forty years." He was also in possession of Nebo, and "the king of Israel" (apparently Omri)
"buil[t] Jahaz and dwelt in it, when he made war with
me."[4] Jahaz was near Dibon. In the time of Eusebius,
it was still "pointed out between Dibon and Medeba."[5]
Mesha says, "And I took it to annex it to Dibon." It
could not, according to Mesha also, have been south of the
Arnon, since Aroer lay between Dibon and the Arnon, and
Mesha would not have annexed to Dibon a town beyond
the deep and difficult ravine of the Arnon, with Aroer lying
between them. It was certainly north of the Arnon, since
Israel was not permitted to come within the border of
Moab, but it was at Jahaz that Sihon met them and fought
the battle in which Israel defeated him and gained possession of his land, *from the Arnon to the Jabbok.*[6] It is said

[1] ‏וירש עמרי את ארץ מה דבא‎.
[2] This lies in the word ‏וירש‎.
[3] A gap in the broken stone probably contained the
subject. I see that Schlottman also supplied, "Israel";
Dr. Ginsburg conjectured, less probably, "the enemy."
[4] In this place only Mesha speaks of the king of Israel's
war with him in the past. Elsewhere he speaks of himself
only as being on the offensive. "I fought against the city"
[Ataroth]; "I fought against it" [Nebo]; "go down, fight
against Horonaim." The king of Israel is apparently the
same throughout, Omri.
[5] S. Jerome de situ loc. Hebr. Opp. iii. 230, v. Ἰεσσά,
"Jassa, where Sihon king of the Amorites is defeated."
[6] Num. xxi. 23–25.

H

also that [1] *Israel dwelt in the land of the Amorites from Aroer which is on the edge of the river Arnon,* [2] *and the city which is in the river* [3] *unto Gilead.* [4] *Aroer on the edge of the river Arnon, and the city which is in the river* Arnon, again occur in describing the southern border of Reuben, among whose towns Jahaz is mentioned, with Beth-Baal-Meon and Kiriathaim, which have been identified.

The afflicting, then, of Moab by Omri, according to Mesha, consisted in this, that he recovered to Israel a portion of the allotment of Reuben, between nine and ten hours in length [5] from north to south, of which, in the time of Israel's weakness through the civil wars which followed on Jeroboam's revolt, Moab must have dispossessed Reuben. Reuben had remained in undisturbed possession of it, from the first expulsion of the Amorites to the time at least of Rehoboam, about five hundred years. "The men of Gad" still "dwelt in Ataroth," Mesha says, "from time immemorial."

The picture which Mesha gives is of a desolation of the southern portion of Reuben. For, "I rebuilt," he says, "Baal-Meon, Kiriathaim, Aroer, Beth-bamoth, Bezer, Beth-Diblathaim, Beth-baal-Meon." Of Beth-Bamoth, and pro-

---

[1] Deut. ii. 36.

[2] "The ruins of Araayr (עראעיר), the Aroer of the Scriptures, standing on the edge of the precipice." Burckhardt, Travels in Syria, p. 372.

[3] "Near the confluence of the Ledjoum and the Mojeb" [Arnon], "about one mile east of the bridge across the Mojeb, there seems to be a fine verdant pasture ground, in the midst of which stands a hill with some ruins upon it." Burckhardt, ib. 373, 374.

[4] Joshua xiii. 16, 18.

[5] The distance is taken from Porter's Handbook, pp. 299–301.

[6] The beginning of Rehoboam's reign is, in the received chronology, 477 B.C.

bably of Bezer, Mesha says, that they had previously been destroyed.[1] But Reuben would not, of course, destroy his own cities. They must then have been destroyed either by Mesha's father, who reigned before him, when invading Reuben, or by Omri, when driving back Moab into his own land, and expelling him from these cities. *Possibly* they were dismantled only, since Mesha speaks only of Omri's occupying Medeba, Ataroth, and Jahaz. He held these three cities only, leaving the rest dismantled, or dismantling them, unable to place defenders in them, and unwilling to leave them as places of aggression for Moab. But whether they ever were fortified towns at all, or how they were desolated, is mere conjecture. Only they were desolated in these wars.

But it appears from Mesha's own statement, that neither Omri nor Ahab invaded Moab proper. For in speaking of his successful war and its results, he mentions no town south of the Arnon. He must have been a tributary king, but not a foot of his land was taken. The subsequent war was not a mere revolt, nor was it a mere refusal to pay tribute, of which Mesha makes no complaint. Nor could the tribute have been oppressive to him, since the spoils, left in the encampment of Moab and his allies shortly after his revolt, is evidence of such great wealth. The refusal to pay tribute would have involved nothing further, unless

---

[1] " I built Beth-Bamoth, for it was destroyed; I built Bezer, for " [the rest is conjecture. There are only two letters, which may be עצ or עז, perhaps עָזֻב " forsaken "] בנה probably, in such simple Hebrew, signifies, in regard to *all* the towns, built. It is the one word used of the king of Israel and of Mesha, "he built;" " I built," although it is rarely used of building on to existing towns and fortifying them (1 Kings xv. 17; 2 Chron. xi. 6). It is probably here used of *re*-building; since the cause of the building was the previous destruction.

Ahaziah had attempted to enforce it, as Hezekiah refused the tribute to Assyria, but remained in his own borders. But Ahaziah, unlike his brother Jehoram who succeeded him, seems to have undertaken nothing, except the building of some ships for trade.[1] Mesha's war was a renewal of the aggression on Reuben.

Heshbon is not mentioned, and therefore must, even after the war, have remained with Reuben.

Mesha's own war was an exterminating war, as far as he records it. "I fought against the city" [Ataroth], he says, "and took it, and killed all the mighty of the city for the well-pleasing of Chemosh and of Moab;" "I fought against it [Nebo] from break of day till noon and took it, and slew all of it, 7000 men; the ladies and maidens I devoted to Ashtar-Chemosh;" to be desecrated to the degradations of that sensual idolatry. The words too, "Israel perished with an everlasting destruction,"[2] stand clear, whether they express Mesha's conviction of the past or his hope of the future.

The war also, on the part of Moab, was a war of his idol Chemosh against God. Chemosh, from first to last, is the agent. "Chemosh was angry with his land;" "Chemosh [was pleased] with it in my days;" "I killed the mighty for the well-pleasing of Chemosh;" "I took captive thence all [ ] and dragged it along before Chemosh at Kiriath;" "Chemosh said to me, Go and take Nebo against Israel;"

[1] 2 Chron. xx. 35, 36.

[2] A break in the stone leaves the subject uncertain, "In my day said [ ], and I will look upon him and upon his house, and Israel perished with an everlasting destruction." Schlottman conjectures, probably, "Chemosh." Ganneau renders as if it were past, אָבַד, so Haug, Geiger, Neubauer, Wright; Schlottman, Nöldeke, and Ginsburg, as future, אֹבַד, though Ginsburg alone renders, "And Israel said, I shall destroy it for ever," which is impossible.

"I devoted the ladies and maidens to Ashtar-Chemosh;"
"I took thence the vessels of IHVH and dragged[1] them
before Chemosh;" "Chemosh drove him [the king of Israel]
out before [my face];" "Chemosh said to me, Go down
against Horonaim." "Chemosh [   ] it in my days."

Contemporary with this aggressive war against Israel
must have been the invasion by *the children of Moab and the
children of Ammon, the great multitude from beyond the sea,
from Syria,*[2] in the reign of Jehoshaphat, which brought such
terror upon Judah. It preceded the invasion of Moab by
Jehoshaphat in union with Jehoram and the king of Edom.
For the invasion of Judah by Moab and Ammon took place,
while Ahab's son, Ahaziah, was still living. For it was *after
this,* that Jehoshaphat joined with Ahaziah in making ships
to go to Tarshish.[3] But the expedition against Moab
was in union with Jehoram who succeeded Ahaziah. The
abundance of wealth which the invaders of Judah brought
with them, and the precious jewels with which they had
adorned themselves, show that this was no mere marauding
expedition, to spoil; but that its object was, to take possession of the land or at least of some portion of it. They
came by entire surprise on Jehoshaphat, who heard of them
first when they were at Hazazon-Tamar or Engedi, some
thirty-six and a half miles from Jerusalem.[4] He felt himself
entirely unequal to meet them, and cast himself upon God.
There was a day of public humiliation of Judah at Jerusalem.
Out of all the cities of Judah they came to seek the Lord.[5]
Jehoshaphat, in his public prayer, owned, *we have no might
against this great company which cometh against us; neither*

---

[1] The word in Hebrew is used of contumelious dragging
along the ground.
[2] 2 Chron. xx. 1, 2.
[3] Ib. xx. 35, 36. "And *after this* did Jehoshaphat king of
Judah join himself with Ahaziah."
[4] 300 stadia. Jos. Ant. ix. 1, 2.   [5] 2 Chron. xx. 4.

know we what to do : but our eyes are upon Thee.[1] He appeals
to God, that He had forbidden Israel to invade Ammon,
Moab, and Mount Seir, so that they turned away from
them and destroyed them not ; and now these rewarded
them by "coming to cast us out of Thy possession which
Thou hast given us to inherit."[2] One of the sons of Asaph
foretold to the congregation, that they might go out fear-
lessly ; for they should not have occasion to fight. A
Psalm, ascribed to Asaph, records a great invasion, the
object of which was the extermination of Israel. *They have
said, Come, and let us cut them off from being a nation, that
the name of Israel may be no more in remembrance.*[3] It had
been a secret confederacy. *They have taken crafty counsel
against Thy people.*[4] It was directed against God Himself,
i.e. His worship and worshippers. *For they have taken counsel
in heart together ; against Thee do they make a covenant.*[5] It
was a combination of the surrounding petty nations ; Tyre
on the north, the Philistines on the west ; on the south the
Amalekites, Ishmaelites, Hagarenes ; eastwards, Edom,
Gebal, Moab, Ammon. But its most characteristic feature
was, that Assur (this corresponds with no period after
Jehoshaphat) occupies a subordinate place to Edom and
Moab, putting them forward and helping *them. Assur also,*
Asaph says,[6] *is joined with them ; they have become an arm to
the children of Lot.* This agrees with the description, *there
is come against thee a great multitude from beyond the sea,
from Syria.*

Scripture does not record on what ground the invasion
of Moab by Jehoram and Jehoshaphat, with the tributary
king of Edom, was directed against Moab proper ; but it
was the result doubtless of the double war of Moab against
Reuben and against Judah. It was a war, in which the

---

[1] 2 Chron. xx. 12. [2] Ib. xx. 11. [3] Ps. lxxxiii. 4.
[4] Ib. lxxxiii. 3. [5] Ib. lxxxiii. 5. [6] Ib. lxxxiii. 8.

strength of Israel and Moab was put forth to the utmost. Jehoram had mustered all Israel ; [1] Moab had gathered all who had reached the age of manhood and upwards, *every one who girded on a girdle and upwards.*[2] The three armies, which had made a seven days' circuit in the wilderness, were on the point of perishing by thirst and falling into the hands of Moab, when Elisha in God's name promised them the supply of their want, and complete victory over Moab. The eager cupidity of Moab, as of many other armies, became the occasion of his complete overthrow. The counsel with which Elisha accompanied his prediction, *ye shall smite every fenced city and every choice city, and every good tree ye shall fell, and all springs of water ye shall stop up, and every good piece of land ye shall waste with stones,*[3] was directed, apparently, to dislodge an enemy so inveterate. For water was essential to the fertility of their land and their dwelling there. We hear of no special infliction of death, like what Mesha records of himself. The war was ended by the king of Moab's sacrificing the heir-apparent of the king of Edom,[4] which naturally created great displeasure against Israel, in whose cause Edom thus suffered, so that they departed to their own land and finally revolted.

Their departure apparently broke up the siege of Ar and the expedition. Israel apparently was not strong enough to carry on the war without Edom, or feared to remain with their armies away from their own land, as in the time of David, of which Edom might take the advantage. We know only the result.

Moab probably even extended her border to the South by the conquest of Horonaim.[5]

After this, Moab is mentioned only on occasion of the

[1] 2 Kings iii. 6.   [2] Ib. iii. 21.   [3] Ib. iii. 19.
[4] See above on Amos ii. 1.
[5] This is marked on the Moabite stone, as a subsequent and distinct expedition.

miracle of the dead man, to whom God gave life, when cast into Elisha's sepulchre, as he came in contact with his bones. Like the Bedaween now, or the Amalekites of old, *the bands of Moab came into the land, as the year came.*[1] Plunder, year by year, was the lot of Israel at the hands of Moab.

On the east of Jordan, Israel must have remained in part (as Mesha says of the Gadites of Aroer) in their old border. For after this, Hazael, in Jehu's reign, smote Israel *from Aroer which is by the river Arnon ;* [2] and at that time probably Ammon joined with him in the exterminating war in Gilead, destroying life before it had come into the world, *that they might enlarge their border.*[3] Jeroboam II., 825 B.C., restored Israel *to the sea of the plain,*[4] i.e. the Dead Sea, and (as seems probable from the limitation of that term in Deuteronomy,[5] *under Ashdoth-Pisgah eastwards*) to its northern extremity, lower in latitude than Heshbon, yet above Nebo and Medeba, leaving accordingly to Moab all which it had gained by Mesha. Uzziah, a few years later, made the Ammonites tributaries,[6] 810 B.C. But forty years later, 771 B.C., Pul, and, after yet another thirty years, 740, Tiglath-pileser having carried away the trans-Jordanic tribes,[7] Moab again possessed itself of the whole territory of Reuben. Probably before. For 726 B.C., when Isaiah foretold that *the glory of Moab should be contemned with all that great multitude,*[8] he hears the wailing of Moab throughout all his towns, and names all those which had once been Reuben's and of whose conquest or possession Moab had boasted,[9] Nebo, Medeba, Dibon, Jahaz, Baiith ; as also those not conquered then, [10] Heshbon, Elealeh ; and those of

[1] 2 Kings xiii. 20.　　　　[2] Ib. x. 33.
[3] See on Amos i. 13.　　　[4] 2 Kings xiv. 25.
[5] Deut. iii. 17.　　　　　[6] 2 Chron. xxvi. 8.
[7] 1 Chron. v. 26.　　　　[8] Isa. xvi. 14.
[9] Ib. xv. 1, 2, 4.　　　　[10] Ib. xv. 4, 5, 1.

Moab proper, Luhith, Horonaim, and its capitals, Ar-Moab
and Kir-Moab.   He hears their sorrow, sees their desolation,
and bewails with their weeping.[1] He had prophesied this
before,[2] and now, three years before its fulfilment by
Tiglath-pileser, he renews it.[3] This tender sorrow for Moab
has more the character of an elegy than of a denunciation;
so that he could scarcely lament more tenderly the ruin
of his own people.   He mentions also distinctly no sin
there except pride.   The pride of Moab seems something
of common notoriety and speech. *We have heard.*[4] Isaiah
accumulates words, to express the haughtiness of Moab;
*the pride of Moab ; exceeding proud ; his pride and his haughti-
ness and his wrath,*[5] pride overpassing bounds, upon others.
His words seem to be formed so as to keep this one bared
thought before us, as if we were to say "pride, prideful,
proudness, pridefulness"; and withal the unsubstantialness
of it all, *the unsubstantiality of his lies.*[6]   Pride is the source
of all ambition ; so Moab is pictured as retiring within her
old bounds, *the fords of Arnon,* and thence asking for aid; her
petition is met by the counter-petition, that, if she would
be protected in the day of trouble, the outcasts of Israel
might lodge with her now : *be thou a covert to her from the
face of the spoiler.*[7] The prophecy seems to mark itself out
as belonging to a time, after the two and a half tribes had
been desolated, as stragglers sought refuge in Moab, and
when a severe infliction was to come on Moab : *the* [8] *remnant*
shall be *small, small not great.*

Yet Moab recovered this too. It was a weakening of
the nation, not its destruction.   Some 126 years after the

---

[1] Isa. xvi. 9.
[2] "That the prophecy must be from any other older
prophet, is an inference from grounds of nought."   Del.
[3] Isa. xvi. 13, 14.
[4] Ib. xvi. 6.   [5] .גאון מואב גא מאד גאותו וגאונו ועברתו
[6] .לא בן בדיו   [7] Isa. xvi. 4, 5.   [8] Ib. xvi. 14.

prophecy of Isaiah, thirty years after the prophecy of Zephaniah, Moab, in the time of Jeremiah, was in entire prosperity, as if no visitation had ever come upon her. What Zephaniah says of the luxuriousness of his people, Jeremiah says of Moab: *Moab is one at ease from his youth; he is resting on his lees; and he hath not been emptied from vessel to vessel, neither hath he gone into captivity.*[1] They *say, We are mighty and strong men for the war.*[2] Moab was a *strong staff*, a *beautiful rod;*[3] he *magnified himself against the Lord;*[4] *Israel* was a *derision* to him; *he skipped for joy* at his distress.[5] Jeremiah repeats and even strengthens Isaiah's description of his pride; *his pride, proud,* he repeats, *exceedingly; his loftiness,* again *his pride, his arrogancy, and the haughtiness of his heart.*[6] Its *strong holds*[7] were unharmed; all its cities, *far and near,* are counted one by one, in their prosperity;[8] its summer-fruits and vintage were plenteous; its vines, luxuriant; all was joy and shouting. Whence should this evil come? Yet so it was with Sodom and Gomorrah just before its overthrow. It was, for beauty, *a paradise of God; well-watered everywhere; as the garden of the Lord, like the land of Egypt.*[9] In the morning *the smoke of the country went up as the smoke of a furnace.*[10] The destruction foretold by Jeremiah is far other than the affliction spoken of by Isaiah. Isaiah prophesies only a visitation, which should reduce her people: Jeremiah foretells, as did Zephaniah, captivity and the utter destruction of her cities. The destruction foretold is complete. Not of individual cities only, but of the whole he saith, *Moab is destroyed.*[11] *The spoiler shall come upon every city, and no city shall escape, and the valley shall perish and the high places*

---

[1] Jer. xlviii. 11.   [2] Ib. xlviii. 14.   [3] Ib. xlviii. 17.
[4] Ib. xlviii. 26.   [5] Ib. xlviii. 27.   [6] Ib. xlviii. 29.
[7] Ib. xlviii. 18.   [8] Ib. xlviii. 1, 3, 5, 21–24.
[9] Gen. xiii. 10.   [10] Ib. xix. 28.   [11] Jer. xlviii. 4.

shall be destroyed, as the Lord hath spoken.[1] Moab himself was to leave his land. *Flee, save your lives, and ye shall be like the heath in the wilderness. Chemosh shall go forth into captivity; his priests and his princes together. Give pinions unto Moab, that it may flee and get away, and her cities shall be a desolation; for there is none to dwell therein.*[2] It was not only to go into captivity, but its home was to be destroyed. *I will send to her those who shall upheave her, and they shall upheave her, and her vessels they shall empty, all her flagons* (all that aforetime contained her) *they shall break in pieces.*[3] *Moab is destroyed and her cities;*[4] *the spoiler of Moab is come upon her; he hath destroyed the strongholds.*[5] The subsequent history of the Moabites is in the words, *Leave the cities and dwell in the rock, dwellers of Moab, and be like a dove which nesteth in the sides of the mouth of the pit.*[6] The purpose of Moab and Ammon against Israel which Asaph complains of, and which Mesha probably speaks of, is retorted upon her. *In Heshbon they have devised evil against it; come and let us cut it off from being a nation. Moab shall be destroyed from being a people, because he hath magnified himself against the Lord.*[7]

Whence should this evil come? They had, with the Ammonites, been faithful servants of Nebuchadnezzar against Judah.[8] Their concerted conspiracy with Edom, Tyre, Zidon, to which they invited Zedekiah,[9] was dissolved. Nebuchadnezzar's march against Judæa did not touch them; for they *skipped with joy*[10] at Israel's distresses. The connection of Baalis, king of the Ammonites, with Ishmael,[11] the assassin of Gedaliah, whom the king of

[1] Jer. xlviii. 8.
[2] Ib. xlviii. 6.
[3] Ib. xlviii. 12.
[4] Ib. xlviii. 15.
[5] Ib. xlviii. 18.
[6] Ib. xlviii. 28.
[7] Ib. xlviii. 2, 42.
[8] 2 Kings xxiv. 2.
[9] Jer. xxvii. 2 sqq.
[10] Ib. xlviii. 27.
[11] Ib. xl. 14; xli. 10.

Babylon made governor over the land¹ out of their own
people, probably brought down the vengeance of Nebuchadnezzar. For Chaldeans too were included in the
slaughter.² The blow seems to have been aimed at the
existence of the people ; for the murder of Gedaliah
followed upon the rallying of the Jews *out of all the places
whither they had been driven.*³ It returned on Ammon itself,
and on Moab who probably on this, as on former occasions,
was associated with it. The two nations, who had escaped
at the destruction of Jerusalem, were warred upon and
subdued by Nebuchadnezzar in the twenty-third year of his
reign,⁴ the fifth after the destruction of Jerusalem.

And then probably followed that complete destruction
and disgraced end, in which Isaiah, in a distinct prophecy,
sees Moab trodden down by God as ⁵ *the heap of straw is
trodden down in the waters* ⁶ *of the dunghill,* and he (Moab)
*stretcheth forth his hands in the midst thereof, as the swimmer
stretcheth forth his hands to swim, and He,* God, *shall bring
down his pride with the treacheries of his hands.* It speaks
much of the continued hostility of Moab, that, in prophesy-
ing the complete deliverance for which Israel waited, the
one enemy whose destruction is foretold, is Moab and those
pictured by Moab. *We have waited for Him and He will save
us—For in this mountain* (Zion) *shall the hand of the Lord rest,
and Moab shall be trodden down under Him.*⁷

After this, Moab, as a nation, disappears from history.
Israel, on its return from the captivity, was again enticed
into idolatry by Moabite and Ammonite wives, as well
as by those of Ashdod and others,⁸ Canaanites, Hittites,
Perizzites, Jebusites, Egyptians, Amorites.⁹ Sanballat also,

---

¹ 2 Kings xxv. 22–26 ; Jer. xl. 5 ; xli. 2.
² Jer. xli. 3.   ³ Ib. xl. 12.
⁴ Jos. Ant. x. 9, 7.   ⁵ Isa. xxv. 10–12.
⁶ בְּמֵי Chethib.   ⁷ Isa. xxv. 9, 10.
⁸ Neh. xiii. 23–26.   ⁹ Ezra ix. 1.

who headed the opposition to the rebuilding of Jerusalem, was a Moabite;[1] Tobiah, an Ammonite.[2] Yet it went no further than intrigue and the threat of war. They were but individuals, who cherished the old hostility. In the time of the Maccabees, the Ammonites, not Moab, *with a mighty power and much people*, were in possession of the Reubenite cities to Jazar.[3] It was again an exterminating war, in which the Jews were to be destroyed.[4] After repeated defeats by Judas Maccabæus, the Ammonites *hired the Arabians*[5] (not the Moabites) *to help them*, and Judas, although victorious, was obliged to remove the whole *Israelite* population, *all that were in the land of Gilead, from the least unto the greatest, even their wives, and their children, and their stuff, a very great host, to the end they might come into the land of Judœa.*[6] The whole population was removed, obviously lest, on the withdrawal of Judas' army, they should be again imperilled. As it was a defensive war against Ammon, there is no mention of any city, south of the Arnon, in Moab's own territory. It was probably with the view to magnify descendants of Lot, that Josephus speaks of the Moabites as being " even yet a very great nation."[7] S. Justin's account, that there is "even now a great multitude of Ammonites,"[8] does not seem to me to imply a national existence. A later writer says, " Now not only the Edomites but the Ammonites and Moabites too are included in the one name of Arabians."[9]

Some chief towns of Moab became Roman towns, connected by the Roman road from Damascus to Elath. Ar and Kir-Moab in Moab proper became Areopolis and Charac-Moab, and, as well as Medeba and Heshbon in the country

[1] Neh. ii. 10 ; iv. 1–8.   [2] Ib. iv. 3, 7.
[3] 1 Macc. v. 6, 8.   [4] Ib. v. 9, 10, 27.
[5] Ib. v. 39.   [6] Ib. v. 45.   [7] Ant. i. 11, 5.
[8] Dial. n. 119, p. 218, Oxf. Tr.
[9] Anon. in Job ap. Origen, i. 852.

which had been Reuben's, preserve traces of Roman occupancy. As such, they became Christian Sees. The towns, which were not thus revived as Roman, probably perished at once, since they bear no traces of any later building.

The present condition of Moab and Ammon is remarkable in two ways: (1) for the testimony which it gives of its former extensive population; (2) for the extent of its present desolation. "How fearfully," says an accurate and minute observer,[1] "is this residence of old kings and their land wasted!" It gives a vivid idea of the desolation, that distances are marked, not by villages which he passes but by ruins.[2] "From these ruined places, which lay on our way, one sees how thickly inhabited the district formerly was."[3] Yet the ground remained fruitful. It was partly abandoned to wild plants, the wormwood and other shrubs;[4]

[1] Seetzen, Reisen, i. 412.

[2] e.g. "Three-quarters of an hour further, we reached the ruins of el-Eale; one and a half hours further we came to Hüsbân; besides some overthrown pillars, nothing important is found here. On the east, about one and a half hours, are the ruins of Shelûl: after an hour on this plain we came to three wasted places, close together; half-an-hour further, we reached the ruins of what formerly was Mádabá; half-an-hour further lay the ruined village of Tuême; above an hour to the west the important ruins of Maéin." Ib. 407, 408.

[3] Ib. 411.

[4] "A little north of el-Eale we came on good soil, which however lay wholly uncultivated and was mostly overgrown with the prickly little Bullân, which gave the country the look of moor-ground" (Seetzen, Travels, i. 406). "The soil here (Heshbon) is in this district excellent, but it lies wholly uncultivated and serves only for pasture to the little herds of sheep, goats, kine, and camels of the Arabs" (ib. p. 407). "The Arabs cultivate a little ground near Mádabá" (p. 409). "The land (the other side the Mujeb [Arnon] and so in Moab proper) had little grass, but there was an extraordinary

partly, the artificial irrigation, essential to cultivation in
this land, was destroyed ;[1] here and there a patch was
cultivated ; the rest remained barren, because the crops

quantity of wormwood on it. Yet the soil seems excellent
for wheat, although no spot was cultivated. Large spots had
the look of our moors from the quantity of wormwood and
other little shrubs " (p. 410). " Here and there, there were
tokens of cultivation, wheatfields ; the wheat was good "
(p. 412).

[1] See Mr. Tristram's picture of " a ruin-covered ridge by
an immense tank of solid masonry, 140 yards by 110 yards,
at Ziza. From the surface of the water to the edge of the
tank was 17 feet 6 inches. The masonry was simply magnificent. The whole system and artificial sluices were pre-
cisely similar to ancient works for irrigation in India and
Ceylon.—Such works easily explain to us the enormous
population, of which the ruined cities give evidence. Everywhere is some artificial means of retaining the occasional
supplies of rain-water. So long as these precious structures
remained in order, cultivation was continuous and famines
remained unknown.—The Islamite invasion left the miserable remnants of a dense and thriving nation entirely dependent on the neighbouring countries for their supply of
corn : a dependence which must continue till these border
lands are secure from the inroad of the predatory bands of
the East " (Land of Moab, pp. 183–186). At Kustul is " a
massive wall in the plain, about 600 yards in length across
the valley, and 18 feet thick, built to dam up the water in the
gentle depression, the head of the wady " (ib. c. 12, p. 220).
" Gôr el Mesráa, as far as the soil can be watered, evinces a
luxuriant fertility. By far the greater part of it is a waste "
(Seetz. ii. 352). " Gôr el Záphia owes its fruitfulness entirely
to the water of the Wady el Hössa, which is guided to the
fields in many canals. But only a very small portion of this
exceedingly rich soil is cultivated, the rest is overgrown with
bushes and shrubs, wherein very many wild boars, hyenas
and other wild animals live " (ib. 355). " This water too [of
the Nimméry] is said formerly to have been used for watering
some fields, of which there is now no trace " (ib. 354).

might become the prey of the spoiler,[1] or the thin population had had no heart to cultivate it. A list of thirty-three
destroyed places, which still retained their names, was given
to Seetzen,[2] " of which many were cities in times of old,
and, besides these, a great number of other wasted villages.
One sees from this, that, in the days of old, this land was
extremely peopled and flourishing, and that destructive
wars alone could produce the present desolation." And
thereon he adds the names of forty more ruined places.
Others say: "The whole of the fine plains in this quarter"
[the south of Moab] "are covered with sites of towns, on every
eminence or spot convenient for the construction of one;
and as all the land is capable of rich cultivation, there can
be no doubt that this country, now so deserted, once presented a continued picture of plenty and fertility."[3] "Every
knoll" [in the highlands of Moab] "is covered with shape-
less ruins.—The ruins consist merely of heaps of squared
and well-fitting stones, which apparently were erected
without mortar."[4] "One description might serve for all
these Moabite ruins. The town seems to have been a
system of concentric circles, built round a central fort, and
outside the buildings the rings continue as terrace-walks,
the gardens of the old city. The terraces are continuous
between the twin hillocks and intersect each other at the
foot."[5] "Ruined villages and towns, broken walls that
once enclosed gardens and vineyards, remains of ancient

---

[1] " True, the land is not ours, but our people are many,
and who shall dare to prevent them from going where they
please? You will find them everywhere, if the land is good
for them." Answer of Beni Sakkr Sheikh—Tristram, Moab.
c. 15, p. 28.

[2] Ib. 416.

[3] Irby and Mangles (May 14), p. 113.

[4] Tristram, Land of Moab, pp. 100, 101.

[5] Ib. 99.

roads; everything in Moab tells of the immense wealth and population, which that country must have once enjoyed."[1]

The like is observed of Ammon.[2] His was direct hatred of the true religion. It was not mere exultation at the

---

[1] Palmer, Desert of the Exodus, ii. 473, 474.

[2] " East of Assalt, including Ammon, are thirty ruined or deserted places of which names are given in Dr. Smith's Arabic lists " (Keith, Prophecy, p. 274). " All this country, formerly so populous and flourishing, is now changed into a vast desert " (Seetzen, Brief Account, &c., p. 34, ib. p. 263). " The far greater part of this country is uninhabited, being abandoned to the wandering Arabs, and the towns and villages are in a state of total ruin " (id. p. 37, ib.). " Two hours from Szalt we came upon some peasants, who were ploughing some little fields near what was a little fountain " (Seetzen, i. 405). " The soil was excellent ; but only here and there we saw a little spot cultivated, and this by the Aduân Arabs " (p. 406). " The country that lay in our route [near Daboah], though now bare of wood, presented a great extent of fertile soil, lying entirely waste, though equal to any of the very best portions of Galilee and Samaria, and capable of producing sustenance for a large population. Around us, in every direction, were remains of more than fifty towns or villages, once maintained by the productive soil, over which they were so thickly studded " (Buckingham, Travels among the Arab Tribes, p. 66). " At Mahanafish we had arrived at a very elevated part of the plain, which had continued fertile throughout the whole distance from Ammon " (p. 81). " SSE. of Yedoody we pushed our way over a continuous tract of fertile soil, capable of the highest cultivation. Throughout the whole extent of the plain were seen ruined towns in every direction, before, behind, on each side, generally seated on small eminences, all at a short distance from each other, and all, as far as we had yet seen, bearing evident marks of former opulence. There was not a tree in sight ; but my guide assured me that the whole of the plain was covered with the finest soil, and capable of being made the most productive corn-land in the world " (ib. p. 85).

I

desolation of an envied people. It was hatred of the worship of God. "Thus saith the Lord God : *Because thou saidst, Aha, against My sanctuary, because it was profaned; and against the land of Israel, because it was desolated; and against the house of Judah, because they went into captivity.*"[1] The like temper is shown in the boast, "*Because that Moab and Seir do say, Behold, the house of Judah is like unto the heathen,*"[2] i.e. on a level with them.

Forbearing and long-suffering as Almighty God is, in His infinite mercy, He does not, for that mercy's sake, bear the direct defiance of Himself. He allows His creatures to forget Him, not to despise or defy Him. And on this ground, perhaps, He gives to His prophecies a fulfilment beyond what the letter requires, that they may be a continued witness to Him. The Ammonites, some 1600 years ago, ceased to "be remembered among the nations." But as Nineveh and Babylon, and the cities of Sodom and Gomorrah, by being what they are, are witnesses to His dealings, so the way in which Moab and Ammon are still kept desolate is a continued picture of that first desolation. Both remain rich, fertile ; but the very abundance of their fertility is the cause of their desolation. God said to Ammon, as the retribution on his contumely : "Therefore, behold, I give thee to the children of the East for a possession, and they shall set their encampments in thee, and place their dwellings in thee; *they* shall eat thy fruit and *they* shall drink thy milk; and I will make Rabbah a dwelling-place of camels, and the children of Ammon a couching-place for flocks."[3] Of Moab He says also, "I will open the side of Moab from the cities, which are on his frontiers, the glory of the country, unto the men of the East with the Ammonites."[4] And this is an exact descrip-

---

[1] Ezek. xxv. 3.   [2] Ib. xxv. 8.
[3] Ib. xxv. 4, 5.   [4] Ib. xxv. 9, 10.

tion of the condition of the land at this day. All travellers describe the richness of the soil. We have seen this as to Moab. But the history is one and the same. One of the most fertile regions of the world, full of ruined towns, destitute of villages or fixed habitations, or security of property, its inhabitants ground down by those who have succeeded the Midianites and the Amalekites, *the children of the East*. "Thou canst not find a country like the Belka," says the Arabic proverb,[1] but "the inhabitants cultivate patches only of the best soil in that territory when they have a prospect of being able to secure the harvest against the invasion of enemies." "We passed many ruined cities," said Lord Lindsay,[2] "and the country has once been very populous, but, in thirty-five miles at least, we did not see a single village; the whole country is one vast pasturage, overspread by the flocks and herds of the Anezee and Beni Hassan Bedouins."

The site of Rabbath Amman was well chosen for strength. Lying "in a long valley"[3] through which a stream passed, "the city of waters" could not easily be taken, nor its inhabitants compelled to surrender from hunger or thirst. Its site, as the eastern bound of Peræa,[4] "the last place where water could be obtained and a frontier fortress against the wild tribes beyond,"[5] marked it for preservation. In Greek times, the disputes for its possession attest the sense of its importance. In Roman, it was one of the chief cities of the Decapolis, though its population was said to be a mixture of Egyptians, Arabians, Phœnicians.[6] The

[1] Burckhardt, Syria, p. 369. "On both sides of the road" (near Naour) "were the vestiges of ancient field-enclosures." Ib. 365.   [2] Travels, p. 279.
[3] Irby and Mangles, June 14, c. 8, p. 146.
[4] Jos. B. J. iii. 3, 3.
[5] Grote in Smith Bibl. Dict. v. Rabbah.
[6] Strabo, xvi. 2, 33, p. 760. Cas.

coins of Roman emperors to the end of the second century
contain symbols of plenty, where now reigns utter desolation.[1]   In the fourth century, it and two other now ruined
places, Bostra and Gerasa, are named as "most carefully
and strongly walled." It was on a line of rich commerce
filled with strong places, in sites well selected for repelling
the invasions of the neighbouring nations.[2]   Centuries
advanced. It was greatly beautified by its Roman masters.
The extent and wealth of the Roman city are attested both
by the remains of noble edifices on both sides of the stream,
and [3] by pieces of pottery, which are the traces of ancient
civilised dwelling, strewed on the earth two miles from
the city.   "At this place, Ammân, as well as Gerasa and
Gamala, three colonial settlements within the compass of a
day's journey from one another, there were five magnificent
theatres and one amphitheatre, besides temples, baths, aque-
ducts, naumachia, triumphal arches." [4]   "Its theatre was
the largest in Syria ; its colonnade had at least fifty
columns." [5]   The difference of the architecture shows that
its aggrandisement must have been the work of different
centuries : its "castle walls are thick, and denote a remote
antiquity ; large blocks of stone are piled up without
cement and still hold together as well as if recently placed."
It is very probably the same which Joab called David to
take, after the city of waters had been taken ; within it are
traces of a temple with Corinthian columns, the largest seen
there, yet "not of the best Roman times."

Yet Amman, the growth of centuries, at the end of our
sixth century was destroyed. For "it was desolate before

---

[1] Ritter, West-Asien, viii. 1157.

[2] Amm. Marc. xiv. 8, 13.

[3] Buckingham, Arab Tribes, pp. 67, 73.

[4] Ib. 77.

[5] See Burckhardt's description of its ruins.   Travels in
Syria, pp. 357–360.

Islam, a great ruin." [1]   "Nowhere else had we seen the
vestiges of public magnificence and wealth in such marked
contrast with the relapse into savage desolation." [2]   But
the site of the old city, so well adapted either for a secure
refuge for its inhabitants or for a secure depository for
their plunder, was, on that very ground, when desolated
of its inhabitants, suited for what God, by Ezekiel, said it
would become, a place where the men of the East should
stable their flocks and herds, secure from straying.   What
a change that its temples, the centre of the worship of its
successive idols, or its theatres, its places of luxury or of
pomp, should be stables for that drudge of man, the camel,
and the stream which gave it the proud title of "city of
waters" their drinking trough !   And yet of the cities
whose destruction is prophesied, this is foretold of Rabbah
alone, as in it alone is it fulfilled !   "Ammon," says Lord
Lindsay, [3] " was situated on both sides of the stream ; the
dreariness of its present aspect is quite indescribable.   It
looks like the abode of death ; the valley stinks with dead
camels ; one of them was rotting in the stream ; and
though we saw none among the ruins, they were absolutely
covered in every direction with their dung."   " Bones and
skulls of camels were mouldering there [in the area of the
ruined theatre] and in the vaulted galleries of this immense
structure."   "It is now quite deserted, except by the
Bedouins, who water their flocks at its little river, descend-
ing to it by a *wady*, nearly opposite to a theatre (in which
Dr. MacLennan saw great herds and flocks) and by the
akiba.   Reascending it, we met sheep and goats by
thousands, and camels by hundreds."   Another says, [4] " The
space intervening between the river and the western hills

[1] Abulf. Tab. Syr., p. 91.
[2] Tristram, Land of Israel, p. 551.
[3] The Holy Land, pp. 279, 281, 283.
[4] G. Robinson's Travels in Palestine and Syria, ii. 175.

is entirely covered with the remains of buildings, now only used for shelter for camels and sheep." Buckingham mentions incidentally that he was prevented from sleeping at night "by the bleating of flocks and the neighing of horses, barking of dogs, &c."[1] Another speaks of "a small stone building in the Acropolis now used as a shelter for flocks."[2] While he was "traversing the ruins of the city, the number of goats and sheep, which were driven in among them, was exceedingly annoying, however remarkable as fulfilling the prophecies."[3] "Before six tents fed sheep and camels."[4] "[5] Ezekiel points just to these (xxv. 5), which passage Seetzen cites.[6] And in fact the ruins are still used for such stalls."

The prophecy is the very opposite to that upon Babylon, though both alike are prophecies of desolation. Of Babylon Isaiah prophesies, "It shall never be inhabited, neither shall it be dwelt in from generation to generation ; neither shall the Arabian pitch tent there, neither shall the shepherds make fold there, but wild beasts of the desert shall lie there, and their houses shall be full of doleful creatures ; and the ostriches shall dwell there, and the jackals shall cry in their desolate houses, and howling creatures in their pleasant palaces."[7] And the ruins are full of wild beasts.[8] Of Rabbah Ezekiel prophesied that it should be "a possession for the men of the East, and I,"[9]

---

[1] Travels among the Arab Tribes, Ruins of Ammon, p. 73.
[2] Lord C. Hamilton in Keith, p. 271.
[3] Id. ib., p. 269.   [4] Seetzen, Reisen, i. 394.
[5] Prof. Kruse, Anmerkung, ib. T. iv. p. 216.
[6] l. 31.
[7] Isa. xiii. 20.
[8] See Rich Mem., pp. 27, 30 ; Buckingham, ii. 307 ; Sir R. K. Porter, Travels, ii. 342, 387 ; Kenneir Memoirs, p. 279 ; Keppel's Narr., i. 179, 180 ; Layard, Nin. and Bab., quoted by Keith on Prophecy, pp. 466, 467.
[9] Ezek. xxv. 4, 5.

9 Therefore *as* I live, saith the Lᴏʀᴅ of hosts, the God of Israel, Surely ᵃ Moab shall be as Sodom, and ᵇ the children of Ammon as Gomorrah, ᶜ *even*

ᵃ Isa. xv. ; Jer. xlviii. ; Ezek. xxv. 9 ; Amos ii. 1.
ᵇ Amos i. 13.
ᶜ Gen. xix. 25 ; Deut. xxix. 23 ; Isa. xiii. 19 and xxxiv. 13 ; Jer. xlix. 18 and l. 40.

God says, "will make Rabbah a stable for camels, and the Ammonites a couching-place for flocks ; " and man's lawlessness fulfils the will and word of God.

9. *Therefore as I live, saith the Lord of hosts.* Life specially belongs to God, since He Alone is Underived Life. *He hath life in Himself.*[1] He is entitled "the living God," as here, in tacit contrast with the dead idols of the Philistines,[2] with idols generally ;[3] or against the blasphemies of Sennacherib,[4] the mockeries of scoffers ;[5] of the awe of His presence,[6] His might for His people ;[7] as the object of the soul's longings,[8] the nearness in the Gospel, *children of the living God.*[9] *Since He can swear by no greater, He sware by Himself.*[10] Since mankind are ready mostly to believe that God means well with them, but are slow to think that He is in earnest in His threats, God employs this sanction of what He says, twice only in regard to His promises or His mercy ;[11] everywhere else to give solemnity to His threats.[12]

[1] S. John v. 26.
[2] 1 Sam. xvii. 26, 36.   [3] Jer. x. 10.
[4] 2 Kings xix. 4, 16.   [5] Jer. xxiii. 36.
[6] Deut. v. 25, 26.   [7] Joshua iii. 10.
[8] Ps. of sons of Korah, xlii. 2 ; lxxxiv. 2.
[9] Hosea i. 10.   [10] Heb. vi. 13.
[11] Isa. xlix. 18 ; Ezek. xxxiii. 11.
[12] Num. xiv. 21 [of the glory which God should have in all the world from his chastisement of Israel], 28 ; Deut. xxxii. 40, [adding לְעוֹלָם] Jer. xxii. 24 ; Ez. v. 11 ; xiv. 16,

the breeding of nettles, and saltpits, and a perpetual

The appeal to the truth of His own being[1] in support of the truth of His words is part of the grandeur of the prophet Ezekiel in whom it chiefly occurs. God says in the same meaning, *by Myself have I sworn,* of promises which required strong faith.[2]

Saith the Lord of Hosts. Their blasphemies had denied the very being of God, as God, to Whom they preferred or likened their idols; they had denied His power or that He could avenge, so He names His Name of power, *the Lord of the hosts* of heaven against their array against His border, I, *the Lord of hosts* Who can fulfil what I threaten, and *the God of Israel* Who Myself am wronged in My people, will make *Moab as Sodom, and the children of Ammon as Gomorrah.* Sodom and Gomorrah had once been flourishing cities, on the borders of that land, which Israel had won from the Amorite, and of which Moab and Ammon at different times possessed themselves, and to secure which Ammon carried on that exterminating war. For they were to the east of the plain *between Bethel and Ai,* where Lot made his choice, *in the plain or circle of Jordan,*[3] the well-known title of the tract through which the Jordan flowed into the Dead Sea. Near this lay Zoar (Ziara[4]), beneath the caves whither Lot, at whose prayer it had been spared, escaped

---

18, 20; xvi. 48 [as Judge]; xvii. 16, 19; xviii. 3 [in rebuke]; xx. 3, 31, 33; xxxiii. 27; xxxiv. 8; xxxv. 11. In the same sense, *I swear by Myself,* Jer. xxii. 5; xlix. 13; *hath sworn by Himself,* Amos vi. 8; by the excellency of Jacob, viii. 7.

[1] Ges. Maurer, &c. [with a strange conception of God] render "ita vi*vam.*" Ewald rightly, "as true as I live."

[2] Gen. xxii. 16 (so often referred to); Isa. xlv. 23, or by Thy Right Hand, i.e. the might which He would put forth.

[3] Gen. xiii. 1, 3, 11.

[4] See the description of Ziara, "once a place of considerable importance," in Tristram, Land of Moab, pp. 328, 330.

desolation : [a] the residue of my people shall spoil them, and the remnant of my people shall possess them.

[a] Ver. 7.

from its wickedness. Moab and Ammon had settled and in time spread from the spot, wherein their forefathers had received their birth. Sodom, at least, must have been in that part of the plain which is to the east of the Jordan, since Lot was bidden to flee to the mountains with his wife and daughters, and there is no mention of the river, which would have been a hindrance.[1] Then it lay probably in that " broad belt of desolation " [2] in the plain of Shittim, as Gomorrah and others of the Pentapolis may have lain in " the sulphur-sprinkled expanse " between El Riha [on the site of Jericho] and the Dead Sea, " covered with layers of salt and gypsum which overlie the loamy subsoil, literally fulfilling the descriptions of Holy Writ (says an eye-witness), *Brimstone and salt and burning, that it is not sown nor beareth, nor any grass groweth therein :* [3] *a fruitful land turned into saltness.*[4] *No man shall abide there, neither shall a son of man dwell in it.*" [5] An elaborate system of artificial irrigation was carried through that cis-Jordanic tract, which decayed when it was desolated of man, and that desolation prevents its restoration.

The doom of Moab and Ammon is rather of entire destruction beyond all recovery, than of universal barrenness. For the imagery, that it should be the *breeding* [lit. *possession*] *of nettles* would not be literally compatible, except in different localities, with that of *saltpits*, which exclude all vegetation. Yet both are united in Moab. The soil continues,

[1] Gen. xix. 17–23.
[2] Tristram, Land of Israel, p. 367.
[3] Deut. xxix. 23.   [4] Ps. cvii. 34.   [5] Jer. xlix. 18.

10 This shall they have ^a for their pride, because

^a Isa. xvi. 6 ; Jer. xlviii. 29.

---

as of old, of exuberant fertility ; yet in part, from the utter
neglect and insecurity of agriculture, it is abandoned to
a rank and encumbering vegetation; elsewhere, from the
neglect of the former artificial system of irrigation, it is
wholly barren. The plant named is one of rank growth,
since outcasts could lie concealed under it.[1] The prepon-
derating authority seems to be for *mollâch*,[2] the Bedawin
name of the "mallow," Prof. E. H. Palmer says,[3] "which,"
he adds, "I have seen growing in rank luxuriance in Moab,
especially in the sides of deserted Arab camps."

*The residue of My people shall spoil them, and the remnant
of My people shall possess them.* Again, a remnant only, but
even these shall prevail against them, as was first fulfilled
in Judas Maccabæus.[4]

10. *This [shall they have for their pride*, lit. *This to them
instead of their pride.* Contempt and shame shall be the
residue of the proud man ; the exaltation shall be gone,
and all which they shall gain to themselves shall be *shame.*
Moab and Ammon are the types of heretics.[5] As they were
akin to the people of God, but hating it ; akin to Abraham
through a lawless birth, but ever molesting the children

---

[1] Job xxx. 7.

[2] Jon. has מַלּוּחִין : the Peschito, מַלּוּחָא, and, remarkably,
does not use a name coincident with the Heb. חרול sc.
חוּרְלָא, a sort of vetch. Abulwalid prefers the מלּוח, but
mentions the חַרְשֶׁף "artichoke" (Höst Nachrichten von
Maroko u. Fez, p. 538) as an "opinion"; R. Tanchum
adopts it, but gives חרמאן as an "opinion," and says that
"altogether it belongs to the prickly plants"; Kimchi says,
that "some count it a nettle ; others, a thistle."   On מלּוח
see Bochart Hieroz. ii. 223–228, ed. Leipz.

[3] MS. letter.   [4] 1 Macc. v. 6–8.   [5] S. Jer. and Rup.

they have reproached and magnified *themselves* against the people of the LORD of hosts.

---

of Abraham, so heretics profess to believe in Christ, to be children of Christ, and yet ever seek to overthrow the faith of Christians. As the Church says, *My mother's children are angry with me*.[1] They seem to have escaped the overthrow of Sodom and Gomorrah (heathen sins), and to have found a place of refuge (Zoar); and yet they are in darkness and cannot see the light of faith; and in an unlawful manner they mingle, against all right, the falsehood of Satan with the truth of God; so that their doctrines become, in part, *doctrines of devils*, in part have some stamp of the original truth. To them, as to the Jews, our Lord says, *Ye are of your father the devil*. While they profess to be children of God, they claim by their names to have God for their Father (Moab) and to be of His people (Ammon), while in hatred to His true children they forfeit both. As Moab seduced Israel, so they the children of the Church. They too enlarge themselves against the borders of the Church, rending off its children and making themselves the Church. They too utter reproaches and revilings against it. " Take away their revilings," says an early father,[2] " against the law of Moses, and the Prophets, and God the Creator, and they have not a word to utter." They too *remove the old landmarks which the fathers* (the Prophets and Apostles) *have set*.[3] And so, barrenness is their portion; as, after a time, heretics ever divide, and do not multiply; they are a desert, being out of the Church of God: and at last the remnant of Judah, the Church, possesses them, and absorbs them into herself.

[1] Cant. i. 6.
[2] Tert. de Præscr. Hær. c. 42, p. 493, Oxf. Tr.
[3] Ib. c. 37, p. 488.

11 The LORD *will be* terrible unto them : for he will * famish all the gods of the earth ; ^a and *men*

* Heb. *make lean.*   ^a Mal. i. 11 ; John iv. 21.

---

11. *The Lord will be terrible unto [upon] them,* i.e. upon Moab and Ammon, and yet not in themselves only, but as instances of His just judgment. Whence it follows, *For He will famish all the gods of the earth.* " [1] Miserable indeed, to whom the Lord is terrible ! Whence is this ? Is not God by nature sweet and pleasurable and serene, and an Object of longing ? For the angels ever desire to look unto Him, and, in a wonderful and unspeakable way, ever look and ever long to look. For miserable they, whose conscience makes them shrink from the face of Love. Even in this life they feel this shrinking, and, as if it were some lessening of their grief, they deny it, as though this could destroy the truth, which they *hold down in unrighteousness.*" [2]

For He will famish [3] *all the gods of the earth,* taking away *the fat of their sacrifices,* and the *wine of their drink offerings.*[4] Within eighty years from the death of our Lord,[5] the governor of Pontus and Bithynia wrote officially to the Roman Emperor, that "the temples had been almost left desolate, the sacred rites had been for a long time intermitted, and that the victims had very seldom found a purchaser," [6] before the persecution of the Christians, and con-

---

¹ Rup.   ² Rom. i. 18.

³ There is no reason to abate the irony by rendering "destroy." נרזה is contrasted with מִשְׁמַן, Isa. xvii. 4, as is רזון, Isa. x. 16 ; רָזֶה, of the land, with שְׁמֵנָה, Num. xiii. 20 ; of the sheep, with בְּרִיָה, Ezek. xxxiv. 20. In Ps. cvi. 15, רזון is used met. for a wasting, emaciating sickness ; in Micah vi. 10, of "an ephah of emaciation," i.e. scant ; in Isa. xxiv. 6, רָזִי is sickness ; (see Ew. Lehrb. 149, g.) [all].

⁴ Deut. xxxii. 38.   ⁵ Between A.D. 103–105.

⁶ Pliny, Epist. x. 32, p. 584, ed. Steph.

shall worship him, every one from his place, *even* all
^a the isles of the heathen.

^a Gen. x. 5.

sulted him as to the amount of its continuance. Towards
the close of the century, it was one of the heathen com-
plaints, which the Christian Apologist had to answer, "they
are daily melting away the revenues of our temples."[1] The
Prophet began to speak of the subdual of Moab and Ammon;
he is borne on to the triumphs of Christ over all the gods
of the heathen, when the worship of God should not be at
Jerusalem only, but *they shall worship Him, every one from
his place.*

Even all the isles of the heathen. For this is the very note
of the Gospel, that "each who through faith in Christ was
brought to the knowledge of the truth, by Him, and with
Him, *worshippeth from his place* God the Father; and God
is no longer known in Judæa only, but the countries and
cities of the heathen, though they be separated by the
intervening sea from Judæa, no less draw nigh to Christ,
pray, glorify, thank Him unceasingly. For formerly *His
Name* was *great in Israel,*[2] but now He is well known to all
everywhere; earth and sea are full of His glory, and so
every one *worshippeth Him from his place;* and this is what
is said, [3] *As I live, saith the Lord, all the earth shall be filled
with the glory of the Lord."* [4]   *The isles* are any distant lands
on the seashore,[5] especially the very distant;[6] but also Asia
Minor [7] and the whole coast of Europe, and even the Indian
Archipelago,[8] since the ivory and ebony came from its *many
isles.* Zephaniah revives the term, by which Moses had

[1] Tert. Apol. c. 42, see p. 90, note *o*, Oxf. Tr.
[2] Ps. lxxvi. 1.   [3] Num. xiv. 21.   [4] S. Cyr.
[5] Jer. xxv. 22 sqq.; Ezek. xxvi. 15 sqq.; Ps. lxxii. 10.
[6] Isa. lxvi. 19.   [7] Dan. xi. 1, 8.
[8] Ezek. xxvii. 15; Ges. Thes. sub v.

12 ¶ [a] Ye Ethiopians also, ye *shall be* slain by
[b] my sword.   *By Cambyses of Persia*

[a] Isa. xviii. 1 and xx. 4 ; Jer. xlvi. 9 ; Ezek. xxx. 9.
[b] Ps. xvii. 13.

---

spoken of the dispersion of the sons of Japhet : " By these
were the *isles of the Gentiles* divided in their lands, every one
after his tongue." [1]   He adds the word, *all ;* all, wherever
they had been dispersed, every one from his place, shall
worship God.   One universal worship shall ascend to God
from all everywhere.   So Malachi prophesied afterwards :
" From the rising up of the sun even to the going down of
the same My Name shall be great among the Gentiles, and
in every place incense shall be offered unto God and a pure
offering ; for My Name shall be great among the heathen,
saith the Lord of hosts." [2]   Even a Jew [3] says here : " This,
without doubt, refers to the time to come, when all the
inhabitants of the world shall know that the Lord is God,
and that His is the greatness and power and glory, and He
shall be called the God of the whole earth."   The *isles* or
coasts of the sea are the more the emblem of the Church, in
that, " lying, as it were, in the sea of this world and encom-
passed by the evil events in it, as with bitter waters, and
lashed by the most vehement waves of persecutions, the
Churches are yet founded, so that they cannot fall, and rear
themselves aloft, and are not overwhelmed by afflictions.
For, for Christ's sake, the Churches cannot be shaken, and
[4] *the gates of hell shall not prevail against them.*" [5]

12. *Ye Ethiopians also, ye shall be slain by My sword ;* lit.
Ye Ethiopians also, the slain of My sword are they.   Having
summoned them to His throne, God speaks *of* them, not *to*

[1] Gen. x. 5.   The phrase אִיֵּי הַגּוֹיִם occurs only in these
two places.
[2] Mal. i. 11.   [3] Abarbanel.
[4] S. Matt. xvi. 18.   [5] S. Cyr.

them any more ;. perhaps in compassion, as elsewhere in indignation.[1] The Ethiopians were not in any direct antagonism to God and His people, but allied only to their old oppressor, Egypt. They may have been in Pharaoh Necho's army, in resisting which, as a subject of Assyria, Josiah was slain : they are mentioned[2] in that army which Nebuchadnezzar smote at Carchemish in the fourth year of Jehoiakim. The prophecy of Ezekiel implies rather, that Ethiopia should be involved in the calamities of Egypt, than that it should be itself invaded. "Great terror shall be in Ethiopia, *when the slain shall fall in Egypt.*"[3] "Ethiopia and Libya and Lydia, &c., and all the men of the land that is in league, shall fall *with these*, by the sword."[4] "They also *that uphold Egypt* shall fall."[5] Syene,[5] the frontier-fortress over against Ethiopia, is especially mentioned as the boundary also of the destruction. "Messengers," God says,[6] "shall go forth from Me to make the careless Ethiopians afraid," while the storm was bursting in its full desolating force upon Egypt. All the other cities, whose destruction is foretold, are cities of lower or upper Egypt.[7]

But such a blow as that foretold by Jeremiah and Ezekiel must have fallen heavily upon the allies of Egypt. We have no details; for the Egyptians would not and did not tell of

[1] Isa. xxii. 16, "What hast thou here, and whom hast thou here, that thou hast hewed thee here a sepulchre ? Hewing him out on high his sepulchre, graving in the rock a dwelling for him." Micah i. 2, "Hear, ye people, all of them." Deut. xxxii. 15, "Thou art waxen fat, art grown thick, art covered with fatness ; and he forsook God Who made him, and lightly esteemed the Rock of his. salvation."

[2] Jer. xlvi. 9.   [3] Ezek. xxx. 4.
[4] Ib. xxx. 5.   [5] Ib. xxx. 6.   [6] Ib. xxx. 9.
[7] Zoan, Aven, Pi-beseth, Tehaphnehes, Sin, on the eastern boundary ; Noph [Memphis], the capital of Lower Egypt ; Pathros, probably a district of Upper Egypt ; No [Thebes], its capital ; Syene, its last town to the south.

the calamities and disgraces of their country.   No one does.
Josephus, however, briefly but distinctly says,[1] that after
Nebuchadnezzar had in the twenty-third year of his reign,
the fifth after the destruction of Jerusalem, "reduced into
subjection Moab and Ammon, he invaded Egypt, with a
view to subdue it," "killed its then king, and having set up
another, captured for the second time the Jews in it and
carried them to Babylon."   The memory of the devastation
by Nebuchadnezzar lived on apparently in Egypt, and is a
recognised fact among the Mohammedan historians, who had
no interest in the fulfilment of Jewish prophecy, of which
it does not appear that they even knew.   Bokht-nasar
[Nebuchadnezzar], they say, "made war on the son of Nechas
[Necho], slew him and ruined the city of Memphis and many
other cities of Egypt : he carried the inhabitants captive,
without leaving one, so that Egypt remained waste forty
years without one inhabitant." [2]   Another says, "The refuge
which the king of Egypt granted to the Jews who fled from
Nebuchadnezzar brought this war upon it : for he took them
under his protection and would not give them up to their
enemy.   Nebuchadnezzar, in revenge, marched against the
king of Egypt and destroyed the country." [3]   "One may be
certain," says a good authority,[4] "that the conquest of
Egypt by Nebuchadnezzar was a tradition generally spread
in Egypt and questioned by no one."   Ethiopia was then
involved, as an ally, and as far as its contingent was con-

[1] Ant. x. 9, 7.   See further Sir G. Wilkinson, Manners and
Customs of the Ancient Egyptians, i. 173-179 ; Pusey's Daniel
the Prophet, pp. 275-277.

[2] Makrizi in De Sacy, Abdallatif Rélation de l'Egypte, p. 247.

[3] Abdallatif, l.c. p. 184.

[4] De Sacy, l.c., who quotes Abulféda [see his Hist. ante-
Islam., p. 102.   He could not find the names of Egyptian kings
between Shishak and the Pharaoh who was the contemporary
of Nebuch.], Masudi, Nosairi, also.

cerned, in the war, in which Nebuchadnezzar desolated Egypt for those forty years. But, although this fulfilled the prophecy of Ezekiel, Isaiah, some sixty years before Zephaniah, prophesied a direct conquest of Ethiopia. *I have given,* God says,[1] *Egypt as thy ransom, Ethiopia and Sheba for thee.* It lay in God's purpose that Cyrus should restore His own people, and that his ambition should find its vent and compensation in the lands beyond. It may be that, contrary to all known human policy, Cyrus restored the Jews to their own land, willing to bind them to himself, and to make them a frontier territory towards Egypt, not subject only but loyal to himself. This is quite consistent with the reason which he assigns : *The Lord God of heaven hath given me all the kingdoms of the earth ; and He hath charged me to build Him an house at Jerusalem which is in Judah ;* [2] and with the statement of Josephus, that he was moved thereto by "reading the prophecy which Isaiah left, 210 years before." [3] It is, alas ! nothing new to Christians to have mixed motives for their actions : the exception is to have a single motive, "for the glory of God." The advantage to himself would doubtless flash at once on the founder of a great empire, though it did not suggest the restoration of the Jews. Egypt and Assyria had always, on either side, wished to possess themselves of Palestine, which lay between them. Anyhow, one Persian monarch did restore the Jews ; his successor possessed himself of "Egypt, and part, at least, of Ethiopia." Cyrus wished, it is related,[4] "to war in person against Babylon, the Bactrians, the Sacæ, and Egypt." He perished, as is known, before he had completed the third of his purposed conquests.[5] Cambyses, although after the conquest of Egypt he planned ill his two more

---

[1] Isa. xliii. 3.
[2] Ezra i. 2, 3.
[3] Ant. xi. 1, 2.
[4] Herod. i. 153.
[5] Ib. 214 and Rawl. notes, p. 350.

K

13 And he will stretch out his hand against the

---

distant expeditions, reduced "the Ethiopians bordering
upon Egypt"[1] ["lower Ethiopia and Nubia"[2]], and these
"brought gifts" permanently to the Persian Sovereign.
Even in the time of Xerxes, the Ethiopians had to furnish
their contingent of troops against the Greeks. Herodotus
describes their dress and weapons, as they were reviewed
at Doriscus.[3] Cambyses, then, did not lose his hold over
Ethiopia and Egypt, when forced by the rebellion of Pseudo-
Smerdis to quit Egypt.

13. Zephaniah began by singling out Judah amid the
general destruction, *I will also stretch out My Hand upon
Judah ;*[4] he sums up the judgment of the world in the same
way : *He will stretch out*, or *Stretch He forth*,[5] *His Hand*

---

[1] Herod. iii. 97.

[2] Sir G. Wilkinson in Rawl. Herod. ii. 487, n. 10.

[3] Her. vii. 69.　　　　　　　[4] i. 4.

[5] וַיֵּשְׂם, וַיֵּט　The ordinary force of the abridged form of
the future with ו is consecutive, viz. that the action so joined
on is the result of the preceding ; "intercede with the Lord
וַיֵּסַר, that He may take away," lit. "and He may take
away." Exod. x. 17. Gesenius' instances are all of this sort.
In Hif. of the regular verb, Judges xiv. 15 ; 1 Sam. vii. 3 ;
Job xi. 6 ; xii. 7 ; Jer. xlii. 3 (Lehrg. p. 321) ; verbs עי, Kal.
Num. xxv. 4 ; Judges vi. 30 ; Isa. l. 2 ; 1 Kings xxi. 10 ;
2 Kings v. 10 ; 2 Chron. xxix. 10 ; xxx. 6, 8 (ib. p. 403) ;
Hif. Exod. viii. 4 ; x. 17 ; Num. xxi. 7 (ib. p. 405) ; verb
לה, Ez. x. 12 ; Isa. ii. 20 ; Isa. xxxviii. 21 ; 1 Kings
xx. 20 ; Jer. xxiii. 18 (ib. p. 428). Such are also Hosea
xiv. 6, 7, 9. Sometimes a prayer seems to be thus interwoven
with prediction, as Num. xxiv. 7, "her seed shall be in many
waters, and exalted be (וְיָרֹם) his king above Amalek, and
exalted shall be his kingdom," and ib. 18, 19, "And Israel doeth
valiantly ; and rule one (וְיֵרְדְּ) from Jacob." Isa. xxxv.
1, 2, "Wilderness and dry place shall be glad for them, and
let the desert rejoice (וְתָגֵל) and it shall blossom as the

north, and [a] destroy Assyria; and will make Nineveh a desolation, *and* dry like a wilderness.

[a] Isa. x. 12; Ezek. xxxi. 3; Nahum i. 1, ii. 10, and iii. 15, 18.

---

against the North and destroy Asshur, and make Nineveh a desolation. Judah had, in Zephaniah's time, nothing to fear from Assyria. Isaiah [1] and Micah [2] had already foretold that the captivity would be to Babylon. Yet of Assyria alone the Prophet, in his own person, expresses his own conformity with the mind of God. Of others he had said, *The word of the Lord is against you, O Canaan, and I will destroy thee; As I live, saith the Lord, Moab shall be as Sodom. Ye also, O Ethiopians, the slain of My sword are they.* Of Assyria alone, by a slight inflection of the word, he expresses that he goes along with this, which he announces. He does not say as an imprecation, "May He stretch forth His hand;" but gently, as continuing his prophecies, *and*, joining on Asshur with the rest; only instead of saying "He will stretch forth," by a form almost insulated in Hebrew, he says, *And stretch He forth His Hand.* In a way not unlike, David having declared God's judgments, *The Lord trieth the righteous; and the wicked and the lover of violence doth His soul abhor*, subjoineth, *On the wicked rain He snares*, signifying that he (as all must be in the Day of judgment) is at one

autumn crocus. It shall blossom abundantly; *and joy it* (וְתָגֵל) yea with joy and jubilee: the glory of Lebanon is given to it; they shall see the glory of the Lord, the excellency of our God." The peculiarity here is, that it stands so apart and independent of the preceding, with which ו connects it. The shade of meaning is so fine that the Verss. and Rabbins pass over it, rendering simply future, as do modern commentators, except Keil, and Ewald who corrects וַיְאַבֵד וַיֵּט arbitrarily and against history.

[1] Isa. xxxix. 6. [2] Micah iv. 10.

14 And [a] flocks shall lie down in the midst of her,
all [b] the beasts of the nations : both the * [c] cor-

a Ver. 6.　　　　　　　　b Isa. xiii. 21, 22.
* Or, *pelican.* - glutton　　c Isa. xxxiv. 11, 14.

---

with the judgment of God. This is the last sentence upon
Nineveh, enforcing that of Jonah and Nahum, yet without
place of repentance now. He accumulates words expressive
of desolateness. It should not only be a *desolation,*[1] as
he had said of Ashkelon, Moab, and Ammon, but a dry,
parched,[2] unfruitful[3] land. As Isaiah, under the same
words, prophesies that the dry and desolate land[4] should,
by the Gospel, be glad, so the gladness of the world should
become dryness and desolation. *Asshur* is named, as though
one individual,[5] implying the entireness of the destruction ;
all shall perish, as one man ; or as gathered into one and
dependent upon one, its evil King. *The North* is not only
Assyria, in that its armies came upon Judah from the
north, but it stands for the whole power of evil,[6] as Nineveh
for the whole, beautiful, evil world. The world with "the
princes of this world" shall perish together.

14. *And flocks shall lie down in the midst of her.* No desolation is like that of decayed luxury. It preaches the
nothingness of man, the fruitlessness of his toils, the
fleetingness of his hopes and enjoyments, and their baffling
when at their height. Grass in a court or on a once beaten

---

[1] שְׁמָמָה Zeph. ii. 4, 9.

[2] צִיָּה of absence of water, Job xxx. 3 ; Ps. lxiii. 1 ; cv. 41‖;
cvii. 35 ; Isa. xli. 18 ; Jer. ii. 6 ; Ez. xix. 13 ; Hosea ii. 3.

[3] Isa. liii. 2.

[4] מדבר וציה Isa. xxxv. 1 ; Jer. joins מדבר ציה וערבה,
l. 12.

[5] Asshur is used in this way of the people, considered in
and with their king, Isa. xxx. 31 ; xxxi. 8.

[6] See Isa. xiv. 13.

morant and the bittern shall lodge in the *upper

Or, knops, or, *chapiters.*

---

road, much more, in a town, speaks of the passing away of
what has been, that man was wont to be there, and is not,
or is there less than he was. It leaves the feeling of void
and forsakenness. But in Nineveh not a few tufts of grass
here and there shall betoken desolation, it shall be one wild
rank pasture, where *flocks* shall not feed only, but *lie down*
as in their fold and continual resting-place, not in the
outskirts only or suburbs, but in the very centre of her
life and throng and busy activity, *in the midst of her,* and
none shall fray them away. So Isaiah had said of the cities
of Aroer, *they shall be for flocks, which shall lie down and none
shall make them afraid,*[1] and of Judah till its restoration
by Christ, that it should be *a joy of wild asses, a pasture of
flocks.*[2] And not only those which are wont to be found in
some connection with man, but *all the beasts of a nation,*[3]
the troops of wild and savage and unclean beasts which
shun the dwellings of man or are his enemies, these in
troops have their lair there.

Both the pelican[4] *and the* [*hedgehog*[5]] *shall lodge in the upper*

---

[1] Isa. xvii. 2.   [2] Ib. xxxii. 14, comp. Jer. vi. 3.

[3] גוֹי "nation," of gregarious creatures, locusts, Jo. i. 6;
ii. 2; עַם, "ants," Prov. xxx. 25, "conies," ib. 26, comp.
ἔθνεα χηνῶν, &c., "apium populi," "equorum gentes," Virg.
Georg. iv. 430, Arab. אֻמָּה. Boch. Hieroz. ii. 468, Leipz.

[4] The most probable rendering, as explaining the ety-
mology. The ό render "pelican," Ps. cii. 6; Lev. xi. 18;
Aq. Symm. Th., Isa. xxxiv. 11; Aq. here. The קוֹק of
the Talmudists (קָקָא Jerus. Targ. ap. Levy Lex.) is probably the same. The pelican retires inland to consume its
food. Tristram, Houghton, in Smith Bibl. Dict. v. Pelican,
note.

[5] There seems a consent that the קִפֹּד is the hedgehog
or porcupine (as in Aram. and Arab.) ό, S. Jer. R. Nathan,

lintels of it ; *their* voice shall sing in the windows ;

---

lintels thereof.   The *chapters* [E.M.] or capitals of the pillars of the temples and palaces shall lie broken and strewn upon the ground, and among those desolate fragments of her pride shall unclean animals haunt.   The pelican has its Hebrew name from vomiting.   It vomits up the shells which it had swallowed whole, after they had been opened by the heat of the stomach, and so picks out the animal contained in them,[1] the very image of greediness and uncleanness.   It dwells also not in deserts only but near marshes, so that Nineveh is doubly waste.

A voice shall sing in the windows.   In the midst of the desolation, the muteness of the hedgehog and the pensive loneliness of the solitary pelican, the musing spectator is even startled by the gladness of a bird, joyous in the existence which God has given it.   Instead of the harmony of music[2] and men-singers and women-singers in their palaces shall be the sweet music of some lonely bird, unconscious that it is sitting *in the windows* of those, at whose name the world grew pale, portions of the outer walls being all which remain of her palaces.   *Desolation* shall be *in the thresholds*, sitting, as it were, in them ; everywhere to be seen in them ; the more, because unseen.   Desolation is something oppressive ; we *feel* its presence.   There, as the warders watch and ward at the empty portals, where once was the fullest throng, shall *desolation sit*, that no one enter.   *For He shall uncover* [*hath uncovered*, E.M.] *the cedar-work ;* in the roofless palaces, the carved *cedar-work* shall be laid open to wind and rain.   Any one must have noticed how piteous and dreary the decay of any house in a town

Rashi, although the Arab. etym. "rolled himself round," seems uncertain.

[1] Aristot. Anim. ix. 10.

[2] אֲרָזָה collective, like עֵצָה Jer. vi. 6.

desolation *shall be* in the thresholds : * for he shall
uncover the [a] cedar work.

---

* Or, *when he hath uncovered.*   [a] Jer. xxii. 14.

---

looks, with the torn paper hanging uselessly on its walls.
A poet of our own said of the beautiful ruins of a wasted
monastery :—

> " For the gay beams of lightsome day
> Gild, but to flout the ruins gray."

But at Nineveh it is one of the mightiest cities of the
world which thus lies waste, and the bared *cedar-work*
had in the days of its greatness, been carried off from the
despoiled Lebanon [1] or Hermon. [2]

15. *This* utter desolation *is the rejoicing city* (so unlike
is it, that there is need to point out that it is the same);
this is she, who was full of joy, exulting exceedingly, [3] but

---

[1] Isa. xiv. 8 ; xxxvii. 24 ; Ezek. xxxi. 16. " In the fragment of another epigraph, we have mention of some objects
also of wood, ' brought from Mt. Lebanon (and taken up to
the mound) from the Tigris ' " (Layard, Nineveh and
Babylon, p. 118). " At that time the countries that are upon
Lebanon, I took possession of, to the great sea of the country
of Akkari " (the Mediterranean), from Inscription (ib. pp. 355,
356). " The conqueror from the upper passage of the Tigris
to Lebanon and the Great Sea " (ib. p. 361). " Standing one
day on a distant part of the mound, I smelt the sweet smell
of burning cedar ; the Arab workmen excavating in the small
temple had dug out a beam, and the weather being cold, had
at once made a fire to warm themselves. The wood was
cedar, probably one of the very beams mentioned in the
inscription, as brought from the forests of Lebanon, by the
king who built the edifice. After a lapse of nearly 3000
years, it had retained its original fragrance " (ib. p. 357).

[2] Rawl. Five Emp. i. 385.

[3] עָלַז (verb, perhaps i.q. ἀλαλάζω) is exulting joy, the
exultation being good or bad, according to its object, in God
or in self and the world ; in God, Ps. xxviii. 7 ; lxviii. 4 ;

15 This *is* the rejoicing city [a] that dwelt carelessly,
[b] that said in her heart, I *am*, and *there is* none beside

[a] Isa. xlvii. 8.   [b] Rev. xviii. 7.

in herself, not in God ; *that dwelt carelessly*, lit. *securely*, and
so carelessly; saying, *Peace and safety*,[1] as though no evil
would come upon her, and so perishing more certainly and
miserably.[2] *That said in her heart*, this was her inmost
feeling, the moving cause of all her deeds : *I am and there
is none beside me ;* literally, *and there is no I besides*,[3] claiming the very attribute of God (as the world does) of self-
existence, as if it alone were *I*, and others, in respect of
her, were as nothing. Pantheism, which denies the being
of God, as Author of the world, and claims the life in the
material world to be God, and each living being to be a
part of God, is only this self-idolatry, reflected upon and
carried out in words. All the pride of the world, all self-
indulgence which says, *Let us eat and drink, for to-morrow we
die*, all covetousness which ends in this world, speaks this
by its acts, *I and no I beside.*

How is she become a desolation, has passed wholly into it,
exists only as a desolation, *a place for beasts to lie down in,*
a mere den for *the wild beasts. Every one that passeth by her
shall hiss* in derision, *and wag* [or *wave*] *his hand* in detesta-
tion, as though putting the hand between them and it,

xcvi. 11, 12 ; cxlix. 5 ; Hab. iii. 18 ; Zeph. iii. 14 ; in good,
Prov. xxiii. 16 ; in God's gifts, Ps. lx. 6 ; cviii. 7 ; in evil,
Ps. xciv. 3 ; Jer. xi. 15 ; xv. 17 ; l. 11 ; li. 39 ; over an
enemy, 2 Sam. i. 20. עָלִיז (intens.) Isa. xxii. 2 ; xxiii. 7 ;
xxiv. 8 ; xxxii. 13, is used, as here, of a city full of its tumul-
tuous, self-confident excitement, as is the verb, Isa. xxiii. 12,
and עָלֵז of an individual, Jer. v. 14 [all].

[1] 1 Thess. v. 3.   [2] See Judges xviii. 27.
[3] As we might say "no second I." This gives an adequate
explanation of the י in אַפְסִי, as no other rendering does.

me : how is she become a desolation, a place for

---

so as not to look at it, or, as it were, motioning it away.
The action is different from that of *clapping the hands* [1] in
exultation.

"It is not difficult," S. Jerome says, " to explain this of
the world, that when the Lord hath stretched forth His
Hand over the North and destroyed the Assyrian, the
Prince of this world, the world also perishes together with
its Princes, and is brought to utter desolation, and is pitied
by none, but all hiss and shake their hands at its ruin.   But
of the Church it seems, at first sight, blasphemous to say
that it shall be a pathless desert, and wild beasts shall
dwell in her, and that afterwards it shall be said insultingly
over her : 'This is the city given up to ill, which *dwelt carelessly and said in her heart, I and none besides.'*   But whoso
should consider that word of the Apostle, wherein he says, *in
the last days perilous times shall come,* [2] and what is written in
the Gospel, that *because iniquity shall abound, the love of many
shall wax cold,* [3] so that then shall that be fulfilled, *When the
Son of Man cometh, shall He find the faith on the earth ?* he
will not marvel at the extreme desolation of the Church,
that, in the reign of Antichrist, it shall be reduced to a desolation and given over to beasts, and shall suffer whatever
the Prophet now describes.   For if for unbelief *God spared not
the natural branches,* but *brake them off,* and *turned rivers into
a wilderness and the water-springs into a dry ground,* and *a
fruitful land into barrenness, for the iniquity of them that dwell
therein,* why not as to those of whom He had said, *He turneth
the wilderness into a standing water, and dry ground into water-
springs, and there He maketh the hungry to dwell :* [4] and as to
those whom *out of the wild olive He hath grafted into the good
olive tree,* why, if forgetful of this benefit, they depart from

[1] Nahum iii. 19.   [2] 2 Tim. iii. 1–5.
[3] S. Matt. xxiv. 12.   [4] Ps. cvii. 33–36.

beasts to lie down in ! every one that passeth by her
^a shall hiss, *and* ^b wag his hand.

^a Job xxvii. 23 ; Lam. ii. 15 ; Ezek. xxvii. 36.
^b Nahum iii. 19.

---

their Maker and worship the Assyrian, should He not undo
them and bring them to the same thirst wherein they were
before ?   Which, whereas it may be understood generally of
the coming of Antichrist or of the end of the world, yet it
may, day by day, be understood of those who feign to be of
the Church of God, and *in works deny it, are hearers of the
word not doers*, who in vain boast in an outward show,
whereas herds, i.e. troops, of vices dwell in them, and brute
animals serving the body, and all the beasts of the field
which devour their hearts [and pelicans, i.e. gluttons,[1] whose
god is their belly] and hedgehogs, a prickly animal full of
spikes which pricketh whatever it toucheth.   After which
it is subjoined, that the Church shall therefore suffer this,
or hath suffered it, because it lifteth itself up proudly and
raised its head like a cedar, given up to evil works, and yet
promising itself future blessedness, and despising others in
its heart, nor thinking that there is any other besides itself,
and saying, *I am, and there is no other beside me*, how is it
become a solitude, a lair of beasts !   For where before
dwelt the Father, and the Son, and the Holy Ghost, and
Angels presided over its ministries, there shall beasts dwell.
And if we understand that, every one that passeth by shall
hiss, we shall explain it thus : when Angels shall pass
through her, and not remain in her, as was their wont, they
shall be amazed and marvel, and shall not support and bear
her up with their hand, when falling, but shall lift up the
hands and shall pass by.   Or they shall make a sound as
those who mourn.   But if we understand this of the devil
and his angels, who destroyed the vine also that was brought

[1] Rib.

CHAPTER III

1 *A sharp reproof of Jerusalem for divers sins.* 8 *An exhortation to wait for the restoration of Israel,* 14 *and to rejoice for their salvation by God.*

WOE to * † her that is filthy and polluted, to the oppressing city !

* Or, gluttonous.   † Heb. craw.

---

out of Egypt, we shall say, that through the soul, which before was the temple of God and hath ceased so to be, the serpent passeth, and hisseth and spitteth forth the venom of his malice in her, and not this only, but setteth in motion his works which figuratively are called *hands.*"

"The earlier and partial fulfilment of prophecy does not destroy, it rather confirms, the entire fulfilment to come. For whoso heareth of the destruction of mighty cities, is constrained to believe the truth of the Gospel, that the fashion of this world passeth away, and that, after the likeness of Nineveh and Babylon, the Lord will in the end judge the whole world also."[1]

CHAP. III. ver. 1. The "woe" having gone round the heathen nations, again circles round where it began, the *Jerusalem that killed the prophets and stoned those that were sent unto her.*[2] Woe upon her, and joy to the holy Jerusalem, the *new Jerusalem,*[3] *the Jerusalem which is from above, the mother of us all,* close this prophecy ; both in figure ; destruction of her and the whole earth, in time, the emblem of the eternal death; and the love of God, the foretaste of endless joy in Him.

[1] Rup.   [2] S. Matt. xxiii. 37.
[3] Rev. iii. 12 ; xxi. 10.

2 She ^aobeyed not the voice; she ^breceived not

ᵃ Jer. xxii. 21.　　　　　　　　ᵇ Ib. v. 3.

---

*Wo*¹ *rebellious and polluted ;* ² *thou oppressive city !* ³ The
address is the more abrupt, and bursts more upon her,
since the Prophet does not name her. He uses as her
proper name, not her own name, "city of peace," but
"rebellious," "polluted"; then he sums up in one, *thou
oppressive city.*

Jerusalem's sin is threefold, actively rebelling against
God; then, inwardly defiled by sin; then cruel to man.
So then, towards God, in herself, towards man, she is
wholly turned to evil, not in passing acts, but in her
abiding state, (1) rebellious, (2) defiled, (3) oppressive.
She is known only by what she has become, and what has
been done for her in vain. She is rebellious, and so had
had the law; defiled, and so had been cleansed ; and therefore her state is the more hopeless.

2. *She obeyed not the Voice,* of God, by the law or the
prophets, teaching her His ways ; and when, disobeying,
He chastened her, *she received not correction,* and when He

---

¹ הוֹי with the partic., as a vocative, as in Amos
v. 18; Isa. xlv. 9, 10; Micah ii. 1 ; Hab. ii. 6, 9, 12, 15,
19, &c.

² מוֹרְאָה from מרא=מרה. This seems more probable than
E.V. (from a meaning given to ראי Nahum iii. 6, and
from מִרְאָה crop of bird, Lev. i. 16) or LXX, ἐπιφανὴς
(as if מַרְאָה as a few MSS. de R.), or S. Jer. "embitter-
ing," provocatrix (as if הַמְרה=מרא), or Abarb. "terrible"
(as from ירא which is expressed by Nif. נורא), or Drus.
"made a spectacle"; παραδειγματιζομένη, cf. מַרְאָה ; but this
is not used elsewhere, though the verb is so common.

³ הָעִיר as a separate vocative, as Num. xv. 15; Cant.
vi. 1 ; Isa. lii. 18; Micah ii. 7, &c., and in the N.T. ὁ βασιλεὺς,
S. Matt. xxvii. 29 ; ὁ υἱὸς, S. Mark x. 47 ; ὁ πατὴρ ib. xiv.
36, &c.

* correction; she trusted not in the LORD; she drew not near to her God.

* Or, *instruction*.

increased His chastisements, she, in the declining age of the state and deepening evil, turned not unto Him, as in the time of the judges, nor ceased to do evil.

In the Lord she trusted not, but in Assyria or Egypt or her idols. Our practical relation to God is summed up in the four words, "Mistrust self; trust God." Man reverses this, and when "self-trust" has of course failed him, then he "mistrusts God." "Such rarely ask of God, what they hope they may obtain from man. They strain every nerve of their soul to obtain what they want; canvass, flatter, fawn, bribe, court favour; and betake themselves to God when all human help fails. They would be indebted, not to God, but to their own diligence. For the more they receive of God, the less, they see, can they exalt their own diligence, the more they are bound to thank God, and obey Him the more strictly." [1]

To her God she drew not nigh, even in trouble, when all draw nigh unto Him, who are not wholly alien from Him; she drew not near by repentance, by faith, hope, or love, or by works meet for repentance, but in heart remained far from Him. And yet He was *her* own *God,* as He had shown Himself in times past, Who changes not, while we change; is faithful to us, while we fail Him; is still our God, while we forget Him; *waits, to have mercy upon us;* shines on us while we interpose our earth-born clouds between us and Him. "Not in body nor in place, but spiritually and inwardly do we approach to the uncircumscribed God," [2] owning Him as our Father, to Whom we daily say "Our Father."

[1] Rib. on Hosea vii. n. 39.   [2] Dion.

3 ^aHer princes within her *are* roaring lions; her judges *are* ^bevening wolves; they gnaw not the bones till the morrow.

^a Ezek. xxii. 27; Micah iii. 9, 10, 11.   ^b Hab. i. 8.

---

3. The Prophet having declared the wickedness of the whole city, rehearses how each in Church and State, the ministers of God in either, who should have corrected the evil, themselves aggravated it. Not enemies, without, destroy her, but

Her princes within her, in the very midst of the flock, whom they should in God's stead *feed with a true heart,* destroy her as they will, having no protection against them. *Her judges are evening wolves;* [1] those who should in the Name of God redress all grievances and wrongs, are themselves like wild beasts, when most driven by famine. *They gnaw not the bones* [2] *till the morrow* or *on the morrow* [lit. *in the morning*]. They reserve nothing till the morning light, but do in darkness the works of darkness, shrinking from the light, and, in extreme rapacity, devouring at once the whole substance of the poor. As Isaiah says, *Thy princes are rebellious and companions of thieves,* [3] and *The Lord will enter into judgment with the ancients of His people and the princes thereof: for ye have eaten up the vineyard:*

[1] See Hab. i. 8.

[2] The meaning of Piel, in Num. xxiv. 8, and met. Ez. xxiii. 34, as denom. from poetic גרם "bone." The Verss. gave the meaning, dropping the metaphor, the LXX and Vulg. rendering "left"; Ch. "deferring to"; Syr. "waiting for." In Arab. مَـ ـعَ signifies "cut off," spec. wool of sheep, fruit of palm-trees, and with لِ p. "gaining for himself or his family." In Syr. it is (1) "cut off"; (2) "decreed"; not "reserved." Abulw., Kim., Menach., render "break" as denom.

[3] Isa. i. 23.

4 Her ^a prophets *are* light *and* treacherous persons ;

^a Jer. xxiii. 11, 32 ; Lam. ii. 14 ; Hosea ix. 7.

---

the spoil of the poor is in your houses.[1]   And Ezekiel, *Her princes in the midst thereof are like wolves, ravening the prey to shed blood, to destroy souls, to get dishonest gain.*[2]

4. *Her prophets* are *light,* boiling and bubbling up, like water boiling over,[3] empty boasters claiming the gift of prophecy, which they have not ; "boldly and rashly pouring out what they willed as they willed;" promising good things which shall not be. So they are *her* prophets, to whom they *prophesy smooth things,* "the prophets of this people"[4] not the prophets of God ; *treacherous persons* [lit. men of treacheries] wholly given to manifold treacheries against God in Whose Name they spake and to the people whom they deceived. "They spake as if from the mouth of the Lord and uttered everything against the Lord."[5]   *The leaders of the people,* those who profess to lead it aright, Isaiah says,[6] *are its misleaders.   Thy prophets,* Jeremiah says,[7] *have seen vain and foolish things for thee; they have seen for thee false visions and causes of banishment.*

Her priests have polluted her sanctuary, lit. *holiness,* and so holy rites, persons,[8] things, places (as the sanctuary), sacrifices. All these they polluted, being themselves polluted ; they polluted first themselves, then the holy things

---

[1] Isa. iii. 14.   [2] Ez. xxii. 27.

[3] פחזות being used by Jeremiah (xxiii. 32) of the false *prophets* who *prophesy false dreams and do tell them and cause My people to err by their lies and by their lightness,* it probably has the same meaning here ; though פחז is used of the boiling over of sensuality (Gen. xlix. 4) and of *empty wanton men,* Judges ix. 4. In Arabic, פחז as well as פהר is used of vainglory ; in Syr. of "impurity."

[4] See Micah ii. 11.   [5] S. Jer.
[6] Isa. ix. 16.   [7] Lam. ii. 14.   [8] Ezra viii. 28.

her priests have polluted the sanctuary, they have done ^a violence to the law.

^a Ezek. xxii. 26.

which they handled, handling them as they ought not; carelessly and irreverently, not as ordained by God; turning them to their own use and self-indulgence, instead of the glory of God; then they polluted them in the eyes of the people, *making them to abhor the offering of the Lord*,[1] since, living scandalously, they themselves regarded the ministry entrusted to them by God so lightly. Their office was to *put difference between holy and unholy and between clean and unclean, and to teach the children all the statutes which the Lord hath spoken unto them by Moses;*[2] that they *should sanctify themselves and be holy, for I the Lord your God am holy.*[3] But they on the contrary, God says by Ezekiel, *have done violence to My law and have profaned My holy things; they have made no difference between holy and profane, and have taught none between clean and unclean.*[4] *Holy* and *unholy* being the contradictory of each other, these changed what God had hallowed into its exact contrary. It was not a mere shortcoming, but an annihilation (so to speak) of God's purposes.

" The Priests of the Church, then, must keep strict watch, not to profane holy things. There is not one mode only of profaning them, but many and divers. For Priests ought to be purified both in soul and body, and to cast aside every form of abominable pleasure. Rather should they be resplendent with zeal in well-doing, remembering what S. Paul saith,[5] *walk in the Spirit and ye shall not fulfil the lust of the flesh.*" [6]

[1] 1 Sam. ii. 17.
[2] Lev. x. 10, 11.
[3] Ib. xi. 44; xix. 2, &c.
[4] Ezek. xxii. 26.
[5] Gal. v. 16.
[6] S. Cyr.

5 ^aThe just LORD ^b*is* in the midst thereof; he will not do iniquity : *every morning doth he bring

^a Deut. xxxii. 4.   ^b Vers. 15, 17. See Micah iii. 11.
* Heb. *morning by morning.*

They have oppressed, done violence, to the law, openly violating it ;[1] or straining it, or secretly wresting and using its forms to wrong and violence, as in the case of Naboth and of Him, of Whom Naboth thus far bore the Image. *We have a law, and by our law He ought to die.*[2] Law exists to restrain human violence ; these reversed God's ordinances ; violence and law changed places : first, they did violence to the majesty of the law, which was the very voice of God, and then, through profaning it, did violence to man.   Forerunners herein of those who, when Christ came, *transgressed the commandment of God,* and *made it of none effect by their traditions ;*[3] omitting also *the weightier matters of the law, judgment and mercy and faith ; full of extortion and excess !*[4]

5. But, besides these *evening wolves in the midst of her,* there standeth Another *in the midst of her,* Whom they knew not, and so, very near[5] to them although they would not draw near to Him.   But He was near, to behold all the iniquities which they did in the very city and place called by His Name and in His very Presence ; He was in her to protect, foster her with a father's love, but she, presuming on His mercy, had cast it off.   And so He was near to punish, not to deliver ; as a Judge, not as a Saviour. " God is everywhere, Who says by Jeremiah, *I fill heaven*

---

[1] The construction with the acc. of person occurs Ezek. xxii. 26 ; Prov. viii. 36 ; Jer. xxii. 3.
[2] S. John xix. 7.   [3] S. Matt. xv. 6.   [4] Ib. xxiii. 23, 25.
[5] The words in Hebrew correspond with each other, being from the same root, קרבה " draw near " ; בקרבה, " in the midst of her " (vers. 2, 3, 5).

L

his judgment to light, he faileth not; but [a] the
unjust knoweth no shame.

[a] Jer. iii. 3, vi. 15, and viii. 12.

---

and earth.[1] But since, as Solomon attesteth, *The Lord is
far from the wicked,*[2] how is He said here to be *in the midst*
of these most wicked men ? Because the Lord is far from
the wicked, as regards the presence of love and grace; still
in His Essence He is everywhere, and in this way He is
equally present to all."[3]

The Lord is in the midst thereof; He will not do iniquity.
" Since He is the primal rule and measure of all righteousness ; therefore from the very fact that He doeth anything,
it is just; for He cannot do amiss, being essentially holy.
Therefore He will give to every man what he deserves.
Therefore we chant, [4] *The Lord is upright, and there is no
unrighteousness in Him.*"[3] Justice and injustice, purity
and impurity, cannot be together. God's Presence then
must destroy the sinners, if not the sin. He was *in the
midst of them,* to sanctify them, giving them His judgments
as a pattern of theirs ; *He will not do iniquity:* but if they
heeded it not, the judgment would fall upon themselves.
It were for God to become *such an one as themselves,*[5] and
to connive at wickedness, were He to spare at last the
impenitent.

Every morning [lit. *in the morning, in the morning*] one
after the other, quickly, openly, daily, continually, bringing
all secret things, all works of darkness, to light, as He said
to David, *Thou didst it secretly, but I will do this thing before
all Israel, and before the sun.*[6] *Doth He bring His judgments
to light,* so that no sin should be hid in the brightness of

[1] Jer. xxiii. 24.   [2] Prov. xv. 29.
[3] Dion.   [4] Ps. xcii. 15.
[5] Ib. l. 21.   [6] 2 Sam. xii. 12.

6 I have cut off the nations : their * towers are

* Or, *corners.*

His Light, as He said by Hosea, *Thy judgments are a light which goeth forth.* "Morning by morning, He shall execute His judgments, i.e. in bright day and visibly, not restraining His anger, but bringing it forth in the midst, and making it conspicuous, and, as it were, setting in open vision what He had foreannounced."[1] Day by day God gives some warning of His judgments. By chastisements which are felt to be His on this side or on that or all around, He gives ensamples which speak to the sinner's heart. *He faileth not.* As God said by Habakkuk, that His promises, although they seem to *linger,* were not *behind*[2] the real time, which lay in the Divine mind, so, contrariwise, neither are His judgments. His hand is never missing[3] at the appointed time. *But the unjust,*[4] he, whose very being and character, *iniquity,* is the exact contrary to what he had said of the perfection of God, [5] *Who doth not iniquity,* or, as Moses had taught them in his song,[6] *all His ways are judgment, a God of truth and without iniquity,*[7] *just and right is He. Knoweth no shame,* as God saith by Jeremiah, *Thou refusedst to be ashamed.*[8] *They were not at all ashamed, neither could they blush.*[9] Even thus they would not be ashamed of their sins, *that they might be converted and God might heal them.*[10]

6. *I have cut off* [the] *nations.* God appeals to His judg-

---

[1] S. Cyr. [2] Hab. ii. 3.

[3] נֶעְדָּר is used of one missing when a muster is made (1 Sam. xxx. 19; 2 Sam. xvii. 22; met. Isa. xxxiv. 16; xl. 26; lix. 15); here only of God, that He does not fail to visit at the time when He ought to be looked for.

[4] עַוָּל. [5] לֹא יַעֲשֶׂה עַוְלָה.

[6] Deut. xxxii. 4. [7] וְאֵין עָוֶל.

[8] Jer. iii. 3. [9] Ib. vi. 15; viii. 12. [10] Isa. vi. 10.

desolate; I made their streets waste, that none
passeth by: their cities are destroyed, so that
there is no man, that there is none inhabitant.

---

ments on heathen nations, not on any particular nation, as
far as we know ; but to past history, whether of those, of
whose destruction Israel itself had been the instrument, or
others. The judgments upon the nations before them were
set forth to them, when they were about to enter on their
inheritance, as a warning to themselves.[1] *Defile not ye yourselves in any of these things; for in all these have the nations
defiled themselves, which I cast out before you : and the land is
defiled ; therefore I do visit the iniquity thereof upon it, and the
land vomiteth out her inhabitants. And ye, ye shall keep My
statutes and My judgments and shall not commit any of these
abominations—And the land shall not spue you out when ye
defile it, as it spued out the nations which were before you.* The
very possession then of the land was a warning to them;
the ruins, which crowned so many of its hilltops,[2] were
silent preachers to them; they lived among the memories
of God's visitations; if neglected, they were an earnest of
future judgments on themselves. Yet God's judgments
are not at one time only. Sennacherib appealed to their
own knowledge, *Behold, thou hast heard what the kings of
Assyria have done to all lands by destroying them utterly. Have
the gods of the nations delivered them which my fathers have destroyed?* [3] Hezekiah owned it as a fact which he knew: *Of
a truth, Lord, the kings of Assyria have laid waste all the nations
and their land.* [4] And God owns him as His instrument:
Now I have brought it to pass, that thou shouldest be to lay

---

[1] Lev. xviii. 24, 25, 26, 28, add ib. xx. 23.

[2] This will be brought out by the "Ordnance survey"
of Palestine, when completed.   Isaiah alludes to them,
xvii. 9.

[3] Isa. xxxvii. 11, 13.   [4] Ib. xxxvii. 18.

7 ^a I said, Surely thou wilt fear me, thou wilt
ᵃ So Jer. viii. 6.

waste defenced cities into ruinous heaps : [1] and, [2] *I will send him
against an ungodly nation, and against the people of My wrath
will I give him a charge, to take the spoil and to take the prey,
and to tread them down as the mire of the streets,* and says of him,
It is in his heart to destroy and to cut off nations not a few.
The king of Babylon too he describes as *the man that made
the earth to tremble, that did shake kingdoms, that made the world
as a wilderness, and destroyed the cities thereof.*[3]   Habakkuk
recently described the wide wasting by the Babylonians,
and the helplessness of nations before him.[4]

Their towers, corner towers,[5] the most carefully fortified
parts of their fortified cities, *are desolate ; I made their streets
waste.* The desolation is complete, within as well as without ;
ruin itself is hardly so desolate as the empty habitations and
forsaken streets, once full of life, where

> " The echoes and the empty tread
>   Would sound like voices from the dead."

7. *I said, surely thou wilt fear Me.* God speaks of things
here, as they are in their own nature. *It could not but be,*
that in the very presence of the Hand of God, destroying
others but as yet sparing them, they must learn to fear
Him ; they must stand in awe of Him for His judgments on others ; they must be in filial fear of Him for His
loving longsuffering towards themselves. "Thou *wilt* receive

[1] Isa. xxxvii. 26.
[2] Ib. x. 6, 7, and the graphic picture ib. 13, 14.
[3] Ib. xiv. 16, 17.   [4] Hab. i. 14–16.
[5] See on i. 16. Since also the subjects spoken of in this
verse are places, the metaph. meaning of פנות "princes,"
i.e. corner-stones, is not probable here, although נשמו is,
in four places, used of men.

receive instruction ;   so their dwelling should not be

---

instruction," corrected and taught through God's correction of others and the lighter judgments on themselves,
as Solomon says, *I looked, I set my heart: I saw, I received
instruction.*[1]   He saith, *receive*, making it man's free act.
God brings it near, commends it to him, exhorts, entreats,
but leaves him the awful power to *receive* or to refuse.
God speaks with a wonderful tenderness. " Surely thou
wilt stand in awe of Me ; thou *wilt* receive instruction; thou
wilt now do what hitherto thou hast refused to do." There
was (so to speak) nothing else left for them,[2] in sight of
those judgments. He pleads their own interests. The
lightning was ready to fall. The Prophet had, in vision,
seen the enemy within the city. Yet even now God lingers,
as it were, *If thou hadst known in this thy day, the things which
are for thy peace.*[3]

So their [her] dwelling should not be cut off. His own holy
land which He had given them. A Jew paraphrases,[4] " And
He will not cut off their dwellings from the land of the
house of My Shechinah " (God's visible Presence in glory).
Judah, who was before addressed *thou*, is now spoken of in
the third person, *her ;* and this also had wonderful tenderness. It is as though God were musing over her and the
blessed fruits of her return to Him ; "it shall not be
needed to correct her further." *Howsoever I punished them :*
lit. *all* (i.e. *all* the offences) *which I visited upon her*, as God
saith of Himself, " *Visiting* the *sins* of the fathers *upon* the
children," [5] and this is mostly the meaning of the words

---

[1] Prov. xxiv. 32.

[2] אַךְ, exclusively of all besides. All the meanings
ascribed to אַךְ are but different ways of expressing in other
languages the primary meaning, " nothing but."

[3] S. Luke xix. 42.   [4] Jon.

[5] Exod. xx. 5 ; xxxiv. 7 ; Num. xiv. 18.

cut off, howsoever I punished them ; but they rose
early, *and* [a] corrupted all their doings.

[a] Gen. vi. 12.

---

visit upon.[1] Amid and notwithstanding all the offences
which God had already chastised, He, in His love and compassion, still longeth, not utterly to remove them from His
Presence, if they would but receive instruction *now;* but
they would not. *How often,* our Lord says,[2] *would I have
gathered thy children together, even as a hen gathereth her chickens
under her wings, and ye would not.* *But indeed,* probably, *Of
a truth* [3] (it is a word strongly affirming what follows) *they
rose early, they corrupted all their doings;* God gave them His
warnings, awaited the result ; they lost no time, they began
with morning light ; they hasted to rise, burthened [4] themselves, made sure of having the whole day before them, to—
seek God as He had sent His prophets, *rising early and
sending them ?* [5] No, nor even simply to do ill, but of set
purpose to do, not this or that corruptly, but to *corrupt all
their doings.* "They with diligence and eagerness rose early,

[1] Exod. xxxii. 34 ; Isa. xiii. 11 ; Jer. xxiii. 2 ; Hosea
i. 4 ; ii. 13 ; iv. 9 ; Amos iii. 2, 14 ; besides the separate
cases of (*a*) visiting upon, or (*b*) visiting the sin. See Ges.

[2] S. Matt. xxiii. 37.

[3] אָכֵן probably (as Ges.)=הָכֵן Jos. iii. 17 ; iv. 5. The
adversative force, which Gesenius (Thes. p. 670) and Ewald
(Lehrb. n. 105, d. p. 274, ed. 8) think to belong to a later
style, lies (as so often in other Heb. particles) in the tacit
contrast of the sentences. Gesenius' instances of this "later
usage" are Ps. xxxi. 23 ; (David's) lxvi. 19 ; lxxxii. 7 ; Job
xxxii. 8 ; Isa. xlix. 4 ; liii. 4 ; Jer. iii. 20, and this place.

[4] The word means originally "placed on the back" ; then
is used of a traveller, who taking his baggage upon him, or
setting it on his camels, sets out in very early dawn, or before
it, as is the practice in hot countries.

[5] Jer. vii. 13, 25 ; xi. 7 ; xxvi. 5 ; xxix. 19.

8 ¶ Therefore ᵃ wait ye upon me, saith the LORD,
until the day that I rise up to the prey : for my

ᵃ Ps. xxvii. 14 and xxxvii. 34 ; Prov. xx. 22.

that, with the same haste wherewith they ought to have
returned to Me, they might show forth in deed what they
had conceived amiss in their mind."[1] There are as many
aggravations of their sin as there are words. The four
Hebrew words bespeak eagerness, wilfulness, completeness,
enormity, in sin. They *rose early*, themselves deliberately
corrupted, of their own mind made offensive, *all* their *doings*,
not slight acts, but *deeds*, great works done with a high
hand.[2]

8. *Therefore wait ye upon [for] Me.* God so willeth not
to punish, but that all should lay hold of His mercy, that
He doth not here even name punishment. Judah had
slighted His mercies ; He was ready to forgive *all* they had
sinned, if they would *now* receive instruction ; they in
return set themselves to corrupt *all* their doings. They
had wholly forsaken Him. *Therefore*—we should have expected, as elsewhere, "Therefore I will visit all your
iniquities upon you." But not so. The chastisement is all
veiled ; the Prophet points only to the mercy beyond.
Therefore wait ye for Me. All the interval of chastisement
is summed up in these words ; i.e. since neither My mercies
towards you, nor My chastisement of others, lead you to
obey Me, *therefore* the time shall be, when My Providence
shall not seem to be over you, nor My Presence among

[1] S. Jer.

[2] עֲלִילוֹת are the "mighty works" of God, or deeds of
man's might, and, as such, mostly great crimes in the sight
of God. So even the heathen have formed from "facio,"
"facinus," of deeds which they too held to involve great
guilt.

determination *is* to ª gather the nations, that I may assemble the kingdoms, to pour upon them mine

ª Joel iii. 2.

---

you;[1] but then, *wait ye for Me*[2] earnestly, intensely, perseveringly, *until the day, that I rise up to the prey. The day* is probably in the first instance, the deliverance from Babylon. But the words seem to be purposely enlarged, that they may embrace other judgments of God also. For the words to *gather the nations, assemble the kingdoms*, describe some array of nations against God and His people; gathering themselves for their own end at that time, but, in His purpose, gathering themselves for their own destruction, rather than the mere tranquil reunion of those of different nations in the city of Babylon, when the Medes and Persians came against *them*. Nor again are they altogether fulfilled in the destruction of Jerusalem, or any other event until now. For although then a vast number of the dispersed Jews were collected together, and were at that time "broken off"[3] and out of covenant with God, they could hardly be called *nations* (which are here and before [4] spoken of in contrast with Judah), much less *kingdoms*. In its fullest sense the prophecy seems to belong to the same events in the last struggle of Anti-Christ, as at

[1] See Hosea iii. 3–5.

[2] חִכָּה is mostly a longing, persevering expectation for a thing or person which as yet comes not, when the delay requires patience; for God, with לְ, Ps. xxxiii. 20; Isa. viii. 17; lxiv. 4; His promise, Hab. ii. 3, and (part. Kal in sense of Pi.) Isa. xxx. 18; with negative, Ps. cvi. 13; for death, Job iii. 21; of endurance, Dan. xii. 12. The only other cases are "lying in wait," Hosea vi. 9, waiting for the end of Job's words, Job xxxii. 4; for the issue of the message to Jehu, 2 Kings ix. 3; till dawn, ib. vii. 9; and of God, waiting for us, till He can show us mercy, Isa. xxx. 18.

[3] Rom. xi. 20.   [4] v. 6.

indignation, *even* all my fierce anger ; for all the earth
ª shall be devoured with the fire of my jealousy.

ª Zeph. i. 18.

the close of Joel[1] and Zechariah.[2] With this agrees the
largeness of the destruction; *to pour out upon them,* in full
measure, emptying out so as to overwhelm them,[3] *Mine
indignation, even all My fierce anger ; for all the earth shall be
devoured with the fire of My jealousy.* The outpouring of *all*
God's wrath, the devouring of the *whole* earth, in the fullest
sense of the words, belongs to the end of the world, when
He shall say to the wicked, "Depart from Me, ye cursed,
into everlasting fire." In lesser degrees, and less fully,
the substance of the prophecy has again and again been
fulfilled to the Jewish Church before Christ, at Babylon
and under the Maccabees; and to the Christian, as when
the Mohammedans hemmed in Christendom on all sides,
and the waves of their conquests on the East and West
threatened to meet, overwhelming Christendom.   The
Church, having sinned, had to *wait* for a while *for God* Who by
His Providence withdrew Himself, yet at last delivered it.

And since the whole history of the Church lies wrapt up
in the Person of the Redeemer, *the day that I rise up to the
prey,* is especially the Day in which the foundation of His
Church was laid, or that in which it shall be completed; the
Day whereon He rose again, as the first-fruits, or that Day
in which He shall *stand again on the earth,*[4] to judge it ; *so
coming even as He went up into Heaven.*[5] Then, *the prey*[6]

---

[1] Joel iii. 2, 9–16.   [2] Zech. xiv.

[3] See Ps. lxix. 24 ; lxxix. 6 ; Jer. vi. 11 ; x. 25 ; xiv. 16 ;
Ezek. xxi. 31 ; Rev. xvi. 1.

[4] Job xix. 25. It is the same word.   [5] Acts i. 11.

[6] עַד commonly signifies "eternity," עַד or לָעַד ; also Gen.
xlix. 27 ; Isa. xxxiii. 23 (as Ch. עָדָא &c.) "prey"; nowhere,
as Ew., "attack."

9 For then will I turn to the people [a] a pure

[a] Isa. xix. 18.

---

must be, what God vouchsafes to account as His gain, *the prey* which is *taken from the mighty*,[1] and *the lawful captivity, the prey of the terrible one*, which shall be delivered ; even that spoil which the Father bestowed on Him *Who made His soul an offering for sin*,[2] the goods of the strong man [3] whom He bound, and spoiled us, His lawful goods and captives, since we had *sold* [4] ourselves *under sin* to him. "Christ lived again having spoiled hell, because [5] *it was not possible* (as it is written) *that He*, being by nature Life, *should be holden of death*." [6]

Here, where spoken of with relation to the Church, *the jealousy* of Almighty God is that love for His people,[7] which will not endure their ill-treatment by those who (as all Anti-Christian power doth) make themselves His rivals in the government of the world.

9. *For then*, in the order of God's mercies. The deliverance from Babylon was the forerunner of that of the Gospel, which was its object. The spread of the Gospel, then, is spoken of in the connection of God's Providence and plan, and time is overlooked. Its blessings are spoken of, as *then* given when the earnest was given, and the people, from whom according to the flesh Christ was to be born, were placed anew in the land where He was to be born. "The Prophet springs, as is his wont, to Christ and the time of the new law." [8] And in Christ, the End of the law, the Prophet ends.

I will turn, contrary to what they had before, *to the people*,

[1] Isa. xlix. 24, 25.   [2] Ib. liii. 10, 12.
[3] S. Matt. xii. 29.
[4] Rom. vii. 14, coll. Isa. l. 1 ; lii. 3.
[5] Acts ii. 24.   [6] S. Cyr.
[7] See on Nahum i. 2.   [8] Lap.

*language, that they may all call upon the name of
the LORD, to serve him with one †consent.

     * Heb. *lip.*   † Heb. *shoulder.*

---

lit. *peoples*, the nations of the earth, *a pure language*, lit. *a
purified lip*. It is a real conversion, as was said of Saul at
the beginning : *God* [lit.] *turned to him another heart.*[1] Before
the dispersion of Babel the world was *of one lip*,[2] but that,

  [1] 1 Sam. x. 9, ‏ויהפך יי לו לב אחר‎, as here ‏אהפך אל עמים‎
‏שׂפה ברורה‎.

  [2] Gen. xi. 1, 6, 7, 9. The Jews also saw that this was a
reversal of the confusion of Babel. "God, blessed for ever,
saith, 'in this world, on account of evil concupiscence (‏יצר‎
‏הרע‎ man's natural corruption), men were divided into
seventy languages ; but in the world to come, all shall agree
with one mind to call upon My Name ; '" alleging this place.
Tanchuma, f. 5, 1, ap. Schoettg. ad loc. "R. Chiia said,
'Thou hearest from Holy Scripture, that all hangeth from the
word of the mouth ; for after the tongues were confounded,
it is added, 'and God dispersed them thence.' But in the
time to come, what is written ? 'Then will I turn, &c.'"
Sohar, Gen. f. 58, col. 217 (Schoettg. loc. gen. n. 37). Again
it is said, "When the days of the Messiah shall come, boys
shall know the hidden things of wisdom ; for then shall all
things be revealed, as is said, Then will I turn, &c." Ib. f. 74,
col. 291 ; ib. ad loc. And of its fulfilment in the conversion
of the world, "Who would have expected that God would
raise up the tabernacle of David, which was fallen ? and yet
it is read, In that day I will raise, &c. (Amos ix. 11). And
who would have hoped that the whole world would be one
band ? as in, Then will I turn, &c." Bereshith rabba, n.
88 fin. Schoettg. loci gen. n. 18, and on Gen. xli. 44 ; "Why
is 'they shall praise Thee' repeated four times in Ps. lxvii.
3, 5 ? He means, 'They shall praise Thee with their heart ;
they shall praise Thee with their mouth ; they shall praise
Thee with their good deeds, and they shall praise Thee with
all these, as it is said, For then will I turn, &c.,' and the Name
of the Lord is no other than the King Messiah, according to,

impure, for it was in rebellion against God. Now it shall
be again of *one lip;* and that, *purified.* The purity is of
faith and of life, *that they may call upon the Name of the
Lord,* not as heretofore on idols, but that every tongue should
confess the one true God, Father, Son, and Holy Ghost, in
Whose Name they are baptized. This is purity of faith.
To *call upon the Name of the Lord Jesus* [1] is the very title of
Christian worship ; *all that called upon the Name* of Jesus,
the very title of Christians.[2] *To serve Him with one consent,*
lit. *with one shoulder,* evenly, steadfastly, *not unequally yoked,*
but all with united strength, bearing Christ's *easy yoke* and
one another's burdens, fulfilling the law of Christ. This is
purity of life. The fruit of the lips is *the sacrifice of praise.*[3]
God gave back one pure language, when, on the Day of
Pentecost, the Holy Spirit, the Author of purity, came
down in fiery tongues upon the Apostles, teaching them
and guiding them *into the whole truth,*[4] and to *speak to every
one in his own tongue, wherein he was born, the wonderful works
of God.*[5] Thenceforth there was to be a higher unity than
that of outward language. For speech is not the outward
sound, but the thoughts which it conveys and embodies.
The inward thought is the soul of the words. The outward
confusion of Babel was to hinder oneness in evil and a
worse confusion. At Pentecost, the unity restored was
oneness of soul and heart, wrought by One Spirit, Whose
gift is the one Faith and the one Hope of our calling, in the

' and the Name of the Lord cometh from far,' " in Mart.
Pug. Fid. f. 327. It is also quoted with other places, as to
be fulfilled in the time of the Messiah, *Tikkune Sohar,* p. 60
(Schoettg. Loc. gen. n. 80), R. Moseh in Ibn Ezra, and Ibn
Ezra himself, of the second temple. Kimchi " after the
wars of Gog."

[1] Acts xxii. 16 ; Rom. x. 13.
[2] Acts ix. 14, 21 ; 1 Cor. i. 2.   [3] Heb. xiii. 15.
[4] S. John xvi. 13.   [5] Acts ii. 8, 11.

10 ᵃ From beyond the rivers of Ethiopia my

ᵃ Ps. lxviii. 31 ; Isa. xviii. 1, 7 and lx. 4, &c. ; Mal. i. 11 ;
Acts viii. 27.

One Lord, in Whom we are one, grafted into the one body,
by our Baptism.[1] The Church, then created, is the One
Holy Catholic Church diffused throughout all the world,
everywhere with one rule of Faith, *the Faith once for all delivered unto the saints,* confessing one God, the Trinity in
Unity, and serving Him in the one law of the Gospel with
one consent. Christians, as Christians, speak the same
language of Faith, and from all quarters of the world, one
language of praise goes up to the one God and Father of
all. " God divided the tongues at Babel, lest, understanding
one another, they should form a destructive unity. Through
proud men tongues were divided; through humble Apostles
tongues were gathered in one. The spirit of pride dispersed
tongues ; the Holy Spirit gathered tongues in one. For
when the Holy Spirit came upon the disciples, they spake
with the tongues of all, were understood by all ; the dispersed tongues were gathered into one. So then, if they
are yet angry and Gentiles, it is better for them to have
their tongues divided. If they wish for one tongue, let
them come to the Church ; for in diversity of the tongues
of the flesh, there is one tongue in the Faith of the heart."[2]
In whatever degree the oneness is impaired within the
Church, while there is yet one Faith of the Creeds, He
Alone can restore it and *turn to her a purified language,* Who
first gave it to those who waited for Him. Both praise and
service are perfected above, where the Blessed, with one
loud voice, *shall cry, Salvation to our God which sitteth upon
the Throne and unto the Lamb ; blessing and glory and wisdom
and thanksgiving and honour and power and might be unto our*

---

[1] Eph. iv. 3–6.　　　　[2] S. Aug. in Ps. liv. 6.

God for ever and ever.[1] And they who *have come out of great tribulation and have washed their robes and made them white in the Blood of the Lamb,* shall be *before the throne of God and serve Him day and night in His Temple.*[2]

10. *From beyond the rivers*[3] *of Ethiopia.* The furthest Southern people, with whom the Jews had intercourse, stand as the type of the whole world beyond. The utmost bound of the known inhabited land should not be the bound of the Gospel. The conversion of Abyssinia is one, but the narrowest fulfilment of the prophecy. The whole new world, though not in the mind of the Prophet, was in the mind of Him Who spake by the Prophet.

My suppliants. He names them as what they shall be when they shall come to Him. They shall come, as needy, to the Fountain of all good, asking for mercy of the unfailing Source of all mercy. He describes the very character of all who come to God through Christ. *The daughter of My dispersed.*[4] God is, in the way of Providence, the Father of all, although, by sin, alienated from Him; whence S. Paul says, *We are the offspring of God.*[5] They were *dispersed,* severed from the oneness in Him and from His house and family; yet still, looking on them as already belonging to Him, He calls them, *My dispersed,* as by Caiaphas, being high-priest, He prophesied that *Jesus should die for that nation; and not for that nation only, but that also He should*

---

[1] Rev. vii. 10, 12.   [2] Ib. vii. 14, 15.

[3] See Isaiah xviii. 1.

[4] Ewald conjectures בת פוט because Nahum speaks of Cush, Phut, and Lubim among the allies of No-Ammon or Thebes, and renders עתרי "my incenses"; first rendering עתר (Ez. viii. 11) "*the smoke of the cloud of incense.*" But this sense is not itself proved (in both Syr. and Arab. incense is עטר not עתר), nor is incense plural; nor is there any parallelism of Cush and Phut in Nahum, but Phut and Lubim are historically named as allies of No.

[5] Acts xvii. 28.

suppliants, *even* the daughter of my dispersed, shall bring mine offering.

---

gather together in one the children of God that were scattered abroad.[1]

Shall bring Mine offering.[2] The offering is the same as that which Malachi prophesies shall continue under the New Testament, which offering was to be offered to the Name of God, not in Jerusalem, but *in every place from the rising of the sun unto the going down of the same.*[3] The dark skin of the Ethiopian is the image of ingrained sin, which man could not efface or change :[4] their conversion, then, declares how those steeped in sin shall be cleansed from all their darkness of mind, and washed white from their sins in baptism and beautified by the grace of God. "The word of prophecy endeth in truth. For not only through the Roman empire is the Gospel preached, but it circles round the barbarous nations. And there are Churches everywhere, shepherds and teachers, guides and instructors in mysteries, and sacred altars, and the Lamb is invisibly sacrificed by holy priests among Indians too and Ethiopians. And this was said plainly by another prophet also,[3] *For I am a great King, saith the Lord, and My Name is great among the heathen,*

[1] S. John xi. 51, 52,

[2] It is possible also to render, "from beyond the rivers of Ethiopia, My suppliants the daughter of My dispersed shall they bring as Mine offering ; " and this some have preferred on account of the like place in Isaiah lxvi. 20, "And they shall bring all your brethren for an offering unto the Lord out of all nations, &c." But the word מנחה alone is common to the two passages, and the words טעבר לנהרי כוש which occur in Isa. xviii. 1, and יובל שי לי ib. 7, make me think that this place rather was in the Prophet's mind.

[3] Mal. i. 11.   [4] Jer. xiii. 23.

11 In that day shalt thou not be ashamed for all thy doings, wherein thou hast transgressed against

---

and in every place incense is offered to My Name and a pure sacrifice." [1]

11. *In that day shalt thou not be ashamed for all thy doings,* because God, forgiving them, will blot them out and no more remember them. This was first fulfilled in the Gospel. "No one can doubt that when Christ came in the flesh, there was an amnesty and remission to all who believed. *For we are justified not by works of righteousness which we have done, but according to His great mercy.* But we have been released from shame. For *He* hath restored us to freedom of access to God, Who for our sakes arose from the dead, and for us ascended to heaven in the presence of the Father. *For Christ, our Forerunner, hath ascended for us now to appear in the presence of God.* So then He took away the guilt of all and freed believers from failures and shame." [1]   S. Peter, even in heaven, must remember his denial of our Lord, yet not so as to be *ashamed* or pained any more, since the exceeding love of God will remove all shame or pain. " [2] Mighty promise, mighty consolation. Now, before that Day comes, the Day of My Resurrection, thou wilt be ashamed and not without reason, since thou ownest by a true confession, *all our righteousnesses are as filthy rags.* [3] But at that Day it will not be so, especially when that shall be which I promise thee in the Prophets and the Psalms, *There shall be a Fountain opened for sin and for uncleanness;* [4] whence David also, exulting in good hope of the Holy Spirit, saith, *Thou shalt wash me and I shall be whiter than snow.* [5] For though he elsewhere saith, *They looked unto Him and were lightened, and their faces were not*

---

[1] S. Cyr.   [2] Rup.   [3] Isa. lxiv. 6.
[4] Zech. xiii. 1.   [5] Ps. li. 7.

M

me : for then I will take away out of the midst of
thee them that ^a rejoice in thy pride, and thou shalt
no more be haughty *because of my holy mountain.

^a Jer. vii. 4 ; Micah iii. 11 ; Matt. iii. 9.
* Heb. *in my holy.*

---

ashamed,[1] yet in this mortal life, when the day of My Resurrection doth not fully shine upon thee, thou art after some
sort ashamed ; as it is written, *What fruit had ye then in
those things whereof ye are now ashamed ?*[2] but that shame
will bring glory, and, when that glory cometh in its place,
will wholly pass away. But when the fulness of that day
shall come, the fulness of My Resurrection, when the
members shall rise, as the Head hath risen, will the memory
of past foulness bring any confusion ? Yea the very memory
of the miseries will be the richest subject of singing, according to that, *My song shall be alway of the loving-kindness of
the Lord.*"[3] For how shall the redeemed forget the mercies
of their redemption, or yet how feel a painful shame even
of the very miseries, out of which they were redeemed by
the fulness of the over-streaming Love of God ?

*For then will I take away out of the midst of thee them that
rejoice in thy pride* [*those of thee who exult in pride*[4]]. All
confusion shall cease, because all pride shall cease, the
parent of sin and confusion. The very gift of God becomes
to the carnal a source of pride. Pride was to the Jew also
the great hindrance to the reception of the Gospel. He
made his *boast of the law,* yea, in God Himself, that he *knew
His will,* and was *a guide of others,*[5] and so was the more
indignant, that the heathen was made equal to him, and

[1] Ps. xxxiv. 5.　　[2] Rom. vi. 21.　　[3] Ps. lxxxix. 1.
[4] It cannot be " those that exult in thy highness " ; for נאוה,
as used of man, always has a bad sense, " self-exaltation."
[5] Rom. ii. 17, 18–20, 23.

12 I will also leave in the midst of thee ᵃan

ᵃ Isa. xiv. 32; Zech. xi. 11; Matt. v. 3; 1 Cor. i. 27, 28;
James ii. 5.

---

that he too was called to repentance and faith in Christ.
So, *going about to establish his own righteousness, he did not
submit himself to the righteousness of God*, but shut himself out
from the faith and grace and salvation of Christ, and rejected Himself. So, [1]*thy pride* may be the pride in being
the people of God, and having Abraham for their father.
And thou shalt no more be haughty [2]*in My holy mountain,* " but thou shalt stand in the great and everlasting
abiding-place of humility, knowing perfectly, that thou now
'knowest in part' only, and confessest truly that no one
ever could or can by his own works be justified in the sight
of God. *For all have sinned and come short of the glory of
God."* [3] Pride, which is ever offensive to God, is yet more
hideous in a holy place or a holy office, *in* Mount Sion
where the temple was or in the Christian priesthood.

12. And *I will also leave* (*over*, as a remnant, it is still the
same heavy prophecy, that *a remnant* only *shall be saved* [4])
an afflicted and poor people. Priests (except that *great*

[1] Rup.

[2] As in E.M., not *because of*. נבה, as a mental quality,
mostly occurs with לב and is used in a bad sense of high-
mindedness = pride; Ps. cxxxi. 1 (David's); Prov. xviii. 12;
Ezek. xxviii. 2, 5, 17; 2 Chron. xxvi. 16; xxxii. 25; absol.
in a bad sense, Isa. iii. 16; Jer. xiii. 15; Ezek. xvi. 50. It
is used of eminence given by God, Job xxxvi. 7, and of the
Messiah as exalted by Him, Isa. lii. 13. Once only, 2 Chron.
xvii. 6, נבה לבו is used in a good sense of Jehoshaphat, that,
being exalted by God, "his heart was elevated in the ways
of the law." The form לְגָבְהָה is like the inf. in Exod. xxix.
29; xxx. 18; xxxvi. 2; Lev. xv. 32, &c.

[3] Rom. iii. 23.

[4] Ib. ix. 27. See above on Micah ii. 12.

afflicted and poor people, and they shall trust in the name of the LORD.

---

company who *were obedient to the faith* [1]), scribes, lawyers, Pharisees, Sadducees were taken away ; and there remained "the people of the land," [2] the *unlearned and ignorant,*[3] *the weak things of the world and the things despised,*[4] who bore the very title of their Master,[5] *the poor and needy; poor in spirit;* [6] poor also in outward things, since *they who had lands, sold them* and they *had all things common.*[7] They were afflicted above measure outwardly in the [8]persecutions, *reproaches, spoiling of* their *goods,* stripes, deaths, which they endured for Christ's sake. They knew too their own poverty; "knowing themselves to be sinners, and that they were justified only by faith in Jesus Christ." [9] When the rest were cast out *of the midst of her,* these should be

[1] Acts vi. 7.

[2] עַם הָאָרֶץ the uneducated, *this people that knoweth not the law* (S. John vii. 49), "one in whom there are moral not intellectual excellences." Rambam in Buxt. Lex. Talm. col. 1626.

[3] Acts iv. 13.

[4] 1 Cor. i. 27, 28.   [5] Ps. xli. 1.

[6] עָנִי is not simply "poor," nor עָנָו simply "meek." עָנִי is one "afflicted," in whom affliction has produced its fruits ; עָנָו, one "meek," but in whom patience has been tried and perfected; as the same class are meant by the πτωχοὶ, S. Luke vi. 20, and the πτωχοὶ τῷ πνεύματι, S. Matt. v. 3 ; and "no humility without humiliation,"· is become a Christian proverb.

[7] Acts ii. 44, 45 ; iv. 32, 35.

[8] Acts viii. 1 ; ix. 2, 13, 14 ; xii. 1, 2 ; xiii. 50 ; xiv. 5, 22 ; xxii. &c. ; Rom. viii. 17, 35, 36 ; xii. 14 ; 1 Cor. ix. 19 ; 2 Cor. i. 8, 9 ; xii. 10 ; 2 Thess. i. 4 ; 2 Tim. iii. 11, 12 ; Heb. x. 32–34 ; S. James ii. 6, 7 ; 1 S. Peter i. 6, 7 ; iv. 13 ; Rev. i. 9 ; vi. 9, &c.

[9] Rup.

13 ^a The remnant of Israel ^b shall not do iniquity,

^a Micah iv. 7 ; Zeph. ii. 7.   ^b Isa. lx. 21.

---

left *in the midst of her* (the words stand in contrast with one another) in the bosom of the Church. *And they shall trust in the name of the Lord.* "As they looked to be justified only in the Name of Christ," and "trusted in the grace and power of God alone, not in any power or wisdom or eloquence or riches of this world, they converted the world to a faith above nature."[1] "Conformed in this too to Christ, Who for our sakes became poor and almost neglected both His divine glory and the supereminence of His nature, to subject Himself to the condition of a servant. So then those instructed in His laws after His example, think humbly of themselves. They became most exceedingly loved of God, and chiefly the divine disciples, who were set as lights of the world."[2]

13. *The remnant of Israel,* the same poor people, the *true Israel* of whom God said, *I leave over* (the word is the same) *a poor people,* few, compared with the rest who were blinded ; of whom the Lord said, *I know whom I have chosen.*[3] These *shall not do iniquity nor speak lies.* "This is a spiritual adorning, a most beautiful coronet of glorious virtues. For where meekness and humility are and the desire of righteousness, and the tongue unlearns vain words and sinful speech, and is the instrument of strict truth, there dawns a bright and most perfect virtue. And this beseems those who are in Christ. For the beauty of piety is not seen in the Law, but gleams forth in the power of Evangelic teaching."[2]

Our Lord said of Nathanael, *Behold an Israelite indeed, in whom is no guile,*[4] and to the Apostles, *I send you forth as sheep among wolves; be ye therefore wise as serpents and*

[1] Dion.   [2] S. Cyr.
[3] S. John xiii. 18.   [4] Ib. i. 47.

ᵃnor speak lies; neither shall a deceitful tongue be

ᵃ Isa. lxiii. 8; Rev. xiv. 5.

harmless as doves: [1] and of the first Christians it is said,
_They, continuing daily with one accord in the temple, and
breaking bread from house to house did eat their meat with
gladness and singleness of heart, praising God and having
favour with all the people._ [2] This is the character of
Christians, as such, and it was at first fulfilled: _Whosoever
is born of God, doth not commit sin;_ [3] _whosoever is born of
God sinneth not; but he that is begotten of God keepeth himself, and that wicked one toucheth him not._ [4] An Apologist,
at the close of the second century, could appeal to the
Roman Emperor, [5] that no Christian was found among
their criminals, "unless it be only as a Christian, or, if he
be anything else, he is forthwith no longer a Christian.
We alone then are innocent! What wonder if this be so,
of necessity? And truly of necessity it is so. Taught
innocence by God, we both know it perfectly, as being revealed by a perfect Master; and we keep it faithfully, as
being committed to us by an Observer, Who may not be
despised." "Being so vast a multitude of men, almost the
greater portion of every state, we live silently and modestly,
known perhaps more as individuals than as a body, and to
be known by no other sign than the reformation of our
former sins." [6] Now in the Church, which "our earth-
dimm'd eyes behold," we can but say, as in regard to the
cessation of war [7] under the Gospel, that God's promises

[1] S. Matt. x. 16.   [2] Acts ii. 46, 47.
[3] 1 S. John iii. 9.   [4] Ib. v. 18.
[5] Tert. Apol. c. 44, 45. See also Justin M. i. n. 34, S.
Athenagoras, n. 2, Minutius Felix, p. 333. Theodoret de cur.
Græc. aff. Disp. xii. circ. med. p. 1021 sqq. ed Schultz;
Lactant. v. 9, quoted ib.
[6] Id. ad Scap. n. 2, p. 145, Oxf. Tr.
[7] See above on Micah iv. 3.

are sure on His part, that still *they that are Christ's have
crucified the flesh with the affections and lusts*,[1] that the
Gospel is *a power of God unto salvation*,[2] that *the preaching of
the Cross is, unto us which are saved, the power of God ;*[3] *unto
them that are called, Christ is the power of God and the wisdom
of God ;*[4] that those who will, *are kept by God through faith
unto salvation ;*[5] but that now too *they are not all Israel,
which are of Israel*,[6] and that *the faithlessness of man does not
make the faith of God of none effect.*[7] "The Church of God
is universally holy in respect of all, by institutions and
administrations of sanctity ; the same Church is really holy
in this world, in relation to all godly persons contained in
it, by a real infused sanctity ; the same is farther yet at
the same time perfectly holy in reference to the saints departed and admitted to the presence of God ; and the same
Church shall hereafter be most completely holy in the world
to come, when all the members, actually belonging to it,
shall be at once perfected in holiness and completed in hap-
piness."[8] Most fully shall this be fulfilled in the Resurrection. "O blessed day of the Resurrection, in whose
fulness no one will sin in word or deed ! O great and
blessed reward to every soul, which, although it hath now
done iniquity and *spoken falsehood*, yet willeth not to do it
further ! Great and blessed reward, that he shall now
receive such immovableness, as no longer to be able to do
iniquity or speak falsehood, since the blessed soul, through
the Spirit of everlasting love inseparably united with God
its Creator, shall now no more be capable of an evil will !"[9]

For they shall feed ; on the hidden manna, "nourished

---

[1] Gal. v. 24.   See Dr. Pusey's Sermon, "The Gospel, the
power of God."   Lenten Sermons, pp. 300–321.

[2] Rom. i. 16.   [3] 1 Cor. i. 18.
[4] Ib. i. 24.   [5] 1 S. Peter i. 5.
[6] Rom. ix. 6.   [7] Ib. iii. 3.
[8] Bp. Pearson on the Creed, Art. ix.   [9] Rup.

found in their mouth : for ^a they shall feed and lie down, and none shall make *them* afraid.

^a Ezek. xxxiv. 28 ; Micah iv. 4 and vii. 14.

most delicately by the Holy Spirit with inward delights, and spiritual food, the bread of life." [1] In the things of the body too was *distribution made unto every man according as he had need.* [2] *And they shall lie down* in the green pastures where He foldeth them ; *and none shall make them afraid,* " [1] for they were ready to suffer and to die for the Name of the Lord Jesus. [3] *They departed from the presence of the council rejoicing that they were counted worthy to suffer shame for His Name.* [4] Before the Resurrection and the sending of the Holy Ghost, how great was the fearfulness, unsteadfastness, weakness of the disciples ; how great, after the infusion of the Holy Spirit, was their constancy and imperturbableness, it is delightsome to estimate in their Acts," when they *bare His Name before the Gentiles and kings, and the children of Israel,* [5] and he who had been afraid of a little maid, said to the High Priest, *We ought to obey God rather than men.* [6] "When Christ the Good Shepherd Who laid down His life for His sheep, shone upon us, we are fed in gardens and pastured among lilies, and lie down in folds ; for we are folded in Churches and holy shrines, no one scaring or spoiling us, no wolf assailing nor lion trampling on us, no robber breaking through, no one invading us, to steal and kill and destroy ; but we abide in safety and participation of every good, being in charge of Christ the Saviour of all." [7]

14. *Sing, O daughter of Sion ; shout, O Israel ; be glad and rejoice with all the heart, O daughter of Jerusalem.* Very remarkable throughout all these verses is the use of the

[1] Dion. [2] Acts iv. 35. [3] Ib. xxi. 13.
[4] Ib. v. 41. [5] Ib. ix. 15.
[6] Ib. v. 29. [7] S. Cyril.

14 ¶ ^a Sing, O daughter of Zion; shout, O Israel; be glad and rejoice with all the heart, O daughter of Jerusalem.

^a Isa. xii. 6 and liv. 1 ; Zech. ii. 10 and ix. 9.

---

sacred number three, secretly conveying to the thoughtful soul the thought of Him, Father, Son, and Holy Ghost, the Holy and Undivided Trinity by Whose operation these things shall be. Threefold is the description of their being freed from sins : (1) they shall *not do iniquity*, (2) *nor speak lies*, (3) *neither shall a deceitful tongue be found in their mouth*. Threefold their blessedness : They shall (1) *feed*, (2) *lie down*, (3) *none make them afraid*. Threefold the exhortation to joy here : "*Sing* to God the father ; *shout* to God the Son ; *be glad and rejoice* in God the Holy Ghost, which Holy Trinity is One God, from Whom thou hast received it that thou art (1) *the daughter of Zion*, (2) *Israel*, (3) *the daughter of Jerusalem; the daughter of Zion* by faith, *Israel* by hope, *Jerusalem* by charity." [1] And this hidden teaching of that holy mystery is continued : [2] *The Lord*, God the Father, *hath taken away thy judgments; He*, God the Son, *hath cast out (cleared quite away) thine enemy; the king of Israel, the Lord*, the Holy Ghost, *is in the midst of thee!* The promise is threefold : (1) *thou shalt not see evil any more;* (2) *fear thou not;* (3) *let not thine hands be slack*. The love of God is threefold: (1) *He will rejoice over thee with joy;* (2) *He will rest in His love;* (3) *He will joy over thee with singing*. Again the words in these four verses are so framed as to be *ful-*filled in the end. All in this life are but shadows of that fulness. First, whether the Church or the faithful soul, she is summoned by all her names, *daughter of Zion* ("the thirsty" athirst for God), *Israel* ("Prince with God"), *Jerusalem* ("City of peace"). By all she is called to the

[1] Rup.   [2] v. 15.

15 The LORD hath taken away thy judgments,
he hath cast out thine enemy: ^a the king of Israel,

^a John i. 49.

---

fullest joy in God with every expression and every feeling.
Sing; it is the inarticulate, thrilling, trembling burst of
joy; *shout;* again the inarticulate yet louder swell of joy,
a trumpet-blast; and then too, deep within, *be glad,* the
calm even joy of the inward soul ; *exult,* the triumph of the
soul which cannot contain itself for joy ; and this, *with the
whole heart,* no corner of it not pervaded with joy. The
ground of this is the complete removal of every evil, and
the full Presence of God.

15. *The Lord hath taken away thy judgments ;* her own,
because brought upon her by her sins. But when God
takes away the chastisements in mercy, He removes and
forgives the sin too. Else, to remove *the judgments* only,
would be to abandon the sinner. *He hath cast out,* lit. *cleared
quite away,*[1] as a man clears away all hindrances, all which
stands in the way, so that there should be none whatever left—*thine enemy;* the one enemy, from whom every
hindrance to our salvation comes, as He saith, *Now shall the
prince of this world be cast out.*[2] *The King of Israel, even the
Lord,* Christ the Lord, *is in the midst of thee,* of Whom it is
said, *He that sitteth on the throne shall dwell among them,*[3] and
Who Himself saith, *Lo I am with you always unto the end
of the world.*[4] *Where two or three are gathered together in My
Name, there am I in the midst of you.*[5] He Who had removed *from the midst of her* the proud, Who had left *in the
midst of her* those with whom He dwelleth, shall Himself

[1] Besides this place, the word is used of " the clearing of a
house," Gen. xxiv. 31 ; Lev. xiv. 36 ; " a way," Isa. xl. 3 ;
lvii. 14 ; lxii. 10 ; Mal. iii. 1 ; " clearing ground," Ps. lxxx. 9.
[2] S. John xii. 31.   [3] Rev. vii. 15.
[4] S. Matt. xxviii. 20.   [5] Ib. xviii. 20.

even the LORD, [a] *is* in the midst of thee : thou shalt
not see evil any more.

[a] Ver. v. 17 ; Ezek. xlviii. 35 ; Rev. vii. 15, and xxi. 3, 4.

dwell *in the midst of her* in mercy, as He had before in
judgment.[1] He cleanseth the soul for His indwelling, and
so dwelleth in the mansion which He had prepared for
Himself. *Thou shalt not see evil any more.* For even the
remains of evil, while we are yet in the flesh, are overruled,
and *work together to good to those who love God.*[2] They cannot
separate between the soul and Christ. Rather, He is nearer
to her in them. We are bidden to *count it all joy when we
fall into divers temptations,*[3] for all sorrows are but medicine
from a father's hand. " And truly our way to eternal joy
is to suffer here with Christ, and our door to enter into
eternal life is gladly to die with Christ, that we may rise
again from death and dwell with Him in everlasting life." [4]
So in the Revelation, it is first said that God should dwell
with His people, and then that all pain shall cease. *Behold
the tabernacle of God is with men, and He will dwell with them
and be their God. And God shall wipe all tears from their
eyes ; and there shall be no more death, neither sorrow nor
crying, neither shall there be any more pain ; for the former
things are passed away.*[5] " [6] In the inmost meaning of the
words, he could not but bid her rejoice and be exceeding
glad and rejoice with her whole heart, her sins being done
away through Christ. For the holy and spiritual Zion, the
Church, the multitude of believers, is justified in Christ
Alone, and we are saved by Him and from Him, escaping
the harms of our invisible enemies, and having in the
midst of us the King and God of all, Who appeared in our
likeness, the Word from God the Father, through Whom

[1] Verses 11, 12, 15, 5.   [2] Rom. viii. 28.
[3] S. James i. 2.   [4] Exhort. in Visit. of the Sick.
[5] Rev. xxi. 3, 4.   [6] S. Cyril.

16 In that day [a] it shall be said to Jerusalem, Fear thou not: *and to* Zion, [b] Let not thine hands be * slack.

[a] Isa. xxxv. 3, 4.   [b] Heb. xii. 12.   * Or, *faint.*

---

we see not evil, i.e. are freed from all who could do us evil. For He is the worker of our acceptableness, our peace, our wall, the bestower of incorruption, the dispenser of crowns, Who lighteneth the assaults of devils, Who giveth us *to tread on serpents and scorpions and all the power of the enemy* [1] —through Whom we are in good hope of immortality and life, adoption and glory, through Whom we shall not see evil any more."

16. *In that day it shall be said to Jerusalem, Fear thou not;* for *perfect love casteth out fear;* [2] whence He saith, *Fear not, little flock: it is your Father's good pleasure to give you the kingdom.* [3] Who then and what should the Church or the faithful soul fear, since *mightier is He that is in her, than he that is in the world? And to Zion, Let not thine hands be slack,* through faint-heartedness, [4] but work with all thy might; be ready to do or bear anything; since Christ worketh with, in, by thee, and *in due time we shall reap, if we faint not.* [5]

17. *The Lord thy God in the midst of thee is mighty; He will save.* What *can* He then not do for thee, since He is Almighty? What *will* He not do for thee, since *He will save?* Whom then should we fear? *If God be for us, who can be against us?* [6] But then was He especially *in the midst of* us, when God *the word became flesh and dwelt among us; and we beheld His Glory, the Glory as of the Only-Begotten of the Father, full of grace and Truth.* [7] Thenceforth He ever

[4] S. Luke x. 19.   [2] 1 S. John iv. 18.
[3] S. Luke xii. 32.   [4] See Heb. xii. 12.   [5] Gal. vi. 9.
[6] Rom. viii. 31.   [7] S. John i. 14.

17 The LORD thy God ᵃ in the midst of thee *is* mighty; he will save, ᵇ he will rejoice over thee

ᵃ Ver. 15.
ᵇ Deut. xxx. 9 ; Isa. lxii. 5 and lxv. 19 ; Jer. xxxii. 41.

---

is in the midst of His own. He with the Father and the Holy Spirit *come unto them and make Their abode with them,*[1] so that they are *the temple of God.   He will save,* as He saith, *My Father is greater than all, and no mar. is able to pluck them out of My Father's hand.   I and My Father are One.*[2] Of the same time of the Christ, Isaiah saith almost in the same words : *Strengthen ye the weak hands and confirm the feeble knees.   Say to them that are of a feeble heart, Be strong, fear not, behold your God will come, He will come and save you ;*[3] and of the Holy Trinity, *He will save us.*[4]

He will rejoice over thee with joy. Love, joy, peace in man, are shadows of that which is in God, by Whom they are created in man.   Only in God they exist undivided, uncreated.   Hence God speaks after the manner of men, of that which truly is in God.   God joyeth " with an uncreated joy " over the works of His Hands or the objects of His Love, as man joyeth over the object of *his* love.   So Isaiah saith,[5] *As the bridegroom rejoiceth over the bride, so shall thy God rejoice over thee.*   As with uncreated love the Father resteth in good pleasure in His Well-beloved Son, so *God is well-pleased with the sacrifices of loving deeds,*[6] and, *the Lord delighteth in thee ;*[7] and, *I will rejoice in Jerusalem and joy in My people :*[8] and, *the Lord will again rejoice over thee for good.*[9] And so in a twofold way God meeteth the longing of the heart of man.   The soul, until it hath found God, is evermore seeking some love to fill it, and can find none,

[1] S. John xiv. 23.
[2] Ib. x. 29, 30.
[3] Isa. xxxv. 3, 4.
[4] Ib. xxxiii. 22.
[5] Ib. lxii. 5.   [6] Heb. xiii. 16.   [7] Isa. lxii. 4.
[8] Ib. lxv. 19.   [9] Deut. xxx. 9.

with joy; *he will rest in his love, he will joy over
thee with singing.

* Heb. *he will be silent.*

---

since the love of God Alone can content it. Then too it
longeth to be loved, even as it loveth. God tells it, that
every feeling and expression of human love may be found
in Him, Whom if any love, he only *loveth Him, because He
first loved us.*[1] Every inward and outward expression or
token of love are heaped together, to express the love of
Him Who broodeth and as it were yearneth *over* (it is twice
repeated) His own whom He loveth. Then too He loveth
thee as He biddeth thee to love Him; and since the love
of man cannot be like the love of the Infinite God, He here
pictures His own love in the words of man's love, to convey
to his soul the oneness wherewith love unites her unto God.
He here echoes in a manner the joy of the Church, to which
He had called her,[2] in words the self-same or meaning the
same. We have *joy* here for *joy* there; *singing* or the un-
uttered, unutterable jubilee of the heart, which cannot
utter in words its joy and love, and joys and loves the
more in its inmost depths because it cannot utter it. A
shadow of the unutterable, because Infinite Love of God,
and this repeated thrice; as being the eternal love of the
Ever-blessed Trinity. This love and joy the Prophet speaks
of, as an exuberant joy, one which boundeth within the
inmost self, and again is wholly *silent in His love,* as the
deepest, tenderest, most yearning, love broods over the object
of its love, yet is held still in silence by the very depth of
its love; and then, again, breaks forth in outward motion,
and leaps for joy, and uttereth what it cannot form in
words; for truly the love of God in its unspeakable love
and joy is past belief, past utterance, past thought. "Truly

[1] 1 S. John iv. 19.   [2] Verse 14.

that joy wherewith *He will be silent in His love*, that exultation wherewith *He will joy over thee with singing*, [1]*Eye hath
not seen nor ear heard, neither hath it entered into the heart of
man.*"[2] The Hebrew word[3] also contains the meaning,
" He in His love shall make no mention of past sins,[4] He
shall not bring them up against thee, shall not upbraid
thee, yea, shall not remember them." It also may express
the still, unvarying love of the Unchangeable God. And
again how the very silence of God, when He seemeth not
to hear, as He did not seem to hear S. Paul, is a very fruit
of His love. Yet that entire forgiveness of sins, and
that seeming absence, are but ways of showing His love.
Hence God speaks of His very love itself, *He will be silent
in His love*, as, before and after, *He will rejoice, He will joy
over thee.*

18–21. In these verses still continuing the number
"three," the prophecy closes with the final reversal of all
which, in this imperfect state of things, seems turned upside
down, when those who now mourn shall be comforted, they
who now bear reproach and shame shall have glory, and
those who now afflict the people of God shall be undone.

18. *I will gather them that are sorrowful*[5] *for*[6] *the solemn*

---

[1] 1 Cor. ii. 9.   [2] Rup.   [3] יחריש

[4] Jer. xxxi. 34 ; xxxiii. 8 ; Micah vii. 18.

[5] This is the common meaning of the root יגה, though
not so frequent in the verb as in nouns, and five out of the
eight cases are in Lam. i. 4 (where the same form נוגות,
Nif. occurs), 12 ; iii. 32, 33 ; the remaining being, this place,
Job xix. 2 ; Isa. li. 23. The other sense "removed" (even
if הגה 2 Sam. xx. 13, implies a פי in this sense) comes to
the same general meaning, though with less force. The
Arab וגי, iv. is wrongly applied (e.g. Ges. Thes. p. 564), as
"procul a se removit." It is simply "abstained from it,"
"refused one's self."

[6] מן is used of the ultimate cause. See Ges. Thes. s. v. 2,
b. p. 802.

18 I will gather *them that* ᵃ *are* sorrowful for the solemn assembly, *who* are of thee, *to whom* * the reproach of it *was* a burden.

19 Behold, at that time I will undo all that afflict

ᵃ Lam. ii. 6.
* Heb. *the burden upon it* was *reproach.*

---

assembly, in which they were to *rejoice* [1] before God and which in their captivity God made to cease.[2] *They were of thee,* the true Israel who were [3] *grieved for the affliction of Joseph; to whom the reproach of it was a burden* [rather,[4] *on whom reproach was laid*]: for this *reproach of Christ is greater riches than the treasures of Egypt,* and such shall inherit the blessing, *Blessed are ye, when men shall hate you, and when they shall separate you from their company, and shall reproach you and cast out your name as evil, for the Son of Man's sake; rejoice ye in that day, and leap for joy ; for, behold your reward is great in heaven.*[5]

19. *Behold, at that time I will undo* [lit. *I deal with* [6]]. While God punisheth not, He seemeth to sit still,[7] be silent,[8] asleep.[9] Then He shall act, He shall *deal* according to their deserts with *all,* evil men or devils, *that afflict thee,* His Church. The prophecy looked for a larger fulfilment than the destruction of Jerusalem, since the Romans who, in God's Hands, avenged the blood of His Saints, themselves were among those who *afflicted her. And will save*

[1] Lev. xxiii. 40 ; Deut. xii. 12, 18 ; xvi. 11 ; xxvii. 7.
[2] Lam. i. 4 ; ii. 6.   [3] Amos vi. 6.
[4] As in Ps. xv. 3, וחרפה לא נשא על קרבו, the construction being like מסתר פנים ממנו, Isa. liii. 3.
[5] S. Luke vi. 22, 23.
[6] As Ru. ii. 19, in a good sense ; Ez. vii. 27 ; xvii. 17 ; xxiii. 25, in a bad ; אותך, אותו, אותם being probably for אתם &c.
[7] Isa. xviii. 4.   [8] Hab. i. 13.   [9] Ps. xliv. 23.

thee : and I will save her that ᵃ halteth, and gather
her that was driven out ; and * I will get them praise
and fame in every land † where they have been put
to shame.

ᵃ Ezek. xxxiv. 36 ; Micah iv. 6, 7.
* Heb. *I will set them for a praise.*
† Heb. *of their shame.*

---

her, the flock or sheep *that halteth,*[1] " imperfect in virtue and
with trembling faith," [2] *and gather,* like a good and tender
shepherd,[3] *her that was driven out;* scattered and dispersed through persecutions. All infirmities within shall
be healed ; all troubles without, removed.

And I will get them praise and fame [lit. *I will make them
a praise and a name*] *in every land where they have been put
to shame.* [4] Throughout the whole world have they been
the offscourings of all things; [5] throughout the whole world
should their praise be, as it is said, *Thou shalt make them
princes in all lands.*[6] One of themselves saith,[7] *Ye see your
calling, brethren, how that not many wise men after the flesh, not
many mighty, not many noble, are called. But God hath chosen
the foolish things of the world to confound the wise ; and God
hath chosen the weak things of the world to confound the things*

[1] See Micah iv. 6, 7.   [2] Dion.   [3] See Isa. xl. 11.
[4] The article is inserted in a way very unusual and probably emphatic. Without it the words would mean, as in
the E.V. " in every land of their shame." But it makes the
meaning of the first words, בכל הארץ, complete in itself ; and
they mean, *in the whole earth.* בשתם then is probably in
apposition, *in the whole earth, their shame,* i.e. the scene of
their shame ; comp. the construction הארון הברית Jos. iii. 14,
17, and those of Deut. viii. 15 ; 1 Kings iv. 13 ; and "Daniel
the Prophet," p. 476. In the next verse, הארץ is un-
doubtedly " the earth."
[5] 1 Cor. iv. 13.   [6] Ps. xlv. 16.   [7] 1 Cor. i. 26–28.

20 At that time ᵃ will I bring you *again*, even
in the time that I gather you : for I will make you

    ᵃ Isa. xi. 12, xxvii. 12, and lvi. 8 ; Ezek. xxviii. 25,
xxxiv. 13, and xxxvii. 21 ; Amos ix. 14.

---

*which are mighty ; and base things of this world, and things
which are despised, hath God chosen, yea, and things which are
not, to bring to nought things that are.* " These He maketh a
praise and a name there, where they were without name
and dispraised, confounding by them and bringing to nought
those wise and strong and mighty, in whose sight they were
contemptible." [1]

    20. *At that time will I bring you in,* i.e. into the one fold,
the one Church, the one *Household of God, even in the time
that I gather you.* " That time" is the whole time of the
Gospel; the one *day of salvation,* in which all who shall
ever be gathered, shall be brought into the new Jerusalem.
These words were fulfilled, when, at our Lord's first Coming,
the remnant, the true Israel, those *ordained to eternal life*
were brought in. It shall be fulfilled again, when "the
fulness of the Gentiles shall be *come in,* and so all Israel
shall be saved." [2] It shall most perfectly be fulfilled at the
end, when there shall be no going out of those once *brought
in,* and those who have gathered others into the Church,
shall be *a name and a praise among all people of the earth,*
those whom God hath *redeemed out of every tribe and tongue
and people and nation,*[3] shining like stars for ever and ever.

    When I turn back your captivity : "that conversion, then
begun, now perfected, when the dead shall rise and they
shall be placed on the right hand, soon to receive the
kingdom prepared for them from the foundation of the
world. O mighty spectacle of the reversed captivity of
those once captives; mighty wonder at their present
blessedness, as they review the misery of their past

    [1] Rup.   [2] Rom. xi. 25, 26.   [3] Rev. v. 9.

a name and a praise among all people of the earth, when I turn back your captivity before your eyes, saith the LORD.

---

captivity ! " [1] *Before your eyes,* so that we shall see what we now believe and hope for, the end of all our sufferings, chastisements, losses, achings of the heart, the fulness of our Redemption. That which our eyes have looked for, *our eyes shall behold and not another,* the everliving God as HE IS, face to Face, *saith the Lord,* Who is the Truth Itself, all Whose words will be fulfilled. *Heaven and earth shall pass away, but My Words shall not pass away,* [2] saith He Who is *God blessed for ever.* And so the Prophet closes in the thought of Him, Whose Name is I AM, the Unchangeable, the everlasting Rest and Centre of those who, having been once captives and halting and scattered among the vanities of the world, turn to Him, to Whom be glory and thanksgiving for ever and ever. Amen.

[1] Rup.   [2] S. Mark xiii. 31.

THE MOABITE STONE (see pp. 113–117)

I MESHA, son of Chemosh-gad, king of Moab the Dibonite. My father reigned over Moab thirty years, and I reigned after my father; and I made this shrine to Chemosh in Korchoh, a shr[ine of deli]verance, because he saved me from all [¹] and because he let me look upon all who hate me, Om[r]i king of Israel; and he afflicted Moab many days, for Chemosh was wroth with his la[n]d; and his son succeeded him, and he too said, I will afflict Moab. In my days said [*Chemosh*²], and I will look upon him and upon his house, and Israel perisheth with an everlasting destruction. And Omri took possession of the land of Moh-deba and there dwelt in it [² Israel in *his days and in*] the days of his son, forty years; [*and looked*] on it Chemosh in my days and I built Baal-Meon and I made in it the ditch [?] and I [built] Kiriathan. And the men of Gad dwelt in the land of [Atar]oth from time immemorial, and the kin[g of I]srael built for him A[ta]roth and I warred against the city; and I took it and I slew all the mi[ghty men] of the city, for the well-pleasing of Chemosh and Moab; and I took captive thence the [   ] and [dr]agged it [or them] before Chemosh in Kiriath and I made to dwell in it the men of Siran, and the men of Macharath. And Chemosh said to me, Go take Nebo against Israel [and I] went by night and I fought against it from the break of the morning to midday and I took it, and I slew the whole of it, seven thousand; [   ] the honourable women [and mai]dens, for

¹ The stone has השלכן, whose meaning is conjectural. Nöldeke conjectures המלכן " the kings."

² Schlottman's conjecture. Likely conjectures I have put in [ ]; mere guesswork I have omitted.

to Ashtar Chemosh [I] dedicated [them] and I took thence
[ves]sels of Yhvh and I dragged them before Chemosh.
And the king of Israel buil[t] Yahats, and dwelt in it when
he warred with me ; and Chemosh drove him from [my]
f[ace and] I took of Moab 200 men, all its chiefs and I took
them against Yahats and took it to add to Dibon.   I built
Korchoh the wall of the forest, and the wall of Ophel [1] and
I built the gates thereof, and I built the towers thereof,
and I built the king's house, and I made prisons for the
gui[lt]y in the mi[dst] of the city ; and there was no cistern
within the city, in Korchoh, and I said to all the people,
make yourselves every man a cistern in his house, and I
cut the cutting for Korchoh by m[en   ] of Israel.
I built [A]roer and I made the high road [2] at the Arnon.   I
built Beth-Bamoth, for it was destroyed.   I built Bezer,
for [it was] forsa[ken]   me[n] of Dibon
              fifty ; for all Dibon was obedience, and I
reig[ned] from Bikran which I added to the land and I
buil[t]— —and Beth Diblathan and Beth-Baal-Meon and
I took there the — of the land and Horonan
dwelt in it — — — — [and] Chemosh said to me, Go fight
against Horonan and I   it—Chemosh in my days and
on   [I] made

---

[1] חומת העפל occurs of Jerusalem, Neh. iii. 27.

[2] המסלת lit. "the way cast up" cannot possibly be a way
over the river.

INTRODUCTION

PROPHET HAGGAI

HAGGAI [1] is the eldest of the threefold band, to whom, after the Captivity, the word of God came, and by whom He consecrated the beginnings of this new condition of the chosen people. He gave them these prophets, connecting their spiritual state after their return with that before the Captivity, not leaving them wholly desolate, nor Himself without witness. He withdrew them about 100 years after, but some 420 years before Christ came, leaving His people to long the more for Him, of Whom all the prophets spake. Haggai himself seems to have

---

[1] His name is explained by S. Jerome "festive." But although there are proper names with *ai* which are adjectives, as בַּרְזִלַּי, שֵׁשַׁי (Ezra x. 40, תַּלְמַי and שֵׁשַׁי are foreign names יְשִׁישַׁי, the termination *ai* is more frequently an abbreviation of the Name of God, which enters so largely into Hebrew names, as indeed we have חֲגִיָּה 1 Chron. vi. 15. And this occurs not only when the first part of the word is a verb, אֲחַסְבַּי, יְאַתְרַי, יְרִיבַי, יִשְׁמְרַי (as אֲחַזַי, אֲחַזַי, יַעֲשַׂי, יַעֲנַי, יִחְמַי, יֶהְדַּי Köhler observes, p. 2), but when it is a noun, as הֹדַי, אֲמִתַּי, שַׁלְמַי, צִלְתַי, מַתְּנַי (coll. מַתַּנְיָה, and שְׁמָשַׁי (מַתַּנְיָהוּ) Ezra iv· פְּעֻלְּתַי (1 Chron. xxvi. 5) perhaps שְׁטָרַי, שַׁבְּתַי or again אִתַּי.

199

almost finished his earthly course, before he was called to be a prophet ; and in four months his office was closed. He speaks as one who had seen the first house in its glory,[1] and so was probably among the very aged men who were the links between the first and the last, and who laid the foundation of the house in tears.[2] After the first two months [3] of his office, Zechariah, in early youth, was raised up to carry on his message ; yet after one brief prophecy was again silent, until the aged prophet had ended the words which God gave him. Yet in this brief space he first stirred up the people in one month to rebuild the temple,[4] prophesied of its glory through the presence of Christ,[5] yet taught that the presence of what was holy sanctified not the unholy,[6] and closes in Him Who, when Heaven and earth shall be shaken, shall abide, and they whom God hath chosen in Him.[7]

It has been the wont of critics, in whose eyes the Prophets were but poets,[8] to speak of the style of Haggai as "tame, destitute of life and power," showing "a marked decline in" [9] what they call "prophetic inspiration." The style of the sacred writers is, of course, conformed to their mission.

---

[1] ii. 3.   [2] Ezra iii. 12.

[3] The prophecies of Haggai and Zechariah are thus intertwined. Haggai prophesies in the sixth and seventh months of the second year of Darius Hystaspis, 520 B.C. (Hag. i. 1 ; ii. 1). Zechariah first prophesies in the eighth month (Zech. i. 1). Haggai resumes at the close of the ninth and there ends (ii. 10, 20). On the same day in the eleventh month, the series of visions were given to Zechariah (Zech. i. 7).

[4] c. i.   [5] ii. 1-9.
[6] Ib. 12.   [7] Ib. 20-23.
[8] Eichhorn, De Wette, Bertholdt, Gesenius (Gesh. d. Hebr. Spr., p. 26), Herzfeldt (Gesch. d. Volkes Israel, ii. 21), Stähelin.
[9] Dr. Davidson, iii. 314.

Prophetic descriptions of the future are but inci-
dental to the mission of Haggai. Preachers do not
speak in poetry, but set before the people their faults
or their duties in vivid, earnest language. Haggai
sets before the people vividly their negligence and
its consequences ; he arrests their attention by his
concise questions ; at one time retorting their excuses ;[1] at another asking them abruptly, in God's
name, to say why their troubles came.[2] Or he puts
a matter of the law to the priests, that they may
draw the inference, before he does it himself.[3] Or he
asks them, what human hope had they,[4] before he
tells them of the Divine. Or he asks them (what
was in their heart), " Is not this house poor ? "[5]
before he tells them of the glory in store for it. At
one time he uses heaped and condensed antitheses,[6]
to set before them one thought ; at another, he
enumerates, one by one, how the visitation of God
fell upon all they had,[7] so that there seemed to be no
end to it. At another, he uses a conciseness, like
S. John Baptist's cry, *Repent ye, for the kingdom of
heaven is at hand,* in his repeated *Set your heart to
your ways ;*[8] and then, with the same idiom, *set
your heart,*[9] viz. to God's ways, what He had done
on disobedience, what He would do on obedience.
He bids them work for God, and then he expresses
the acceptableness of that work to God, in the three
words, *And-I-will-take-pleasure in-it and-will-be-
glorified.*[10] When they set themselves to obey, he
encouraged them in the four words, *I with-you saith
the-Lord.*[11] This conciseness must have been still

[1] i. 4. [2] i. 9. [3] ii. 12, 13.
[4] ii. 19. [5] ii. 3. [6] i. 6.
[7] i. 11. [8] i. 5–7. [9] ii. 15–18.
[10] i. 8. [11] i. 13.

more impressive in his words, as delivered.[1] We use many words, because our words are weak. Many of us can remember how the House of Lords was hushed, to hear the few low, but sententious words of the aged general and statesman. But conceive the suggestive eloquence of those words, as a whole sermon, *Set your-heart on-your-ways.*

Of distant prophecies there are but two,[2] so that the portion to be compared with the former prophets consists but of at most seven verses. In these the language used is of the utmost simplicity. Haggai had but one message as to the future to convey, and he enforced it by the repeated use of the same word,[3] that temporal things should be shaken, the eternal should remain, as S. Paul sums it up.[4] He, the long-longed for, the chosen of God, the signet on His Hand, should come ; God would fill that house, so poor in their eyes, with glory, and there would He give peace. Haggai had an all-containing but very simple message to give from God. Any ornament of diction would but have impaired and obscured its meaning. The two or three slight idioms, noticed by one after another, are, though slight, forcible.[5]

The office of Haggai was mainly to bring about one definite end, which God, Who raised him up and inspired him, accomplished by him. It is in the light of this great accomplishment of the work entrusted to him at the verge of man's earthly course, that his power and energy are to be estimated. The words which are preserved in his book are doubtless (as indeed was the case as to most of the prophets)

---

[1] See on ii. 5, 9.   [2] ii. 6–9, 21–23.
[3] מרעיש, ii. 6, 21 ; והרעשתי, ii. 7.   [4] Heb. xii. 26.
[5] See on ii. 3, 5, 17. The junction of אחת מעט, ii. 6, is a mistake of the critics.

the representatives and embodiment of many like words, by which, during his short office, he roused the people from their dejection, indifference, and irreligious apathy, to the restoration of the public worship of God in the essentials of the preparatory dispensation.

Great lukewarmness had been shown in the return. The few looked mournfully to the religious centre of Israel, the ruined temple, the cessation of the daily sacrifice, and, like Daniel, *confessed* their *sin and the sin of* their *people Israel, and presented* their *supplication before the Lord* their *God for the holy mountain of* their *God*.[1] The most part appear, as now, to have been taken up with their material prosperity, and, at best, to have become inured to the cessation of their symbolical worship, connected, as it was, with the declaration of the forgiveness of their sins. Then too, God connected His declaration of pardon with certain outward acts : *they* became indifferent to the cessation of those acts. For few returned. The indifference was even remarkable among those most connected with the altar. Of the twenty-four orders[2] of priests, one-sixth] only, four orders[3] returned ; of the Levites only seventy-four individuals ;[4] while of those assigned to help them, the Nethinim and the children of Solomon's servants, there were 392.[5] This coldness continued at the return of Ezra. The edict of Artaxerxes,[6] as suggested by Ezra, was more pious than those appointed to the service of God. In the first instance, no Levite answered to the invitation ;[7] on the special urgency and message of Ezra, *by the good hand of*

---

[1] Dan. ix. 20. [2] 1 Chron. xxiv. 3–19.
[3] Ezra ii. 36–39. [4] Ib. ii. 40.
[5] Ib. ii. 58. [6] Ib. vii. 13–14. [7] Ib. viii. 15.

God upon us they brought us a man of understanding,[1]
of the sons of Levi ; some three or four chief Levites ;
their sons and brethren ; in all, thirty-eight ; but
of the Nethinim, nearly six times as many, 220.[2]
Those who thought more of temporal prosperity
than of their high spiritual nobility and destination,
had flourished doubtless in that exile as they have
in their present homelessness, as *wanderers among
the nations.*[3] Haman calculated apparently on being
able to *pay* out of their spoils *ten thousand talents
of silver,*[4] some £300,000,000, two-thirds of the annual
revenue of the Persian Empire [5] *into the king's
treasuries.*

The numbers who had returned with Zerubbabel
had been (as had been foretold of all restorations)
a remnant only. There were 42,360 free men, with
7337 male or female slaves.[6] The whole population
which returned was not above 212,000 free-men and
women and children. The proportion of slaves is
about one-twelfth, since in their case adults of both
sexes were counted. The enumeration is minute,
giving the number of their horses, mules, camels,

---

[1] Ezra viii. 18, 19.   [2] Ib. viii. 20.
[3] See on Hosea ix. 17.
[4] Esther iii. 9. Ahasuerus apparently, in acceding to
Haman's proposal, made over to him the lives and property
of the Jews. *The silver* is *given unto thee, the people also, to
do with them as it seemeth good to thee* (ib. 11). The Jews'
property was confiscated with their lives. On the contrary,
it was noticed that the Jews, when permitted to defend their
lives, did *not lay their hands on the prey,* which, by the king's
decree, was granted to them, with authority to take the lives
of those who *should assault them.* Esther viii. 11 ; ix. 10, 15, 16.
[5] 14,560 silver talents. Herod. iii. 95.
[6] Ezra ii. 64, 65 ; Neh. vii. 66, 67. In the time of Augustus
it was no uncommon thing for a person to have 200 slaves
(Hor. Sat. i. 3, 11); it is said that very many Romans possessed 10,000, or 20,000 slaves. Athenæus, vi. p. 272.

asses.[1] The chief of the fathers, however, were not poor, since (though unspeakably short of the wealth won by David and consecrated to the future temple) *they offered freely for the house of God, to set it up in its place*,[2] a sum about £117,100 [3] of our money. They had, beside, a grant from Cyrus, which he intended to cover the expenses of the building, the height and breadth whereof were determined by royal edict.[4]

The monarch, however, of an Eastern empire had, in proportion to its size, little power over his subordinates or the governors of the provinces, except by their recall or execution, when their oppressions or peculations notably exceeded bounds. The returned colony, from the first, were in fear of the nations, *the peoples of those countries*,[5] their old enemies probably; and the first service, *the altar to offer burnt-offerings thereon*, was probably a service of fear rather than of love, as it is said, *they set up the altar upon its bases; for it was in fear upon them from the peoples of the lands, and they offered burnt-offerings thereon unto the Lord*.[5] They hoped apparently to win the favour of God, that He might, as of old, protect them against their enemies. However, the work was carried on *according to the grant that they had of Cyrus king of Persia;*[6] and the foundations of the temple were laid amidst mixed joy at the carrying on of the work thus far, and sorrow

---

[1] 736 horses, 245 mules, 435 camels, 6720 asses. Ezra ii. 66, 67; Neh. vii. 68, 69.

[2] Ezra ii. 68, 69.

[3] The golden daric being estimated at £1, 2s., the 61,000 darics would be £67,100; the "maneh" being 100 shekels, and the shekel about 2s., the 5000 maneh of silver would be about £50,000.

[4] Ezra i. 2–4.   [5] Ib. iii. 3.   [6] Ib. iii. 7.

at its poverty, compared to the first temple.[1] The hostility of the Samaritans discouraged them. Mixed as the religion of the Samaritans was—its better element being the corrupt religion of the ten tribes, its worse the idolatries of the various nations, brought thither in the reign of Esarhaddon—the returned Jews could not accept their offer to join in their worship, without the certainty of admitting, with them, the idolatries, for which they had been punished so severely. For the Samaritans pleaded the identity of the two religions. *Let us build with you, for we serve your God, as ye do ; and we do sacrifice unto Him since the days of Esarhaddon which brought us up hither.*[2] But in fact this mixed worship, in which *they feared the Lord and served their own gods,*[3] came to this, that *they feared not the Lord, neither did they after the law and commandment which the Lord commanded the children of Jacob.*[4] For God claims the undivided allegiance of His creatures ; *these feared the Lord and served their graven images, both their children and their children's children : as did their fathers, so do they to this day.*[5] But this worship included some of the most cruel abominations of heathendom, the sacrifice of their children to their gods.[6]

The Samaritans, thus rejected, first themselves harassed the Jews in building, apparently by petty violence, as they did afterwards in the rebuilding of the walls by Nehemiah. [7] *The people of the land weakened the hands of the people of Judah, and wore them out*[8] *in building.* This failing, they *hired counsellors* (doubtless at the Persian court), *to*

---

[1] Ezra iii. 11–13. [2] Ib. iv. 2. [3] 2 Kings xvii. 33.
[4] Ib. xvii. 34. [5] Ib. xvii. 41. [6] Ib. xvii. 31.
[7] בְּלֵה Cheth. [8] Ezra iv. 4.

frustrate their purpose, all the days of Cyrus king of Persia, until the reign of Darius king of Persia.[1] The object of the intrigues was probably to intercept the supplies, which Cyrus had engaged to bestow, which could readily be effected in an Eastern Court without any change of purpose or any cognisance of Cyrus.

In the next reign of Ahashverosh (i.e. Khshwershe, a title of honour of Cambyses) they wrote accusations against the Jews, seemingly without any further effect, since none is mentioned.[2] Perhaps Cambyses, in his expedition to Egypt, knew more of the Jews than the Samaritans thought, or he may have shrunk from changing his father's decree, contrary to the fundamental principles of Persism, not to alter any decree, which the sovereign (acting, as he was assumed to do, under the influence of Ormuzd) had written.[3] Pseudo-Smerdis (who doubtless took the title of honour, Artachshatr) may, as an impostor, have well been ignorant of Cyrus' decree, to which no allusion is made.[4] From him the Samaritans, through Rehum the chancellor, obtained a decree prohibiting, until further notice, the rebuilding of *the city*. The accusers had overreached themselves; for the ground of their accusation was, the former rebellions of the city;[5] the prohibition accordingly extended only to the *city*,[6] not to the temple. However, having obtained the decree, they were not scrupulous about its application, and *made* the Jews *to cease by arm and power*,[7] the governor of the Jews being apparently unable, the governor of the cis-Euphratensian pro-

---

[1] Ezra iv. 5.   [2] Ib. iv. 6.
[3] See Daniel the Prophet, pp. 445–447.
[4] Ezra iv. 7 sqq.   [5] Ib. iv. 12, 13, 15, 16.
[6] Ib. iv. 19, 21.   [7] Ib. iv. 23.

vinces being unwilling, to help. As this, however, was, in fact, a perversion of the decree, the Jews were left free to build, and in the second year of Darius Hystaspis, *Haggai, and* then *Zechariah, prophesied in the name of the God of Israel* to Zerubbabel, the native Governor, and Joshua the high-priest, and *the Jews in Judah and Jerusalem ; and they began to build the house of God in Jerusalem.*[1] Force was no longer used. Those engaged in building appealed to the edict of Cyrus ; the edict was found at Ecbatana,[2] and the supplies which Cyrus had promised were again ordered. The difficulty was at the commencement. The people had been cowed perhaps at first by the violence of Rehum and his companions ; but they had acquiesced readily in the illegal prohibition, and had *run each to his own house,*[3] some of them to their *ceiled houses.*[4] All, employers or employed, were busy on their husbandry. But nothing flourished. The labourers' wages disappeared, as soon as gained.[5] East and west wind alike brought disease to their corn ; both, as threatened upon disobedience in the law.[6] The east wind scorched and dried it up ;[7] the warm west wind turned the ears yellow[8] and barren ; the hail smote the vines, so that when the unfilled and mutilated

---

[1] Ezra v. 1, 2.　　[2] Ib. vi. 2.　　[3] Hag. i. 9.
[4] Ib. i. 4.　　[5] Ib. i. 6.　　[6] Deut. xxviii. 22.

[7] שִׁדָּפוֹן comp. שְׁדוּפוֹת קָדִים Gen. xli. 6, 23, 27.

[8] יֵרָקוֹן Forskäl (in Niebuhr, Beschreibung v. Arabien, Pref., p. xlv.) took down from the mouth of " Muri, a Jew of Mecca, that, in the month Marchesvan, a warm wind sometimes blew, which turned the ears yellow and they yielded no grain ; it was an unsteady wind, but spoils all it touches." " M. Forskäl remarks that the fields near the canal of Alexandria are sown in October and reaped in Feb." Id. In Arabic the disease is called ירקאן. Ges. Thes.

clusters were pressed out, two-fifths only of the hoped-for produce was yielded; of the corn, only one-half.[1]

In the midst of this, God raised up an earnest preacher of repentance. Haggai was taught, not to promise anything at the first, but to set before them what they had been doing, what was its result. [2] He sets it before them in detail; tells them that God had so ordered it for their neglect of His service, and bids them amend. He bids them quit their wonted ways : *Go up into the mountain ; bring wood ; build the house.* Conceive in Christian England, after some potato-disease, or foot-and-mouth-disease (in Scripture language " *a murrain* among the cattle "), a preacher arising and bidding them, *consider your ways*, and as the remedy, not to look to any human means, but to do something which should please Almighty God ; and not preaching only, but effecting what he preached. Yet such was Haggai. He stood among his people, his existence a witness of the truth of what he said ; himself one, who had lived among the outward splendours of the former temple ; a contemporary of those, who said *the temple of the Lord, the temple of the Lord, the temple of the Lord* are *these ;* [3] who had held it to be impossible that Judah should be carried captive ; who had prophesied the restoration of the vessels of God,[4] which had been carried away, not, as God foretold, after the captivity, but as an earnest that the fuller captivity should not be ; [5] yet who had himself, according to the prophecies of the prophets of those days, been carried into captivity, and was now a part of that restoration which God had pro-

---

[1] Hag. ii. 16.   [2] Ib. i. 5–11.   [3] Jer. vii. 4.
[4] Ib. xxvii. 16 ; xxviii. 3.   [5] Ib. xxviii. 2.

O

mised. He stood among them "in gray-haired might," bade them do, what he bade them, in the name of God, to do ; and they did it. When they had set about the work, he assured them of the presence of God with them.[1] A month later, when they were seemingly discouraged at its poorness, he promised them in God's name, that its glory should be greater than that of Solomon's.[2] Three days after, in contrast with the visitations up to that time, while there was as yet no token of any change, he promised them in the name of God, *From this day will I bless you.*[3]

He himself apparently saw only the commencement of the work ; for his prophecies lay within the second year of Darius and the temple was not completed till the sixth.[4] Even the favourable rescript of Darius must have arrived after his last prophecy, since it was elicited by the inquiry of the governor, consequent upon the commenced rebuilding,[5] three months only before his office closed.[6]

While this restoration of the public worship of God in its integrity was his main office, yet he also taught by parable [7] that the presence of what was outwardly holy did not, in itself, hallow those among whom it was ; but was itself unhallowed by inward unholiness.

Standing too amid the small handful of returned exiles, not, altogether, more than the inhabitants of Sheffield, he foretold, in simple all-comprehending words, that central gift of the Gospel, *In this place will I give peace, saith the Lord.*[8] So had David, the

1 Hag. i. 13.
2 Ib. ii. 3–9.
3 ii. 19.
4 Ezra vi. 15.
5 Ib. v. 3 sqq.
6 Hag. i. 15 ; ii. 10, 20.
7 ii. 10–14.
8 ii. 9.

sons of Korah, Micah, Isaiah, Ezekiel prophesied ; [1]
but the peace was to come, not then, but in the days
of the Messiah. Other times had come, in which
the false prophets had said,[2] *Peace, peace, when there
was no peace ;* when God had taken away His peace
from *this people.*[3] And now, when the chastisements
were fulfilled, when the land lay desolate, when every
house of Jerusalem lay burned with fire,[4] and the
"blackness of ashes" alone "marked where they
stood" ; when the walls were broken down so that,
even when leave was given to rebuild them, it seemed
to their enemies a vain labour to *revive the stones
out of the heaps of rubbish which were burned ;* [5] when
*the place of their fathers' sepulchres lay waste, and
the gates thereof were consumed with fire ;* [6] when, for
their sakes, Zion was *ploughed as a field* and *Jerusalem*
was *become heaps* [7]—let any one picture to himself
the silver-haired prophet standing, at first, alone,
rebuking the people, first through their governor
and the high-priest, then the collected multitude,
in words, forceful from their simplicity, and obeyed !
And then let them think whether anything of human
or even Divine eloquence was lacking, when the
words flew straight like arrows to the heart, and
roused the people to do at once, amid every obstacle,
amid every downheartedness or outward poverty,
that for which God sent them. The outward ornament of words would have been misplaced, when
the object was to bid a downhearted people, in the
Name of God, to do a definite work. Haggai sets

[1] Ps. lxxii. 3–7 ; lxxxv. 8, 10 ; Micah v. 5 ; Isa. ix. 6, 7 ;
xxvi. 12 ; xxxii. 17 ; lii. 7 ; liii. 5 ; liv. 10, 13 ; lvii. 19 ;
lx. 17 ; lxvi. 12 ; Ezek. xxxiv. 25 ; xxxvii. 26.
[2] Jer. vi. 14 ; viii. 11 ; xiv. 13.　　[3] Ib. xvi. 5.
[4] 2 Chron. xxxvi. 19.　　[5] Neh. iv. 2.
[6] Ib. ii. 3.　　[7] Micah iii. 12.

before his people cause and effect ; that they denied
to God what was His, and that God denied to them
what was His to give or to withhold. His sermon
was, in His words Whom he foretold : *Seek ye first
the kingdom of God and His righteousness, and all
these things shall be added unto you.* He spake in
the name of God, and was obeyed.

"The Holy Ghost, Who spake by the mouth of
the prophets, willed that he by a foreboding name
should be called Haggai, i.e. 'festive,' according to
the subject whereof He should speak by his mouth.
Yet was there not another festiveness in the prophet's
heart, than the joy which he had or could have with
the people, from the rebuilding of that temple made
with hands, again to be defiled and burned with
fire irrecoverably ? Be it that the rebuilding of that
temple, which he saw before him, was a matter of
great festive joy ; yet not in or for itself, but for
Him, the festive joy of saints and angels and men,
Christ ; because when the temple should be rebuilt,
the walls also of the city should be rebuilt and the
city again inhabited and the people be united in one,
of whom Christ should be born, fulfilling the truth of
the promise made to Abraham and David and confirmed by an oath. So then we, by aid of the Holy
Spirit, so enter upon what Haggai here speaketh,
as not doubting that he altogether aimeth at Christ.
And so may we in some sort be called or be Haggais,
i.e. 'festive,' by contemplating that same, which
because he should contemplate, he was, by a Divine
foreboding, called Haggai." [1]

[1] Rup.

HAGGAI

CHAPTER I

1 *Haggai reproveth the people for neglecting the building of the house.* 7 *He inciteth them to the building.* 12 *He promiseth God's assistance to them
being forward.*

In [a] the second year of Darius the king, in the sixth
month, in the first day of the month, came the word

[a] Ezra iv. 24 and v. 1 ; Zech. i. 1.

CHAP. I. ver. 1. *In the second year of Darius,* i.e. Hystaspis. The very first word of prophecy after the Captivity
betokens that they were restored, not yet as before, yet so,
as to be hereafter, more than before. The earthly type, by
God's appointment, was fading away, that the Heavenly
truth might dawn. The earthly king was withdrawn, to
make way for the Heavenly. God had said of Jeconiah, *No
man of his seed shall prosper, sitting upon the throne of David,
and ruling any more in Israel :* [1] and so now prophecy begins
to be dated by the years of a foreign earthly ruler, as in
the Baptism of the Lord Himself.[2] Yet God gives back in
mercy more than He withdraws in chastisement. The
earthly rule is suspended, that men might look out more
longingly for the Heavenly.

[1] Jer. xxii. 30.   [2] S. Luke iii. 1.

of the Lord *by Haggai the prophet unto ªZerub-

* Heb. *by the hand of Haggai.*

ª 1 Chron. iii. 17, 19 ; Ezra iii. 2 ; Matt. i. 12 ; Luke iii. 27.

In the sixth month. They counted by their own months, beginning with Nisan, the first of the ecclesiastical year (which was still used for holy purposes and in sacred history), although, having no more any kings, they dated their years by those of the empire, to which they were subject.[1] In the sixth month, part of our July and August, their harvest was past, and the dearth, which they doubtless ascribed (as we do) to the seasons, and which Haggai pointed out to be a judgment from God, had set in for this year also. The months being lunar, *the first day of the month* was the festival of the new moon, a popular feast [2] which their fore-fathers had kept,[3] while they neglected the weightier matters of the law, and which the religious in Israel had kept, even while separated from the worship at Jerusalem.[4] *In* its very *first day*, when the grief for the barren year was yet fresh, Haggai was stirred to exhort them to *consider their ways ;* a pattern for Christian preachers, to bring home to people's souls the meaning of God's judgments. God directs the very day to be noted, in which He called the people anew to build His temple, both to show the readi-ness of their obedience, and a precedent to us to keep in memory days and seasons, in which He stirs our souls to build more diligently His spiritual temple in our souls.[5]

By the hand of Haggai. God doth well-nigh all things which He doeth for man through the hands of men. He committeth His words and works for men into the hands of men as His stewards, to dispense faithfully to His house-

---

[1] See Zech. i. 7 ; vii. 1.   [2] Prov. vii. 20.

[3] Isa. i. 13, 14.

[4] 2 Kings iv. 23, add Amos viii. 5 ; Hosea ii. 11.

[5] Castro.

babel the son of Shealtiel, *governor of Judah, and

* Or, *captain.*

---

hold.[1] Hence He speaks so often of the law, which He
commanded *by the hand of Moses;* [2] but also as to other
prophets, Nathan,[3] Ahijah,[4] Jehu,[5] Jonah,[6] Isaiah,[7] Jeremiah,[8] and the prophets generally.[9] The very prophets of
God, although gifted with a Divine Spirit, still were willing
and conscious instruments in speaking His words.

Unto Zerubbabel (so called from being born in Babylon)
the son of Shealtiel. By this genealogy Zerubbabel is known
in the history of the return from the captivity in Ezra and
Nehemiah.[10] God does not say by Jeremiah, that Jeconiah
should have no children, but that he should in his lifetime
be childless, as it is said of those married to the uncle's or
brother's widow, *they shall die childless.*[11] Jeremiah rather
implies that he should have children, but that they should
die untimely before him. For he calls Jeconiah, *a man who
shall not prosper in his days; for there shall not prosper a
man of his seed, sitting on the throne of David, and ruling any
more in Israel.*[12] He should die (as the word means) *bared* [13]
of all, alone and desolate. The own father of Shealtiel

---

[1] S. Luke xii. 42.

[2] Twelve times in the Pent. ; five times in Joshua ; in
Judges once ; in 1 Kings viii. ; 2 Chron. twice ; Neh. ix. 14 ;
Ps. lxxvii. 20.

[3] 2 Sam. xii. 25.

[4] 1 Kings xii. 15 ; xiv. 18 ; 2 Chron. x. 15.

[5] 1 Kings xvi. 7.   [6] 2 Kings xiv. 25.

[7] Isa. xx. 2.   [8] Jer. xxxvii. 2.

[9] Hosea vii. 20 ; 2 Chron. xxix. 25.

[10] Ezra iii. 2, 8 ; v. 2 ; Neh. xii. 1.

[11] Lev. xx. 20, 21.   [12] Jer. xxii. 30.

[13] עֲרִירִי from עָרַר, as the Samar. Vers. renders it in Lev.
xx. 20, 21, "naked." Abraham uses it of his desolation in
having no son. Gen xv. 2 [all].

to ^aJoshua the son of ^bJosedech, the high priest, saying,

^a Ezra iii. 2 and v. 2.　　　　　^b 1 Chron. vi. 15.

appears to have been Neri,[1] of the line of Nathan son of David ; not, of the line of the kings of Judah. Neri married, one must suppose, a daughter of Assir, son of [2]Jeconiah, whose grandson Shealtiel was ; and Zerubbabel was the own son of Pedaiah, the brother of Shealtiel, whose son he was in the legal genealogy inscribed according to the law as to those who die childless ;[3] or as having been adopted by Shealtiel, being himself childless, as Moses was called the son of the daughter of Pharaoh.[4] So broken was the line of the unhappy Jehoiachin, two-thirds of whose own life was passed in the prison,[5] into which Nebuchadnezzar cast him.

Governor of Judah. The foreign name [6] betokens that

[1] S. Luke iii. 27.　　　　[2] 1 Chron. iii. 17–19.
[3] Deut. xxiii. 5–10.　　　[4] Exod. ii. 10.
[5] Jer. lii. 31.

[6] See in Daniel the Prophet, pp. 570–572. Keil adduces a conjecture of Spiegel, " that *pechah* is from *pâvan*, ' protector ' (from *pâ*), which in Sanskrit and old Persian occurs in compounds as *Khshatrapâvan*, Satrap, but in the Avesta occurs in the abridged form *pâvan*. Thence *might* be developed *pagvan*, as *dregvat* from *drevaṭ*, *huôgva* from *huôva*." Max Müller kindly informs me : " Phonetically *pavâo* could hardly become *pagvâo*, and even this would still be considerably different from Pechah. The insertion of a *g* before a *v* in Zend is totally anomalous. It rests entirely on the uncertain identification of *dregvanṭ*, ' bad,' with *drvanṭ*, for in the second instance, *huova* is much more likely a corruption of *huogva*, than *vice versâ*. *Pavâo* in Zend would mean ' protector,' but like the Sanskrit *pâvân*, it occurs only at the end of compounds. The one passage, quoted in support of its occurring as a separate noun, seems to me to contain an etymological play, where *pavâo* is used as an independent noun in order

the civil rule was now held from a foreign power, although
Cyrus showed the Jews the kindness of placing one of
themselves, of royal extraction also, as his deputy over
them. The lineage of David is still in authority, connecting the present with the past, but the earthly kingdom had
faded away. Under the name *Sheshbazzar* Zerubbabel is
spoken of both as *the prince* [1] and the *governor* [2] of Judah.
With him is joined *Joshua the son of Josedech, the high priest,*
whose father went into captivity,[3] when his grandfather
Seraiah was slain by Nebuchadnezzar.[4] The priestly line
also is preserved. Haggai addresses these two, the one of
the royal, the other of the priestly, line, as jointly respon-
sible for the negligence of the people; he addresses the
people only through them. Together, they are types of
Him, the true King and true Priest, Christ Jesus, Who by
the Resurrection raised again the true temple, His Body,
after it had been destroyed.[5]

2. *Thus speaketh the Lord of hosts, saying, This people say.*
Not Zerubbabel or Joshua, but *this people.* He says not,
My people, but reproachfully *this people,* as, in acts, dis-
owning Him, and so deserving to be disowned by Him.

to explain the two compounds, *paçça-paváo* and *pará-paváo,*
i.e. protecting behind and protecting in front, as if we were
to say, ' he is a *tector,* both as a *pro-tector* and *sub-tector.*' "

[1] Ezra i. 8. In relation to Cyrus, he is called by his
Persian name Sheshbazzar, by which name he is mentioned
in Tatnai's letter to Darius, as having been commissioned by
Cyrus to rebuild the temple and as having done so (Ezra
vi. 14–16), while, in the history of the restoration, he is related
to have done it under his domestic name Zerubbabel. On
these changes of names by their masters, see Daniel the
Prophet, p. 16.

[2] Ezra v. 14.   [3] 1 Chron. vi. 15.
[4] 2 Kings xxv. 18–21.   [5] S. Jer.

people say, The time is not come, the time that the
Lord's house should be built.

The time is not come, lit. *It is not time to come, time for the
house of the Lord to be built.*[1] They might yet sit still ; the
time for them *to come* was not yet ; for not yet was the *time
for the house of the Lord to be built.* Why it was not time,
they did not say. The government did not help them ; the
original grant by Cyrus [2] was exhausted ; the Samaritans
hindered them, because they would not own them (amid
their mishmash of worship, *worshipping*, our Lord tells
them, they *know not what* [3]) as worshippers of the same God.
It was a bold excuse, if they said, that the seventy years
during which the temple was to lie waste, were not yet
ended. The time had long since come, when, sixteen years
before, Cyrus had given command that the house of God
should be built. The prohibition to build, under Artaxerxes
or Pseudo-Smerdis, applied directly to the city and its
walls, not to the temple, except so far as the temple itself,
from its position, might be capable of being used as a fort,
as it was in the last siege of Jerusalem. Yet in itself a
building of the size of the temple, apart from outer buildings, could scarcely so be used. The prohibition did not
hinder the building of stately private houses, as appears
from Haggai's rebuke. The hindrances also, whatever they
were, had not begun with that decree. Anyhow, the death
of Pseudo-Smerdis had now, for a year, set them free, had
they had any zeal for the glory and service of God. Else
Haggai had not blamed them. God, knowing that He
should bend the heart of Darius, as He had that of Cyrus,
requires the house to be built without the king's decree.
It was built in faith, that God would bring through what

[1] The first sentence being left incomplete, for, "It is not
time to come to build the Lord's house."
[2] Ezra iii. 7.   [3] S. John iv. 22.

He had enjoined, although outward things were as adverse now as before. And what He commanded He prospered.[1]

There was indeed a second fulfilment of seventy years, from the destruction of the temple by Nebuchadnezzar 586 B.C., to its consecration in the sixth year of Darius, 516 B.C. But this was through the wilfulness of man, prolonging the desolation decreed by God, and Jeremiah's prophecy relates to the people, not to the temple.

"The Prophet addresses his discourse to the chiefs [in Church and State] and yet accuses directly, not their list-lessness, but that of the people, in order both to honour them before the people and to teach that their sins are to be blamed privately not publicly, lest their authority should be injured, and the people incited to rebel against them; and also to show that this fault was directly that of the people, whom he reproves before their princes, that, being openly convicted before them, it might be ashamed, repent, and obey God; but that indirectly this fault touched the chiefs themselves, whose office it was to urge the people to this work of God." [2] "For seldom is the Prince free from the guilt of his subjects, as either assenting to, or winking at them, or not coercing them, though able." [3]

Since also Christians are the temple of God, all this prophecy of Haggai is applicable to them. "When thou seest one who has lapsed thinking and preparing to build through chastity the temple which he had before destroyed through passion, and yet delaying day by day, say to him, 'Truly thou also art of the people of the captivity, and sayest, *The time is not yet come for building the house of the Lord.*' Whoso has once settled to restore the temple of God, to him every time is suited for building, and the prince, Satan, cannot hinder, nor the enemies around. As soon as being thyself converted, thou callest upon the name of the Lord, He will

---

[1] Ezra v., vi.   [2] Lap.   [3] à Castro from Alb.

3 Then came the word of the LORD [a] by Haggai
the prophet saying,

[a] Ezra v. 1.

---

say, *Behold Me.*" [1] " To him who willeth to do right, the
time is always present ; the good and right-minded have
power to fulfil what is to the glory of God, in every time
and place." [2]

3. *And the word of the Lord came.* " Before, he prophesied
nothing, but only recited the saying of the people ; now he
refutes it in his prophecy, and repeats, again and again,
that he says this not of himself, but from the mind and
mouth of God." [3] It is characteristic of Haggai to inculcate
thus frequently, that his words are not his own, but the
words of God. Yet " the prophets, both in their threats
and prophecies, repeat again and again, *Thus saith the Lord*,
teaching us, how we should prize the word of God, hang
upon it, have it ever in our mouth, reverence, ruminate on,
utter, praise it, make it our continual delight." [3]

4. *Is it time for you* [*you* [4]], being what you are, the
creatures of God, *to dwell in your ceiled houses*,[5] more emphatically, *in your houses*, and those *ceiled*, probably with
costly woods, such as cedar.[6] But where then was the
excuse of want of means ? They imitated, in their alleged
poverty, what is spoken of as magnificent in their old kings,
Solomon and Shallum, but not having, as Solomon first did,
covered the house of God *with beams and rows of cedar*.[7]
" Will ye dwell in houses artificially adorned, not so much
for use as for delight, and shall My dwelling-place, wherein
was the Holy of holies, and the Cherubim, and the table of

---

[1] S. Jer.   [2] S. Cyr.   [3] Lup.
[4] לכם אתם, the pers. pron. repeated emphatically.
[5] The force of מפונים in appos. to בתיכם.
[6] ספון בארז 1 Kings vii. 6, 7 ; Jer. xxii. 14.
[7] 1 Kings vi. 9, ויספן.

4 [a] *Is it* time for you, O ye, to dwell in your ceiled houses, and this house *lie* waste ?

[a] 2 Sam. vii. 2 ; Ps. cxxxii. 3, &c.

---

shewbread, be bestreamed with rains, desolated in solitude, scorched by the sun ? " [1]

" With these words carnal Christians are reproved, who have no glow of zeal for God, but are full of self-love, and so make no effort to repair, build, or strengthen the material temples of Christ, and houses assigned to His worship, when aged, ruinous, decaying or destroyed, but build for themselves curious, voluptuous, superfluous dwellings.   In these the love of Christ gloweth not ; these Isaiah threateneth, [2] *Woe to you who join house to house and field to field, and regard not the work of the Lord !* " [3]

To David and Solomon the building of God's temple was their heart's desire ; to early Christian emperors, to the ages of faith, the building of churches ; now mostly, owners of lands build houses for this world's profit, and leave it to the few to build in view of eternity, and for the glory of God.

5. *And now, thus saith the Lord of Hosts, Consider* [lit. *set your heart upon*] *your ways,* what they had been doing, what they were doing, and what those doings had led to, and would lead to.   This is ever present to the mind of the prophets, as speaking God's words, that our acts are not only *ways* in which we go, each day of life being a continuance of the day before ; but that they are *ways* which lead somewhither in God's Providence and His justice ; to some end of the *way,* good or bad.   So God says by Jeremiah, *I set before you the way of life and the way of death ;* [4] and David,[5] *Thou wilt shew me the path of life,* where it follows,

[1] S. Jer.   [2] Dion.   [3] Isa. v. 8, 12.
[4] Jer. xxi. 8.   [5] Ps. xvi. 11.

5 Now therefore thus saith the Lord of hosts,
* ª Consider your ways.

> * Heb. *Set your heart on your ways.*
> ª Lam. iii. 40 ; ver. 7.

---

*In Thy Presence is the fulness of joy and at Thy Right Hand
there are pleasures for evermore;* and Solomon, *Reproofs of
instruction are the way of life;*[1] and, he is in *the way of life
who keepeth instruction; and he who forsaketh rebuke, erreth;*[2]
and, *The way of life is above to the wise, that he may depart
from hell beneath;*[3] and of the adulterous woman, *Her house
are the ways of hell, going down to the chambers of death;*[4]
and *her feet go down unto death; her steps take hold on hell;
lest thou shouldest ponder the path of life.*[5] Again, *There is a
way that seemeth right unto a man, and the end thereof are the
ways of death;*[6] and contrariwise, *The path of the righteous is
a shining light, shining more and more until the midday.*[7] *The
ways of darkness*[8] are the ways which end in darkness; and
when Isaiah says, *The way of peace hast thou not known,* he
adds, *whosoever goeth therein shall not know peace.*[9] They who
choose not peace for their way, shall not find peace in and
for their end.

On these your ways, Haggai says, *set your hearts,* not
thinking of them lightly, nor giving a passing thought to
them, but fixing your minds upon them; as God says to
Satan, *Hast thou set thy heart on My servant Job?*[10] and God
is said to set His eye or His face upon man for good[11] or
for evil.[12] He speaks also, not of setting the mind, applying
the understanding, giving the thoughts, but of *setting the*

[1] Prov. vi. 23.
[2] Ib. x. 17.
[3] Ib. xv. 24.
[4] Ib. vii. 27.
[5] Ib. v. 5, 6.
[6] Ib. xiv. 12 ; xvi. 25.
[7] Ib. iv. 18.
[8] Ib. ii. 13.
[9] Isa. lix. 8.
[10] Job i. 8.
[11] Jer. xxiv. 6.
[12] Ib. xxi. 10.

heart, as the seat of the affections. It is not a dry weighing
of the temporal results of their ways, but a loving dwelling
upon them ; for repentance without love is but the gnawing
of remorse.

" *Set your heart on your ways:* i.e. your affections,
thoughts, works, so as to be circumspect in all things; as
the Apostle says, *Do nothing without forethought,*[1] i.e. without
previous judgment of reason; and Solomon, *Let thine eyes
look right on, and let thine eyelids look straight before thee ;*[2]
and the son of Sirach, *Son, do nothing without counsel, and
when thou hast done it thou wilt not repent.*[3] For since, according to a probable proposition, nothing in human acts
is indifferent, i.e. involving neither good nor ill deserts,
they who do not thus *set* their *hearts upon* their *ways,* do
they not daily incur well-nigh countless sins, in thought,
word, desire, deed, yea and by omission of duties? Such
are all fearless persons who heed not to fulfil what is
written, *' Keep your heart with all watchfulness.*"[5]

" He *sows much* to his own heart, but *brings in little,*
who by reading and hearing knows much of the heavenly
commands, but by negligence in deeds bears little fruit.
He eats and is not satisfied, who, hearing the words of God,
coveteth the gains or glory of the world. Well is he said
not to be *satisfied,* who *eateth* one thing, hungereth after
another. *He* drinks and is not inebriated, who inclineth
his ear to the voice of preaching, but changeth not his
mind. For through inebriation the mind of those who
drink is changed. He then who is devoted to the knowledge of God's word, yet still desireth to gain the things
of the world, *drinks and is not inebriated.* For were he
inebriated, no doubt he would have changed his mind and
no longer seek earthly things, or love the vain and passing

[1] 1 Tim. v. 21. [2] Prov. iv. 25.
[3] Ecclus. xxxii. 19, Vulg. [4] Prov. iv. 23. [5] Dion.

6 Ye have ^a sown much, and bring in little; ye
eat, but ye have not enough; ye drink, but ye are
not filled with drink; ye clothe you, but there is

^a Deut. xxviii. 38; Hosea iv. 10; Micah vi. 14, 15;
Hag. ii. 16.

---

things which he *had* loved. For the Psalmist says of the
elect, *They shall be inebriated with the richness of Thy house,*[1]
because they shall be filled with such love of Almighty
God, that, their mind being changed, they seem to be
strangers to themselves, fulfilling what is written, [2] *If
any will come after Me, let him deny himself.*" [3]

6. *Ye have sown much.* The Prophet expresses the
habitualness of these visitations by a vivid present. He
marks no time and so expresses the more vividly that it
was at all times. It is one continually present evil. *Ye
have sown much and there is a bringing in little; there is
eating and not to satisfy; there is drinking and not to ex-
hilarate; there is clothing and not to be warm.*[4] It is not
for the one or the other years, as, since the first year of
Darius Hystaspis; it is one continued visitation, co-ordinate
with one continued negligence. As long as the sin lasted,
so long the punishment. The visitation itself was twofold;
impoverished harvests, so as to supply less sustenance;
and various indisposition of the frame, so that what would,
by God's appointment in nature, satisfy, gladden, warm,
failed of its effect. *And he that laboureth for hire, gaineth
himself hire into a bag full of holes* [lit. *perforated*]. The
labour pictured is not only fruitless, but wearisome and
vexing. There is a seeming result of all the labour, some-

---

[1] Ps. xxxvi. 8. [2] S. Matt. xvi. 24.
[3] S. Greg. in Ezek. Hom. i. 10, n. 7, Opp. i. 1266.
[4] לֹא חֹם. The לֹ is not pleonastic, but from the imper-
sonal לֹ חֹם 1 Kings i. 1, 2; Eccl. iv. 11 (*bis*).

none warm; and ^a he that earneth wages earneth wages *to put it* into a bag * with holes.

7 ¶ Thus saith the LORD of hosts, Consider your ways.

^a Zech. viii. 10.   * Heb. *pierced through.*

---

thing to allure hopes; but forthwith it is gone. The heathen assigned a like baffling of hope as one of the punishments of hell. "Better and wiser to seek to be blessed by God, Who bestoweth on us all things. And this will readily come to those who choose to be of the same mind with Him and prefer what is for His glory to their own. For so saith the Saviour Himself to us, ¹ *Seek ye first the kingdom of God and His righteousness, and all these things shall be added unto you.*" ²

"*He* loses good deeds by evil acts, who takes account of his good works, which he has before his eyes, and forgets the faults which creep in between; or who, after what is good, returns to what is vain and evil." ³ "Money is seen in the pierced bag, when it is cast in; but when it is lost, it is not seen. They then who look how much they give, but do not weigh how much they gain wrongly, cast their rewards into a pierced bag. Looking to the Hope of their confidence they bring them together; not looking, they lose them." ⁴

"*They* lose the fruit of their labour, by not persevering to the end, or by seeking human praise, or by vainglory within, not keeping spiritual riches under the guardianship of humility. Such are vain and unprofitable men, of whom the Saviour saith, ⁵ *Verily I say unto you, they have their reward.*" ⁶

¹ S. Matt. vi. 33.   ² S. Cyr.   ³ Lap.
⁴ S. Greg. Reg. Past. iii. 21, fin. Opp. ii. 68.
⁵ S. Matt. vi. 2, add 5, 16.   ⁶ Dion.

P

8 Go up to the mountain, and bring wood, and

8. *Go up into the mountain.* Not Mount Lebanon, whence the cedars had been brought for the first temple; whence also Zerubbabel and Joshua had procured some out of Cyrus' grant,[1] at the first return from the captivity. They were not required to buy, expend, but simply to give their own labour. They were themselves to *go up to the mountain,* i.e. the mountainous country where the trees grew, *and bring* them. So, in order to keep the feast of tabernacles, Ezra made a proclamation *in all their cities and in Jerusalem, Go ye up to the mountain and bring leafy branches of vines, olives, myrtles, palms.*[2] The palms, anyhow, were timber. God required not goodly stones, such as had been already used, and such as hereafter, in the temple which was built, were the admiration even of disciples of Jesus,[3] but which were, for the wickedness of those who rejected their Saviour, *not to be left, one stone upon another.* He required not costly gifts, but the heart. The neglect to build the temple was neglect of Himself, Who ought to be worshipped there. His worship sanctified the offering; offerings were acceptable, only if made with a free heart.

And I will have pleasure in it. God, Who has declared that He has no *pleasure in thousands of rams, or ten thousands of rivers of oil,*[4] had delight in *them that feared Him,*[5] that are *upright in their way,*[6] that *deal truly,*[7] in the *prayer* of the *upright;*[8] and so in the temple too, when it should be built to His glory.

And will be glorified.[9] God is glorified in man, when

---

[1] Ezra iii. 7.   [2] Neh. viii. 15.   [3] S. Matt. xxiv. 1, 2.
[4] Micah vi. 7.   [5] Ps. cxlvii. 11.   [6] Prov. xi. 20.
[7] Ib. xii. 22.   [8] Ib. xv. 8.
[9] There is no ground for the Kri וְאֶכָּבְדָה, *and so should I be glorified* or *honoured.* It is a positive promise that G̊d̊

build the house ; and I will take pleasure in it, and I
will be glorified, saith the LORD.

---

man serves Him; in Himself, when He manifests aught
of His greatness; in His great doings to His people,[1] as
also in the chastisement of those who disobey Him.[2] God
allows that glory, which shines ineffably throughout His
creation, to be obscured here through man's disobedience,
to shine forth anew on his renewed obedience. The glory
of God, as it is the end of the creation, so is it His
creature's supreme bliss. When God is really glorified,
then can He show forth His glory, by His grace and accept-
ance. "The glory of God is our glory. The more sweetly
God is glorified, the more it profits us :"[3] yet not our
profit, but the glory of God is itself our end ; so the
Prophet closes in that which is our end, *God will be
glorified*.

"Good then and well-pleasing to God is zeal in fulfilling

would show forth His glory, as in וְאֶרְצֶה immediately before.
God says, "Do this, and I will do that." Comp. Zech. i. 3.
Of sixty-five instances which Böttcher (Lehrb. n. 965, c)
gives of הָ after the imperative, sixty-one relate to some
wish of the human agent; four only relate to God. Deut. v.
31, "Stand here by Me, וַאֲדַבְּרָה, that I may speak unto
thee ; " Isa. xli. 22, 23, irony, including men, " that we may
consider and know ; that we may know ; " Ps. l. 7, " hear
Me and *I would speak*, and *testify* ; " Mal. iii. 7, " Return to
Me, and I would return unto you ; " the return of the creature
being a condition that God could return to it. On the other
hand, the Ch. Lam. v. 21, " Turn Thou us unto Thee, וְנָשׁוּב,
and we will return," expresses the absolute will to return ;
Ruth iv. 4, "Tell me, וְאֵדַע, and I shall know," the certainty
of the knowledge, upon which Boaz would act.

[1] Isa. xxvi. 15 ; xliv. 23 ; lx. 21 ; lxi. 3.
[2] Exod. xiv. 4 ; Ezek. xxviii. 22.
[3] S. Aug. Serm. 380, n. 6.

9 ᵃ Ye looked for much, and, lo, *it came* to little ;
and when ye brought *it* home, ᵇ I did * blow upon it.

ᵃ Hag. ii. 16.   ᵇ Ib. ii. 17.
* Or, *blow it away.*

---

whatever may appear necessary for the good condition of
the Church and its building-up, collecting the most useful
materials, the spiritual principles in inspired Scripture,
whereby he may secure and ground the conception of God,
and may show that the way of the Incarnation was well-
ordered, and may collect what appertains to accurate knowledge of spiritual erudition and moral goodness.   Nay,
each of us may be thought of, as the temple and house
of God.   For Christ *dwelleth in us* by the Spirit, and we
are *temples of the living God,* according to the Scripture.[1]
Let each then build up his own heart by right faith, having
the Saviour as the *precious foundation.*   And let him add
thereto other materials, obedience, readiness for anything,
courage, endurance, continence.   So *being framed together
by that which every joint supplieth,* shall we *become a holy
temple, a habitation of God through the Spirit.*[2]   But those
who are slow to faith, or who believe but are sluggish in
shaking off passions and sins and worldly pleasure, thereby
cry out in a manner, *The time is not come to build the house
of the Lord.*"[3]

9. *Ye looked,* lit. *a looking;* as though he said, it has
all been one looking, *for much,* for increase, the result of
all sowing, in the way of nature : *and behold it came to little,*
i.e. less than was sown ; as Isaiah denounced to them of
old by God's word, *the seed of a homer shall yield an ephah,*[4]
i.e. one-tenth of what was sown.   *And ye brought it home,
and I blew upon it,* so as to disperse it, as, not the wheat,
but the chaff is blown before the wind.   This, in whatever

[1] 2 Cor. vi. 16.   [2] Eph. iv. 16 ; ii. 21, 22.
[3] S. Cyr.   [4] Isa. v. 10.

Why? saith the LORD of hosts. Because of mine
house that *is* waste, and ye run every man unto his
own house.

---

way it came to pass, was a further chastisement of God.
The little seed which they brought in lessened through
decay or waste. *Why? saith the Lord of hosts.* God asks
by his Prophet, what He asks in the awakened conscience.
God with rebukes chastens man for sin.[1] Conscience, when
alive, confesses for *what* sin; or it asks itself, if memory
does not supply the special sin. Unawakened, it murmurs
about the excess of rain, the drought, the blight, the
mildew, and asks, not itself, but why, in God's Providence,
these inflictions came in these years? They felt doubtless
the sterility in contrast with the exceeding fruitfulness
of Babylonia,[2] as they contrasted the *light bread*,[3] the
manna, with the plenteousness of Egypt.[4] They ascribed,
probably, their meagre crops (as we mostly do) to mere
natural causes, perhaps to the long neglect of the land
during the captivity. God forces the question upon their
consciences, in that Haggai asks it in His Name, in Whose
hands all powers stand, *saith the Lord of hosts.* They have
not to talk it over among themselves, but to answer
Almighty God, *why?* That *why?* strikes into the inmost
depths of conscience!

Because of My house which is waste, and ye run, lit. *are
running,* all the while, *each to his own house.*[5] They were

[1] Ps. xxxix. 11.

[2] Herod. i. 193; Theophr. Hist. Plant. viii. 7; Berosus
Fr. 1; Strabo, xvi. 1, 14; Pliny, Nat. Hist. xviii. 17; Amm.
Marc. xxiv. 9.

[3] Num. xxi. 5.   [4] Ib. xi. 5.

[5] רוץ with לְ is used of the direction whither a man goes;
if used of an action, hasting to do it; as *runneth to evil* (Isa.
lix. 7; Prov. i. 16). Here לביתו cannot be " on account of
his house," but to it, viz. for his business there.

10 Therefore [a] the heaven over you is stayed from dew, and the earth is stayed *from* her fruit.

[a] Lev. xxvi. 19 ; Deut. xxviii. 23 ; 1 Kings viii. 35.

absorbed in their material interests, and had no time for those of God. When the question was of God's house, they stir not from the spot; when it is of their own concerns, they run. Our Lord says, *Seek ye first the kingdom of God and His righteousness, and all these things shall be added unto you.*[1] Man reverses this, seeks his own things first, and God withholds His blessing.

"This comes true of those who prefer their own conveniences to God's honour, who do not thoroughly uproot self-love, whose penitence and devotion are shown to be unstable; for on a slight temptation they are overcome. Such are they who are bold, self-pleasing, wise and great in their own eyes, who do not ground their conversation on true and solid humility."[2]

"To those who are slow to fulfil what is for the glory of God, and the things whereby His house, the Church, is firmly stayed, neither the heavenly dew cometh, which enricheth hearts and minds, nor the fruitfulness of the earth—i.e. right action; not food nor wine nor use of oil. But they will be ever strengthless and joyless, unenriched by spiritual oil, and remain without taste or participation of the blessing through Christ."[3]

10. *Therefore, for you,* on your account ;[4] for your sins,[5] He points out the moral cause of the drought, whereas men think of this or that cause of the variations of the seasons, and we, e.g. take into our mouths Scripture-words, as *murrain of cattle,* and the like, and think of nothing less than why it was sent, or Who sent it. Haggai directs the mind to the higher Cause, that as they withheld their service

[1] S. Matt. vi. 33.   [2] Dion.   [3] S. Cyr.
[4] As in Ps. xliv. 22.   [5] Jon.

11 And I [a] called for a drought upon the land, and upon the mountains, and upon the corn, and upon the new wine, and upon the oil, and upon *that* which the ground bringeth forth, and upon men, and upon cattle, and [b] upon all the labour of the hands.

[a] 1 Kings xvii. 1 ; 2 Kings viii. 1.   [b] Hag. ii. 17.

from God, so, on their account and by His will, His creatures withheld[1] their service from them.

11. *And I called for a drought upon the land.* God called to the people and they would not hear. It is His ever-repeated complaint to them. *I called unto you, and ye would not hear.* He called to His inanimate creatures to punish them, and *they* obeyed. So Elisha tells the woman, whose son he had restored to life, *The Lord hath called to the famine, and it shall also come to the land seven years.*[2]

And upon men, in that the drought was oppressive to man. The Prophet may also allude to the other meaning of the word, "waste," "desolation." They had left the house of the Lord[3] waste, therefore God called for waste, desolation, upon them.

12. *Then Zerubbabel, and all the remnant of the people,* not, "the rest of the people" but "the remnant,"[4] those who

[1] כָּלָא being everywhere transitive, and in this V. also, is probably transitive here.

[2] 2 Kings viii. 1.

[3] חָרֵב, Hag. i. 4, 9 ; חֹרֶב, i. 11.

[4] This is the almost uniform usage of שְׁאֵרִית, "remnant which remains over," mostly after the rest have been destroyed or carried captive. See above on Amos i. 8 ; add, *the remnant of Judah,* Jer. xl. 11 ; xlii. 19 ; xliii. 5 ; xliv. 12, 14 ; *of Israel,* Zeph. iii. 13 ; Ezek. xi. 13 ; *whole remnant of the people,* Jer. xli. 10, 16 ; *of Ashdod,* Jer. xxv. 20 ; *of the coast of Caphtor,* Ib. xlvii. 4 ; *of their valley,* ib. 5 ; *of the coast of the sea,* Ezek. xxv. 16 ; *of the nations,* ib. xxxvi. 3, 4, 5 ; *of*

12 ¶ ᵃ Then Zerubbabel the son of Shealtiel, and
Joshua the son of Josedech, the high priest, with all
the remnant of the people, obeyed the voice of the
LORD their God, and the words of Haggai the prophet,

ᵃ Ezra v. 2.

---

remained over from the captivity, the fragment of the two
tribes, which returned to their own land, *hearkened unto the
voice of the Lord.* This was the beginning of a conversion.
In this one thing they began to do, what, all along, in their
history, and most in their decay before the captivity they
refused to do—obey God's word. So God sums up their
history, by Jeremiah, *I spake unto thee in thy prosperity, thou
saidst, I will not hear. This is thy way from thy youth, that
thou hearkenedst not unto My voice.*[1] Zephaniah still more
briefly, *she hearkened not unto* [any] *voice.*[2] Now in reference,
it seems, to that account of their disobedience, Haggai says,
using the self-same formula, [3] *they hearkened unto the voice of
the Lord,* [4] *according to the words of Haggai.* They obeyed,
not vaguely, or partly, but exactly, *according to the words*
which the messenger of God spake.

And they feared the Lord. "Certainly the presence of the

the land, אדמה, Isa. xv. 9 ; *of My people,* Zeph. ii. 9 ;
of His heritage, Micah vii. 18 ; *thy remnant,* Isa. xiv. 30 ;
Ezra v. 10 ; *its remnant,* Isa. xliv. 17 ; *their remnant,* Jer.
xv. 9 ; and of those who had actually returned, Zech. viii. 6,
11, 12. In two places in which it signifies " the rest " (Jer.
xxxix. 3 ; 1 Chron. xii. 38), it is at least the rest of a whole,
already mentioned. A third only, Neh. vii. 72, is uncertain.
The word is used almost exclusively by the prophets.

[1] Jer. xxii. 21.
[2] לא שמעה בקול. See Introduction to Zeph.
[3] וישמע בקול יי.
[4] This is the only place in which שמע על דברי is used.

as the LORD their God had sent him, and the people
did fear before the LORD,

13 Then spake Haggai the LORD'S messenger in
the LORD'S message unto the people, saying, ^a I *am*
with you, saith the LORD.

^a Matt. xxviii. 20 ; Rom. viii. 31.

Divine Majesty is to be feared with great reverence." [1] " The
fear of punishment at times transports the mind to what is
better, and the infliction of sorrows harmonises the mind to
the fear of God ; and that of the Proverbs comes true, *He
that feareth the Lord shall be recompensed,*[2] and *the fear of the
Lord* tendeth *to life ;* [3] and Wisdom, *The fear of the Lord is
honour and glory,*[4] and *the fear of the Lord shall rejoice the
heart, and giveth joy and gladness and a long life.*[5] See how
gently and beseemingly God smites us." [6]

" See how the loving-kindness of God forthwith goes along
with all changes for the better. For Almighty God changes
along with those who will to repent, and promises that He
will be with them ; which what can equal ? For when God
is with us, all harm will depart from us, all good come in
to us." [6]

13. *And Haggai, the Lord's messenger.* Malachi, whose
own name was framed to express that he was *the Lord's
messenger,* and Haggai alone use the title, as the title of a
prophet ; perhaps as forerunners of the great prophet whom
Malachi announced. Malachi also speaks of the priest, as
the messenger of the Lord of hosts,[7] and prophesies of John
Baptist as *the messenger* [8] of the Lord, who should *go before
His face.* Haggai, as he throughout repeats that his words
were God's words, frames a new word,[9] to express, in the

[1] Dion.   [2] Prov. xiii. 13.   [3] Ib. xix. 23.
[4] Ecclus. i. 11.   [5] Ib. i. 12.   [6] S. Cyr.
[7] Mal. ii. 7.   [8] Ib. iii. 1.   [9] סלאכות.

HAGGAI

234 **HAGGAI**

14 And [a] the LORD stirred up the spirit of Zerubbabel the son of Shealtiel, [b] governor of Judah, and
the spirit of Joshua the son of Josedech, the high
priest, and the spirit of all the remnant of the people ;

[a] 2 Chron. xxxvi. 22 ; Ezra i. 1.   [b] Hag. ii. 21.

---

language of the New Testament,[1] that he had an embassy
from God; *in the Lord's message.*

I am with you. All the needs and longings of the creature
are summed up in those two words, *I with-you.* "Who art
Thou and who am I?   Thou, He Who Is ; I, he who am
not ;" nothing, yea worse than nothing. Yet *if God be for
us,* S. Paul asks, *who can be against us?*[2] Our Blessed Lord's
parting promise to the Apostles, and in them to the Church,
was, *Lo I am with you alway,* even *to the end of the world.*[3]
The all-containing assurance goes beyond any particular
promise of aid, as, "I will help you, and will protect you, so
that your building shall have its completion."[4] This is one
fruit of it ; "since I am in the midst of you, no one shall
be able to hinder your building."[5] But, more widely, the
words bespeak *His* presence in love, Who knows all our
needs, and is Almighty to support and save us in all. So
David says, *When I walk through the valley of the shadow of
death, I will fear no evil; for Thou art with me :*[6] and God
says by another, *I* will be *with him in trouble,*[7] and by Isaiah,
When thou passest through the waters, I will be *with thee.*[8]

14. *And the Lord stirred up the spirit.* The words are used
of any strong impulse from God to fulfil His will, whether
in those who execute His will unknowingly as Pul,[9] to carry
off the trans-Jordanic tribes, or the Philistines and Arabians

[1] 2 Cor. v. 20.   [2] Rom. viii. 31.   [3] S. Matt. xxviii. 20.
[4] Dion.   [5] S. Jer.   [6] Ps. xxiii. 4.
[7] Ib. xci. 15.   [8] Isa. xliii. 2.   [9] 1 Chron. v. 26.

ᵃ and they came and did work in the house of the
LORD of hosts, their God.

15 In the four and twentieth day of the sixth
month, in the second year of Darius the king.

ᵃ Ezra v. 2, 8.

---

against Jehoram,[1] or the Medes against Babylon;[2] or
knowingly, as of Cyrus to restore God's people and rebuild
the temple,[3] or of the people themselves to return.[4] "The
spirit of Zerubbabel and the spirit of Joshua were stirred,
that the government and priesthood may build the temple
of God: the spirit of the people too, which before was
asleep in them; not the body, not the soul, but the spirit,
which knoweth best how to build the temple of God."[5]
"The Holy Spirit is stirred up in us, that we should enter
the house of the Lord, and do the works of the Lord."[6]

"Again, observe that they did not set themselves to
choose to do what should please God, before He was with
them and stirred up their spirit. We shall know hence
also, that although one choose zealously to do good and be
in earnest therein, yet he will accomplish nothing, unless
God be with him, raising him up to dare, and sharpening
him to endure, and removing all torpor. For so the
wondrous Paul says of those entrusted with the divine
preaching, *I laboured more abundantly than they all*, yet
added very wisely, *yet not I, but the grace of God which was
with me*,[7] and the Saviour Himself saith to the holy Apostles,
Without Me ye can do nothing.[8] For He is our desire, He,
our courage to any good work; He our strength, and, if He
is with us, we shall do well, *building ourselves to a holy temple,*

[1] 2 Chron. xxi. 16.   [2] Jer. li. 11.
[3] Ezra i. 1.   [4] Ib. i. 5.
[5] S. Jer.   [6] Ap. Lap.
[7] 1 Cor. xv. 10.   [8] S. John xv. 5.

CHAPTER II

1 *He encourageth the people to the work, by promise
of greater glory to the second temple than was in
the first.* 10 *In the type of holy things and unclean he sheweth their sins hindered the work.*
20 *God's promise to Zerubbabel.*

IN the seventh *month*, in the one and twentieth *day*
of the month, came the word of the LORD * by the
prophet Haggai, saying,

* Heb. *by the hand of.*

---

a habitation of God in the Spirit; [1] if He depart and withdraws, how should any doubt, that we should fail, overcome
by sluggishness and want of courage ? " [2]

15. *In the four and twentieth day of the month.* The interval
of twenty-three days must have been spent in preparation,
since the message came on the first of the month, and the
obedience was immediate.

CHAP. II. ver. 1. *In the seventh month, in the one and twentieth
day of the month.* This was the seventh day of the feast
of tabernacles,[3] and its close. The eighth day was to be
a sabbath, with its *holy convocation*,[4] but the commemorative
feast, the dwelling in booths, in memory of God's bringing
them out of Egypt, was to last seven days. The close, then,
of this feast could not but revive their sadness at the
glories of their first deliverance by God's *mighty hand and
outstretched arm,* and their present fewness and poverty.
This depression could not but bring with it heavy thoughts
about the work, in which they were, in obedience to God,

[1] Eph. ii. 21, 22.   [2] S. Cyr.
[3] Lev. xxiii. 34, 36, 40–42.   [4] Ib. xxiii. 36, 39.

· 2 Speak now to Zerubbabel the son of Shealtiel, governor of Judah, and to Joshua the son of Josedech, the high priest, and to the residue of the people, saying,

3 [a] Who *is* left among you that saw this house in her first glory ? and how do ye see it now ? [b] *is it* not in your eyes in comparison of it as nothing ?

[a] Ezra iii. 12.   [b] Zech. iv. 10.

---

engaged ; and that, all the more, since Isaiah and Ezekiel had prophesied of the glories of the Christian Church under the symbol of the temple. This despondency Haggai is sent to relieve, owning plainly the reality of its present grounds, but renewing, on God's part, the pledge of the glories of this second temple, which should be thereafter.

3. *Who is left among you?* The question implies that there were those among them who had seen the first house in its glory, yet but few. When the foundations of the first temple were laid, there were many. *Many of the priests and Levites and chief of the fathers, ancient men, that had seen the first house, when the foundations of this house were laid before their eyes, wept with a loud voice.*[1] Fifty-nine years had elapsed from the destruction of the temple in the eleventh year of Zedekiah to the first of Cyrus ; so that old men of seventy years had seen the first temple, when themselves eleven years old. In this second year of Darius seventy years had passed, so that those of seventy-eight or eighty years might still well remember it. Ezra's father, Seraiah, was slain in the eleventh year of Zedekiah ; so he must have been born at latest a few months later ; yet he lived to the second year of Artaxerxes.

[1] Ezra iii. 12.

4 Yet now ᵃ be strong, O Zerubbabel, saith the
_____
ᵃ Zech. viii. 9.
_____

Is not such as it is,[1] *as nothing?* Besides the richness of
the sculptures in the former temple, everything, which admitted of it, was overlaid with gold; *Solomon overlaid the*
whole house with gold, until he had finished all the house, the
whole altar by the oracle, the two cherubim, the floor of the house,
the doors of the holy of holies and the ornaments of it, *the*
cherubims thereon and *the palm trees he covered with gold fitted*
upon the carved work;[2] *the altar of gold and the table of gold,*
whereupon the shewbread was, the ten candlesticks of pure gold,
with the flowers and the lamps and the tongs of gold, the bowls,
the snuffers and the basons and the spoons and the censers of
pure gold, and hinges of pure gold for all the doors of the temple.[3]
The porch that was in the front of the house, twenty cubits broad
and 120 cubits high, was overlaid within with pure gold;[4] the
house glistened with precious stones; and the gold (it
is added) was *gold of Parvaim,* a land distant of course
and unknown to us. *Six hundred talents of gold* (about
£4,320,000 [5]) were employed in overlaying the Holy of
holies. *The upper chambers were also of gold; the weight of*
the nails was fifty shekels of gold.

[1] Such is probably the force of כמוהו.   Comp. כמוך כפרעה
[Gen. xliv. 18] "one such as thou is like Pharaoh," and
perhaps כמהו, Exod. ix. 18, and אשר כמוני, 2 Sam. ix. 8,
הוא כאין (which Ewald says older writers would have used)
would have been weaker.

[2] 1 Kings vi. 22, 28, 30, 32, 35.

[3] Ib. vii. 48–50.   [4] 2 Chron. iii. 4–9.

[5] Reckoning the silver shekel at 2s., the talent of silver
= 3000 shekels, would be £300 ; reckoning the gold talent,
as, in weight, double the silver talent, and the relation of
gold to silver as 12 to 1 (H. W. Poole in Smith Bibl. Dict.,
pp. 1734, 1735), the gold talent would be £300 × 24 = £7200 ;
and 600 gold talents £4,320,000.   This would not be so much
as Solomon imported yearly, 666 talents = £4,795,200.

LORD; and be strong, O Joshua, son of Josedech, the high priest; and be strong, all ye people of the land, saith the LORD, and work: for I *am* with you, saith the LORD of hosts :

---

4. *Yet now be strong—and work.* They are the words with which David exhorted Solomon his son to be earnest and to persevere in the building of the first temple. *Take heed now, for the Lord hath chosen thee to build an house for the sanctuary: be strong and do.*[1] *Be strong and of good courage, and do.*[2] This combination of words occurs once only elsewhere,[3] in Jehoshaphat's exhortation to *the Levites and priests and the chiefs of the fathers of Israel,*[4] whom he had set as judges in Jerusalem. Haggai seems then to have adopted the words, with the purpose of suggesting to the downhearted people, that there was need of the like exhortation, in view of the building of the former temple, whose relative glory so depressed them. The word *be strong* (elsewhere rendered, *be of good courage*) occurs commonly in exhortations to persevere and hold fast, amid whatever obstacles.[5]

5. *The word which I covenanted.* The words stand more

---

[1] 1 Chron. xxviii. 10.   [2] Ib. xxviii. 20.
[3] 2 Chron. xix. 11.   [4] Ib. xix. 8.
[5] Gesenius (v. חזק) refers to the following: 2 Sam. x. 12 (Joab to Abishai in the war with the Syrians); 2 Chron. xxv. 8 (the prophet to Amaziah); 2 Sam. xiii. 28 (Absalom to his servants about the murder of Amnon); Ps. xxvii. 14; xxxi. 24 (with the corresponding promise that God would *establish their hearts*); Isa. xli. 6 (in mockery of the laborious process of making an idol). It occurs also, supported by וֶאֱמָץ Jos. i. 6, 7, 9, 18 (God's words to Joshua); Deut. xxxi. 7 (Moses to Joshua); ib. 6 (to Israel); Josh. x. 25 (Joshua to the people); 2 Chron. xxxii. 7 (Hezekiah to the people); חזק itself is repeated Dan. x. 19, חֲזַק וַחֲזָק.

5 ^a *According to* the word that I covenanted with

^a Exod. xxix. 45, 46.

forcibly, because abruptly.¹ It is an exclamation which
cannot be forced into any grammatical relation with the
preceding. The more exact idiom would have been " Remember," " take to heart." But the Prophet points to it
the more energetically, because he casts it, as it were, into
the midst, not bound up with any one verb. This would be
the rather done in speaking to the people, as David to his
followers,² *That which the Lord hath given us and hath preserved*

¹ Less probable seems to me (1) To make את הדבר
depend on עשׂו in v. 4, as Kim. A. E. (*a*) on account of the
idiom in 1 Chron. in which, as here, עשׂה stands absolutely,
" do work " ; (*b*) Haggai is exhorting them to this one work
of rebuilding the temple, not to obedience to the law generally ;
(*c*) he speaks of what God had promised them, not of their
duties to God. (2) To supply זכרו " remember," or any
like word, is arbitrary, unless it means that *we* should fill up
the meaning by some such word. (3) To construe, " Remember the word which I covenanted with you, fear not "
(Ew.) ; (*a*) gives undue prominence to the absence of fear,
which was one consequence of God's covenant that He would
be their God, they His people, not the covenant itself ;
(*b*) *Fear not*, is elsewhere the counterpart and supplement
of the exhortation, " be strong," 2 Chron. xxv. 8 ; Isa.
xxxv. 4. (*c*) In Exod. xx. 20 (referred to by Ew.) " fear
not " is only Moses' exhortation on occasion of the terrors of
the manifestation of God on Mt. Sinai. (4) It is doubly improbable, that it, as well as רוחי, should be the subject of
the sing. עמֶדֶת. The את הדבר and the רוחי seem to be
different constructions, in order to prevent this. Böttcher
terms it, " an acc. abs. of the object," and cites Deut. xi.
2 ; Ezek. xliii. 7 ; xlvii. 17–19 (" unless one correct זאת for
ואת "); Zech. viii. 17. (Lehrb. n. 516, *e*.)

² 1 Sam. xxx. 23, which Ewald compares. Lehrb. n. 329,
a, p. 811, ed. 8, and in his Die Proph. iii. 183. Only he, not
very intelligibly, makes it a sort of oath, *By the word, By that*

you when ye came out of Egypt, so [a]my spirit re-
maineth among you : fear ye not.

[a] Neh. ix. 20 ; Isa. lxiii. 11.

---

us and given the company against us into our hands! i.e.
" Would you deal thus with it ? " The abrupt form rejects
it as shocking. So here, *The word which I covenanted with
you,* i.e. this *I will be with you,* was the central, all-containing
promise, to which God pledged Himself when He brought
them out of Egypt. He speaks to them as being one with
those who came up out of Egypt, as if they were the very
persons. The Church, ever varying in the individuals of
whom it is composed, is, throughout all ages, in God's sight,
one; His promises to the fathers are made to the children
in them. So the Psalmist says, *There* (at the dividing
of the Red Sea and the Jordan) *do we rejoice in Him,* as
if present there ; and our Lord promises to the Apostles,
I am with you always even to the end of the world,[1] by an ever-
present Presence with them and His Church founded by
them in Him.

My Spirit abideth among you, as the Psalmist says, *They
[the heavens] perish and Thou abidest;*[2] *The counsel of the
Lord standeth for ever;*[3] *His righteousness endureth for ever.*[4]
The Spirit of God is God the Holy Ghost, with His manifold
gifts. Where He is, is all good. As the soul is in the
body, so God the Holy Ghost is in the Church, Himself its
life, and bestowing on all and each every good gift, as each
and all have need. As S. Paul says of the Church of Christ :
*There are diversities of gifts, but the same Spirit ; and there are
diversities of operations, but it is the same God, Who worketh all
in all. All these worketh one and the self-same Spirit, dividing*

which the Lord hath given us. But he suggests the like broken
sentence, Zech. vii. 7.

[1] S. Matt. xxviii. 20.   [2] Ps. cii. 26.
[3] Ib. xxxiii. 11.   [4] Ib. cxi. 3.

Q

6 For thus saith the LORD of hosts; ^a Yet once,

a Ver. 21; Heb. xii. 26.

---

to every man severally as He will.[1] But above and beyond all
gifts He is present as the Spirit of holiness and love, making
the Church and those in whom He individually dwells, acceptable to God. Special applications, such as *the Spirit of
wisdom and might;* a spirit such as He gave to Moses to
judge His people:[2] the spirit of prophecy;[3] or the spirit
given to Bezaleel and Aholiab for the work of the sanctuary[4]
—these recognise in detail the one great truth, that all
good, all wisdom, from least to greatest, comes from God
the Holy Ghost; though one by one they would exclude
more truth than they each contain.

6. *Yet once, it is a little while.* This, the rendering of
S. Paul to the Hebrews, is alone grammatical.[5] *Yet once.*
By the word *yet* he looks back to the first great shaking of
the moral world, when God's revelation by Moses and to His
people broke upon the darkness of the pagan world, to be a
monument against heathen error till Christ should come;
once looks on, and conveys that God would again shake the
world, but *once* only, under the one dispensation of the
Gospel, which should endure to the end.

It is a little while. "The 517 years, which were to elapse
to the birth of Christ, are called *a little time,* because to the
prophets, ascending in heart to God and the eternity of
God, all times, like all things of this world, seem, as they

---

[1] 1 Cor. xii. 4, 6, 11.   [2] Alb. quoting Num. xi. 25.

[3] Jon. "My prophets shall teach you, fear not."

[4] Included by Lap.

[5] אחת 2 Kings vi. 10; Ps. lxii. 11; Job xl. 5; אחד, as
an adj., follows the noun. In the only exception alleged
by Ges., Dan. viii. 13, it is used of one certain angel, as contrasted with another. מעט is used of time, Job x. 20; xxiv.
24. עוד אחת ו is the like construction as עוד מעט ו, Exod.
xvii. 4; Ps. xxxvii. 10; Hosea i. 4.

are, only a little thing, yea, a mere point,"[1] which has neither length nor breadth. So S. John calls the time of the new law, *the last hour: Little children, it is the last hour.*[2] It was *little* also in respect to the time which had elapsed from the fall of Adam, upon which God promised the Saviour Christ ;[3] little also in respect to the Christian law, which has now lasted above 1800 years, and the time of the end does not seem yet nigh.

I will shake the heavens and the earth, and the sea and the dry land. It is one universal shaking of all this our world and the heavens over it, of which the Prophet speaks. He does not speak only of *signs in the sun and in the moon and in the stars,*[4] which might be, and yet the frame of the world itself might remain. It is a shaking, such as would involve the dissolution of this our system, as S. Paul draws out its meaning : *This word, once more, signifieth the removing of the things that are shaken, that those things which cannot be shaken may remain.*[5] Prophecy, in its long perspective, uses a continual foreshortening, speaking of things in relation to their eternal meaning and significance, as to that which shall survive, when heaven and earth and even time shall have passed away. It blends together the beginning and the earthly end ; the preparation and the result ; the commencement of redemption and its completion ; our Lord's coming in humility and in His Majesty. Scarce any prophet but exhibits things in their intrinsic relation, of which time is but an accident. It is the rule, not the exception. The Seed of the woman, Who should bruise the serpent's head, was promised on the fall ; to Abraham, the blessing through his seed ; by Moses, the prophet like unto him ; to David, an everlasting covenant.[6] Joel unites the outpouring of the Spirit of God on the Day of Pentecost, and the hatred

---

[1] Lap.
[2] 1 S. John ii. 18.
[3] Gen. iii. 15.
[4] S. Luke xxi. 25.
[5] Heb. xii. 27.
[6] 2 Sam. xxiii. 5.

it *is* a little while, and [a] I will shake the heavens, and the earth, and the sea, and the dry *land ;*

[a] Joel iii. 16.

---

of the world till the Day of Judgment ; [1] Isaiah, God's judgments on the land and the Day of final judgment ; [2] the deliverance from Babylon, and the first coming of Christ ; [3] the glories of the Church, the new heavens and the new earth which shall remain for ever, and the unquenched fire and undying worm of the lost ; [4] Daniel, the persecutions of Antiochus Epiphanes, of Anti-Christ, and the Resurrection; [5] Obadiah, the punishment of Edom, and the everlasting kingdom of God; [6] Zephaniah, the punishment of Judah and the final judgment of the earth ; [7] Malachi, our Lord's first and second Coming.[8]

Nay, our Lord Himself so blends together the destruction of Jerusalem and the days of Anti-Christ and the end of the world, that it is difficult to separate them, so as to say what belongs exclusively to either.[9] The prophecy is an answer to two distinct questions of the Apostles, (1) *When shall these things* (viz. the destruction of the temple) *be ?* (2) *and what shall be the sign of Thy coming and of the end of the world ?* Our Lord answers the two questions in one. Some things seem to belong to the first Coming, as *the*

[1] Joel ii. 28–32 ; iii.
[2] Isa. xxiv.
[3] Ib. xl.–lxvi.
[4] Ib. lxvi. 22–24.
[5] Dan. xi. xii.
[6] Obad. 18–21.
[7] See on Zeph. i. 2, 3.
[8] Mal. iii. 1–5, 17, 18 ; iv.
[9] The second question about the end of the world occurs only in S. Matthew (xxiv. 3) ; the first, *When shall these things be ?* occurs in S. Mark also (xiii. 4) and S. Luke (xxi. 7). The words in S. Mark, *This generation shall not pass till all these things be done* (xiii. 30), seem to me to be cast in the form of their question, *When shall these things be ?* viz. the things about which they had asked.

abomination of desolation spoken of by Daniel,[1] and the flight from *Judæa into the mountains.*[2] But the exceeding deceivableness is authoritatively interpreted by S. Paul[3] of a distant time ; and our Lord Himself, having said that *all these things,* of which the Apostles had inquired, should take place in that generation,[4] speaks of His absence as of a man taking a far journey,[5] and says that *not the angels in heaven knew that hour, neither the Son ;* [6] which precludes the idea, that He had just before declared that the whole would take place in that generation. For this would be to make out, that He declared that the Son knew not the hour of His Coming, which He had just (on this supposition) declared to be in that generation.

So then, here. There was a general shaking upon earth before our Lord came. Empires rose and fell. The Persian fell before Alexander's ; Alexander's world-empire was ended by his sudden death in youth ; of his four successors, two only continued, and they too fell before the Romans ; then were the Roman civil wars, until, under Augustus, the temple of Janus was shut. "For it greatly beseemed a work ordered by God, that many kingdoms should be confederated in one empire, and that the universal preaching might find the peoples easily accessible who were held under the rule of one state."[7] In the Heavens was the star, which led the wise men, the manifestation of Angels to the shepherds ; the preternatural darkness at the Passion ; the Ascension into the highest Heaven, and the descent of the Holy Ghost with *a sound from heaven as* [*of*] *a rushing mighty wind.*[8] "God had moved them [heaven and earth] before,

---

[1] S. Matt. xxiv. 15, 16.   [2] Ib. xxiv. 16.
[3] 2 Thess. ii. 2–10.   [4] S. Mark xiii. 30.
[5] Ib. xiii. 34.   [6] Ib. xiii. 32.
[7] S. Leo Hom. 82 in Nat. Ap. Petri et Pauli. c. 2, col. 322, Ball.
[8] Acts ii. 2.

when He delivered the people from Egypt, when there was in heaven a column of fire, dry ground amid the waves, a wall in the sea, a path in the waters, in the wilderness there was multiplied a daily harvest of heavenly food [the manna], the rock gushed into fountains of waters. But He moved it afterwards also in the Passion of the Lord Jesus, when the heaven was darkened, the sun shrank back, the rocks were rent, the graves opened, the dead were raised, the dragon, conquered in his waters, saw the fishers of men, not only sailing in the sea, but also walking without peril. The dry ground also was moved, when the unfruitful people of the nations began to ripen to a harvest of devotion and faith,—so that *more were the children of the forsaken, than* of *her which had a husband,* and, [1] *the desert flourished like a lily."* [2] " He moved earth in that great miracle of the birth from the Virgin : He moved the sea and dry land, when in the islands and in the whole world Christ is preached. So we see all nations moved to the faith." [3]

And yet, whatever preludes of fulfilment there were at our Lord's first Coming, they were as nothing to the fulfilment which we look for in the Second, *when* [4] *the earth shall be utterly broken down ; the earth, clean, dissolved ; the earth, moved exceedingly ; the earth shall reel to and fro like a drunkard, and shall be removed like a hanging-cot in a vineyard,* [5] *and the transgression thereof is heavy upon it ; and it shall fall and not rise again ;* whereon follows an announcement of the final judgment of men and angels, and the everlasting kingdom of the blessed in the presence of God.

Of that *day of the Lord,* S. Peter uses our Lord's image,

[1] Isa. xxxv. 1.

[2] S. Ambr. Ep. 30 ad Iren. n. 11, 12 ; Opp. ii. 913, Ben.

[3] S. Aug. de Civ. Dei, xviii. 25.

[4] Isa. xxiv. 19, 20.

[5] מלונה. See a picture of one in Niebuhr.

7 And I will shake all nations, ^a and the desire of
ᵃ Gen. xlix. 10 ; Mal. iii. 1.

---

[1] that it *shall come as a thief in the night, in which the
heavens shall melt with fervent heat, the earth also and the
works therein shall be burned up.*[2]

7. *And the desire of all nations shall come.* The words
can only mean this, *the* central longing of all nations ;[3]

---

[1] S. Matt. xxiv. 43.   [2] 2 S. Peter iii. 10.

[3] חמד is " coveted." It is the passion forbidden in the
tenth commandment, Exod. xx. 17 (*bis*) ; Deut. v. 18 ; vii. 21 ;
Exod. xxxiv. 24 ; Jos. vii. 21 ; Prov. vi. 25 ; Micah ii. 2.
In Prov. xii. 12, it is a passionate desire which ends in choice.
It is united with " loved " and " hated," ib. i. 22 ; of the
passionate idolatry, Isa. i. 29. It is used of God's passionless
good-pleasure in that which He chooses, yet speaking after
the manner of men, Ps. lxviii. 17, and of man's not longing
for Jesus, Isa. liii. 2. The Piel is used once of intense longing, Cant. ii. 3. Men covet things for some real or seeming
good ; and so the passive form of the verb, חָמוּד or נֶחְמָד,
are things which are the object of coveting, and so things
desirable ; חמור Job xx. 20 ; Ps. xxxix. 12 ; Isa. xliv. 9 ;
נחמד Gen. ii. 9 ; iii. 6 ; Ps. xix. 10 ; Prov. xxi. 20. מַחְמַד
with the gen. is " the desire of the eye," what it covets or
desires, 1 Kings xx. 6 ; Ezek. xxiv. 16, 21, 25 ; Lam. ii. 4 ;
or desirable things, belonging to one, Jo. iv. 5 ; Isa. lxiv. 11 ;
Lam. i. 10 ; 2 Chron. xxxvi. 19, or from it, מחמדי בטנם,
Hosea ix. 16, "the desires of the womb," "the desired children that their womb had borne," or with ל, " the desired
things consisting in their silver," מחמד לכספם, ib. ix. 6, or
abs. Cant. v. 16, מחמד occurs in the same sense, Lam. i. 7,
11 ; חֲמֻדוֹת or איש ח. of Daniel, as the object of the love
of God, Dan. ix. 23 ; x. 11, 19 ; and of desirable things,
Gen. xxvii. 15 ; 2 Chron. xx. 25 ; Dan. x. 3 ; xi. 38, 43 ;
Ezra viii. 27.

As to חֶמְדָה itself, two idioms have been confused : (1)
that in which it is accessory to another word, as כלי חמדה
"vessels of desire," Hosea xiii. 15 ; Jer. xxv. 34 ; 2 Chron

all nations shall come : and I will fill this house with glory, saith the LORD of hosts.

He whom they longed for, either through the knowledge of Him spread by the Jews in their dispersion, or mutely by the aching craving of the human heart, longing for the restoration from its decay. *The earnest expectation of the creature* did not begin with the Coming of Christ, nor was

xxxii. 27; Dan. xi. 8; Nahum ii. 9; ארץ חמדה, "land of desire," Ps. cvi. 24; Jer. iii. 19; Zech. vii. 14; בתי חמדתך "houses of thy desire," or "thy houses of desire," Ezek. xxvi. 12 ; חלקת חמדתי " my portion of desire," Jer. xii. 10. These we might paraphrase "pleasant vessels," "pleasant land," as we might say "desirables." Not that the word חמדה means, in itself, "pleasant things," any more than the word "coveted" signifies *pleasant*, though those things only are "coveted," which are thought to be pleasant. The original sense of the root to "desire," is obviously brought out the more, when the idea is not subsidiary, but the chief. There are four cases, in which *Chemdah* is so used. (1) "Jehoram died בלא חמדה, unregretted," we should say ; "no one longing for him," 2 Chron. xxi. 20; (2) "To whom is כל חמדת ישראל, the whole longing of Israel ? " 1 Sam. ix. 20 ; (3) The well-known words חמדת נשים, *Chemdath Nashim*, "the desire of women," Dan. xi. 37. If (as this is now generally understood) this means "the object of the longing of women," so much the more must חמדת כל הגוים mean, "the object of the longing of all nations." They cannot mean, "the most desirable of all nations," "die liebsten aller Völker," Ew. formerly ; "die edelsten aller Völker," Hitzig ; "die auserlesensten derselben," Umbreit. This must have been expressed by aid of the passive parti- ciple in any of the forms, by which a superlative is expressed. Nor can it mean "the costly things of all people" (",die höhen Schätzen aller der Völker," Ewald; "die Köstbarkeiten aller Nationen," Scholz). This, if expressed by the word at all, would have been, מַחֲמַדֵּי כל הגוים. Rashi, A. E., Kimchi, explain as if ב were omitted. R. Isaac (Chizzuk Emunah,

it limited to those who actually came to Him. *The whole creation*, S. Paul saith, *groaneth and travaileth in pain together until now.*[1] It was enslaved, and the better self longed to be free; every motion of grace in the multitudinous heart of man was a longing for its Deliverer; every weariness of what it was, every fleeting vision of what was better, every sigh from out of its manifold ills were notes of the one varied cry, "Come and help us." Man's heart, formed in the image of God, could not but ache to be re-formed by and for Him, though *an unknown God*, Who should reform it.

This longing increased as the time drew nigh, when Christ should come. The Roman biographer attests the existence of this expectation, not among the Jews only, but in the East;[2] this was quickened doubtless among the heathen by the Jewish Sibylline book, in that, amid the expectations of one sent from heaven, who should found a kingdom of righteousness, which the writer drew from the Hebrew prophets, he inserted denunciations of temporal vengeance upon the Romans, which Easterns would share. Still, although written 170 years before our Lord came,[3] it had not apparently much effect until the time when, from the prophecies of Daniel, it was

in Wagens, Tela ignea, p. 288) quotes 2 Kings xii. 11, where בית " stands as the acc. of place ; R. Tanchum omits the verse, Abulwalid the instance. It is not noticed by R. Parchon, Kimchi, Menahem ben Saruk, David b. Abraham, in their dictionaries. Abarbanel retains the meaning, "the desire of all nations," interpreting it of the holy land. He paraphrases ויבואו ח. כלם הנ. "that they shall come to the holy land and there shall He be avenged of them, and then at that time 'I will fill this house with glory,'" v. p. רעח, 4. The Anon. Arab. (Hunt. 206) renders "the most precious things of all nations shall come."

[1] Rom. viii. 19–22.   [2] Suet. Vesp. c. 4.
[3] See Pusey's Daniel the Prophet, pp. 364–368.

clear that He must shortly come.[1] Yet the attempt of
the Jewish [2] and heathen [3] historian to wrest it to Ves-
pasian, shows how great must have been the influence of
the expectation, which they attempted to turn aside. The
Jews, who rejected our Lord Whom Haggai predicted,
still were convinced that the prediction must be fulfilled
before the destruction of the second temple. The impulse
did not cease even after its destruction. R. Akiba, whom
they accounted "the first oracle of his time, the first and
greatest guardian of the tradition and old law," [4] of whom
they said, that "God revealed to him things unknown to
Moses," [5] was induced by this prophecy to acknowledge
the imposter Bar-cochab, to the destruction of himself
and of the most eminent of his time; fulfilling our Lord's
words, *I am come in My Father's name, and ye receive Me
not; if another shall come in his own name, him ye will
receive.*[6] Akiba, following the traditional meaning of the
great prophecy which riveted his own eyes, paraphrased
the words, "Yet a little, a little of the kingdom, will I
give to Israel upon the destruction of the first house,
and after the kingdom, lo! I will shake heaven, and
after that will come the Messiah." [7]

[1] See Pusey's Daniel the Prophet, pp. 230–233.

[2] Jos. B. J. vi. 5, 4.

[3] Tac. Hist. v. 13.

[4] "He was President of the academies of Lidda and
Jafna, disciple and successor of Rabban Gamaliel, and a
man of such learning and repute, that he was accounted
among the Hebrews the first oracle, &c." De Rossi Diz. stor.
d. Autori Ebr. sub v.

[5] R. Bechai.   [6] S. John v. 43.

[7] Sanhedrin. dist. *chelek* in Mart. Pug. fid., p. 305. R.
Gedaliah B. Yechaiah quotes R. Akiba, rejecting his interpretation. "And not as Rabbi Akibah, who was interpreting
this section ; ' *Yet once, it is a little and I shake the heaven
and the earth.*' He interprets, that when Israel went to the

Since the words can only mean "the Desire of all nations," he or that which all nations long for, the construction of the words does not affect the meaning. Herod doubtless thought to advance his own claims on the Jewish people by his material adorning of the temple ; yet, although mankind do covet gold and silver, few could seriously think that, while a heathen immoral but observant poet could speak of "gold undiscovered and so better placed," [1] or our own of the "pale and common drudge 'Tween man and man," a Hebrew prophet could recognise gold and silver as *the desire of all nations.* R. Akiba and S. Jerome's Jewish teachers, after our Lord came, felt no difficulty in understanding it of a person. We cannot in English express the delicacy of the phrase, whereby manifoldness is combined in unity, the Object of desire containing in itself many objects of desire. To render " the desire of all nations" or " the desire*s* of all nations" alike fail to do this. A great heathen master of language said to his wife, "fare you well, my longings," [2] i.e. I suppose, if he had analysed his feelings, he meant that she manifoldly met the longings of his heart ; she had in herself manifold gifts to content them. So S. Paul sums up all the truths and gifts of the Gospel, all which God shadowed out in the law and had given us in Christ, under the name of "the good things to come." [3] A pious modern writer [4]

captivity of Babylon, Haggai the prophet spake this section, and its meaning is, that in this house there will be little glory, and after this I will bring the desire of the heathen to Jerusalem." Shalsheleth Hakkabbala extracted in the Carm. R. Lipmanni confut., p. 619, in Wagenseil Tela ignea satanæ.

[1] " Aurum irrepertum et sic melius situm." Hor. Od. iii. 3, 49.

[2] " Valete, mea desideria, valete." Cic. Ep. ad Famil. xiv. 2, fin.

[3] Heb. x. 1, τῶν μελλόντων ἀγαθῶν.

[4] Dr. Watts, vol. i., Serm. 4.

speaks of "the unseen *desirables* of the spiritual world." A psalmist expresses at once the collective, "God's Word" and the "words" contained in it, by an idiom like Haggai's, joining the feminine singular as a collective with the plural verb: *How sweet are Thy word unto my taste*, lit. *palate.*[1] It is God's word, at once collectively and individually, which was to the Psalmist so *sweet*. What was true of the whole, was true, one by one, of each part; what was true of each part, was true of the whole. So here, the object of this longing was manifold, but met in one, was concentrated in One, *in Christ Jesus, Who of God is made unto us wisdom and righteousness and sanctification and redemption.*[2] That which the whole world sighed and mourned for, knowingly or unknowingly, light to disperse its darkness, liberty from its spiritual slavery, restoration from its degradation, could not come to us without some one, who should impart it to us.

But if Jesus was *the longed-for of the nations* before He came, by that mute longing of need for that which it wants (as the parched ground thirsteth for the rain[3]) how much more afterwards! So Micah and Isaiah describe many peoples inviting one another, *Come ye, and let us go up to the mountain of the Lord, to the house of the God of Jacob; and He will teach us of His ways, and we will walk in His paths.*[4] And in truth He became the *desire of the nations*, much more than of the Jews; as S. Paul says,[5] God foretold of old; *Moses saith, I will provoke you to jealousy by them that are not a people; by a foolish nation I will anger you. But Esaias is very bold and saith, I was found of them that sought Me not.*

---

[1] Ps. cxix. 103, ‏מה נמלצו לחכי אמרתך‎.
[2] 1 Cor. i. 30.
[3] Euripides so uses ἐρᾶν, of the ground longing for the rain.
[4] Micah iv. 2; Isa. ii. 3.
[5] Rom. x. 19, 20; quoting Deut. xxxii. 21; Isa. lxv. 1-3.

So till now and in eternity, "[1] Christ is the longing of all holy souls, who long for nothing else, than to please Him, daily to love Him more, to worship Him better. So S. John longed for Him, *Come, Lord Jesus.*[2] So Isaiah, *The desire of our soul is to Thy Name and to the remembrance of Thee: with my soul have I desired Thee in the night; yea, with my spirit within me, will I seek Thee early.*[3] So S. Ignatius, "Let fire, cross, troops of wild beasts, dissections, rendings, scattering of bones, mincing of limbs, grindings of the whole body, ill tortures of the devil come upon me, only may I gain Jesus Christ.—I seek Him Who for us died; I long for Him Who for us rose."[4]

"Hungerest thou and desirest food? Long for Jesus! He is the bread and refreshment of Angels. He is manna, *containing in Him all sweetness and pleasurable delight.* Thirstest thou? Long for Jesus! He is the well of *living water,* refreshing, so that thou shouldest thirst no more. Art thou sick? Go to Jesus. He is the Saviour, the physician, nay, salvation itself. Art thou dying? Sigh for Jesus! He is *the resurrection and the life.* Art thou perplexed? Come to Jesus! He is *the Angel of great counsel.* Art thou ignorant and erring? Ask Jesus; He is *the way, the truth and the life.* Art thou a sinner? Call on Jesus! For *He shall save His people from their sins.* To this end He came into the world: *This is all His fruit, to take away sin.* Art thou tempted by pride, gluttony, lust, sloth? Call on Jesus! He is humility, soberness, chastity, love, fervour: *He bare our infirmities, and carried,* yea still beareth and carrieth, *our griefs.* Seekest thou beauty? He is *fairer than the children of men.* Seekest thou wealth? In Him are *all treasures,* yea in Him *the fulness of the Godhead dwelleth.* Art thou ambitious of

---

[1] Lap.   [2] Rev. xxii. 20.
[3] Isa. xxvi. 8, 9.
[4] Ep. ad Rom. in Ruinart Acta Mart. p. 703.

honours? *Glory and riches are in His house. He is the King of glory.* Seekest thou a friend? He hath the greatest love for thee, Who for love of thee came down from heaven, toiled, endured the Sweat of Blood, the Cross and Death; He prayed for thee by name in the garden, and poured forth tears of Blood! Seekest thou wisdom? He is the Eternal and Uncreated Wisdom of the Father! Wishest thou for consolation and joy? He is the sweetness of souls, the joy and jubilee of Angels. Wishest thou for righteousness and holiness? He is *the Holy of holies;* He is *everlasting Righteousness,* justifying and sanctifying all who believe and hope in Him. Wishest thou for a blissful life? He is *life eternal,* the bliss of the saints. Long then for Him, love Him, sigh for Him! In Him thou wilt find all good; out of Him, all evil, all misery. Say then with S. Francis, ' My Jesus, my love and my all!' O Good Jesus, burst the cataract of Thy love, that its streams, yea seas, may flow down upon us, yea, inebriate and overwhelm us." [1]

And I will fill this house with glory. The glory, then, was not to be anything which came from man, but directly from God. It was the received expression of God's manifestation of Himself in the tabernacle,[2] in Solomon's temple,[3] and of the ideal temple [4] which Ezekiel saw, after the likeness of that of Solomon, that *the glory of the Lord filled the house.* When then of this second temple God uses the self-same words, that He will *fill it with glory,* with what other glory should He fill it than His own? In the history it is said, *the glory of the Lord filled the temple;* for there man relates what God did. Here it is God Himself Who speaks; so He says not, *the glory of the Lord,* but, *I will fill the house with glory,* glory which

---

[1] Lap.   [2] Exod. xl. 34, 35.
[3] 1 Kings viii. 11; 2 Chron. v. 14; vii. 1-12.
[4] Ezek. xliii. 5; xliv. 4.

8 The silver *is* mine and the gold *is* mine, saith the LORD of hosts.

---

was His to give, which came from Himself. To interpret that *glory of* anything material, is to do violence to language, to force on words of Scripture an unworthy sense, which they refuse to bear.

The gold upon the walls, even had this second temple been adorned like the first, did not fill the temple of Solomon. However richly any building might be overlaid with gold, no one could say that it is filled with it. A building is filled with what it contains; a mint or treasure-house may be filled with gold: the temple of God was *filled*, we are told, *with the glory of the Lord.* His creatures bring Him such things as they can offer; they bring *gold and incense;*[1] they *bring presents* and *offer gifts;*[2] they do it, moved by His Spirit, as acceptable to Him. God is nowhere said, Himself to give these offerings to Himself.

8. *The silver is Mine, and the gold is Mine.* These words, which have occasioned some to think that God, in speaking of the glory with which He should fill the house, meant our material riches, suggest the contrary. For silver was no ornament of the temple of Solomon. Everything was overlaid with gold. In the tabernacle there were bowls of silver,[3] in Solomon's temple they and all were of gold.[4] Silver, we are expressly told, *was nothing accounted of* [5] *in the days of Solomon: he made silver to be in Jerusalem as stones — for abundance.*[6] Rather, as God says by the Psalmist, *Every beast of the forest is Mine, so are the cattle upon a thousand*

[1] Isa. lx. 6. [2] Ps. lxxii. 10.
[3] Num. vii. 19, 25, 31, &c. The "charger" (קערה) which in the tabernacle was of silver (Num. vii. 13, &c.), does not appear in the temple of Solomon.
[4] 1 Kings vii. 50; 2 Chron. iv. 8.
[5] 1 Kings x. 21. [6] Ib. x. 27.

9 [a] The glory of this latter house shall be greater

[a] John i. 14.

---

hills: I know all the fowls of the mountains, and the wild beasts of the field are Mine. If I were hungry, I would not tell thee: for the world is Mine and the fulness thereof: [1] so here He tells them, that for the glory of His house He needed not gold or silver: for all the wealth of the world is His. They had no ground "to grieve then, that they could not equal the magnificence of Solomon who had abundance of gold and silver." [2] All was God's. He would fill it with divine glory. The Desire of all nations, Christ, should come, and be a glory, to which all created glory is nothing.

"God says really and truly, that the silver and gold is His, which in utmost bounty He created, and in His most just government administers, so that, without His will and dominion, neither can the bad have gold and silver for the punishment of avarice, nor the good for the use of mercy. Its abundance does not inflate the good, nor its want crush them: but the bad, when bestowed, it blinds: when taken away, it tortures." [3]

"It is as if He would say, Think not the temple inglorious, because, maybe, it will have no portion of gold or silver, and their splendour. I need not such things. How should I? *For Mine is the silver and Mine the gold, saith the Lord Almighty.* I seek rather true worshippers: with their brightness will I gild this temple. Let him come who hath right faith, is adorned by graces, gleams with love for Me, is pure in heart, poor in spirit, compassionate and good." [4] "These make the temple, i.e. the Church, glorious and renowned, being glorified by Christ. For they have learned to pray, *The glory of the Lord our God be upon us.*" [5]

[1] Ps. l. 10–12.   [2] Lap.
[3] S. Aug. Serm. 50 (de Ag. 2), n. 4, 5.
[4] S. Cyr.   [5] Ps. xc. 17.

9. *The glory of this latter house shall be greater than of the former*, or, perhaps, more probably, *the later glory of this house shall be greater than the former ;* for he had already spoken of the present temple, as identical with that before the captivity ; " Who is left among you that saw *this house* in her first glory, and how do you see *it* now ? " [1] He had spoken of its *first glory.* Now he says, in contrast, its later glory should be greater than that of its most glorious times.[2] In this case the question, whether the temple of Herod was a different material building from that of Zerubbabel, falls away. In either case, the contrast is between two things, either the temple in that its former estate, and this its latter estate after the captivity, or the two temples of Solomon and Zerubbabel. There is no room for a third temple. God holds out no vain hopes. To comfort those distressed by the poverty of the house of God which they were building, God promises a glory to this house greater than before. A temple, erected, after this

---

[1] ii. 3. So the LXX. " Wherefore great will be the last glory of this house above the first [glory]." In the other case, the order would have probably been, כבוד הבית האחרון הזה as in Exod. iii. 3; Deut. ii. 7; iv. 6; 1 Sam. xii. 16; 1 Kings iii. 9; xx. 13, 28; Jon. i. 12; but, as Köhler observes, this is not quite uniform, as in 2 Chron. i. 10.

[2] This interpretation involves a change in the wording of the argument from this prophecy, as to the time of our Lord's first coming. For thus interpreted, it does not speak of a second house, and so does not, in terms, speak of the material building which was destroyed. R. Isaac made use of this : " A difficulty need not be raised, that he said, ' this house ' of the house which is to be built, since of the first house, which in their time was of old waste, he said ' this house ' in the words, ' who is left among you, who hath seen this house in its first glory ? ' and as ' this house ' is spoken of the house of the sanctuary which was then desolate, which was passed away, so he saith, ' this house,' of the house which shall be." Chizzuch Emunah, c. 34, Wagens, p. 292.

than of the former, saith the LORD of hosts : and in
this place will I give [a] peace, saith the LORD of hosts.

[a] Ps. lxxxv. 8, 9 ; Luke ii. 14 ; Eph. ii. 14.

had lain waste above 1800 years, even if Anti-Christ were to
come now and to erect a temple at Jerusalem, could be no
fulfilment of this prophecy.

In material magnificence the temple of Solomon, built
and adorned with all the treasures accumulated by David
and enlarged by Solomon, far surpassed all which Herod,
amid his attempts to give a material meaning to the prophecy, could do. His attempt shows how the eyes of the
Jews were fixed on this prophecy, then when it was about
to be fulfilled. While taking pains, through the slowness
of his rebuilding, to preserve the identity of the fabric, he
lavished his wealth, to draw off their thoughts from the
king, whom the Jews looked for, to himself. The friendship of the Romans, who were lords of all, was to replace
the *all nations*, of whom Haggai spoke ; he pointed also to
the length of peace, the possession of wealth, the greatness
of revenues, the surpassing expenditure beyond those
before.[1] A small section of Erastians admitted these
claims of the murderer of his sons. The Jews generally
were not diverted from looking on to *Him Who should come.*
Those five things, the absence whereof they felt, were con-

[1] In his oration to the Jews, " Our forefathers built this
temple to the supreme God after the return from Babylon,
yet in size it lacks 60 cubits in height ; for so much did the
first, which Solomon built, exceed.—But since, by the counsel
of God, I now rule, and we have a long peace, and ample
funds and large revenues ; and chief of all, the Romans,
who, so to speak, are lords of all, are our friends and kindly
disposed " (Joseph, Ant. xv. 11, 1), and a little later (n. 3)
" exceeding the expenditure of those aforetime, in a way
in which no other appears to have adorned the temple."
See Hengst. Christ. iii. 257, 258, ed. 2.

nected with their atoning worship or God's Presence among them : "the ark with the mercy-seat and the Cherubim, the Urim and Tummim, the fire from heaven, the Shechinah, the Holy Ghost."[1] Material magnificence could not replace spiritual glory. The explanations of the great Jewish authorities,[2] that the second temple was superior to the

---

[1] Yoma, 21, b.

[2] "Rab and Samuel disputed hereon, or, as others, R. Jochanan and R. Eliezer. The former said, 'it shall be more glorious in structure ; ' the latter, 'in years.' " Baba bathra, c. 1, f. 30. R. Asariah quotes also from the Shir hashshirim Rabba on Cant. ii. 12 and viii. 1, and adds, "We have found that the best interpreters explained this prophecy literally as to the second house." This is followed by Kimchi, Rashi, A. E., Lipmann (Nizz. n. 260), Manasseh ben Israel (De Term. Vitæ), iii. 4 (Hilpert, De Gloria Templi Post., Thes. Theol.-Phil. p. 1086 sqq.), Tanchum. Of the magnificence of the building they allege only that the building was in *size* equal to that of Solomon, while even in material magnificence it was beyond measure inferior. The relative duration they underrate : "the first, 410 years ; the second, 420 ; " for from the eleventh of Solomon's reign, 1005 B.C., to the burning of the temple in the eleventh of Zedekiah, were 417 years ; but from the sixth of Darius, when the second temple was finished, 515 B.C., to the burning of the temple under Titus, A.D. 70, were 585 years. But mere duration is not glory. R. Isaac says as Abarbanel ; "But it is a difficulty in what they say, that Scripture says not, 'great shall be the building of the house,' or, 'the time of the house,' only 'great shall be the glory of the house ; ' for though the second house stood ten years more than the first, this was not such great glory, that for this the prophet should say what he said ; and again though the days during which the second house stood were 100 years more than the duration of the first house, and though in its building it were twofold greater than the first house, how saith Scripture of it on this account, that its glory was greater than the first, since the glory which dwelt in the first house did not dwell in it ? " Chizz. Em. l.c. pp. 287, 288. "Wherefore it is rather the true glory

first in structure (which was untrue) or in duration, were laid aside by Jews who had any other solution wherewith to satisfy themselves. "The Shechinah and the five precious things," says one,[1] "which, according to our wise of blessed memory, were in it, and not in the second house, raised and exalted it beyond compare." Another [2] says, "When Haggai saith, 'Greater shall be the glory of this later house than the first,' how is it, that the house which Zerubbabel built through the income which the king of Persia gave them was more glorious than the house which Solomon built? And though it is said that the building which Herod made was exceeding beautiful and rich, we should not think that it was in its beauty like to the house which Solomon built. For what the wise of blessed memory

which is the abiding of the glory of the Shechinah in this house for ever; which did not abide continually in the first house; but in the second house the glory did not dwell at all; for they had not the ark and the mercy-seat and the cherubim, or the Urim and Tummim, nor the Holy Spirit, nor the heavenly fire, nor the anointing oil, as it was in the first house." Ib. p. 293. Others made the glory to consist in the absence of idolatry, quoted Ib. p. 286. R. Lipmann, Nizz. p. 42, makes it to consist in the uninterruptedness of the worship of God there, whereas the temple was shut by Ahaz and Manasseh (as was the second at least desecrated by Antiochus Epiphanes for three years, 1 Macc. i. 54; iv. 59).

[1] R. Asariah de Rossi, *Imre Binah*, c. 51, in Hilpert, l.c. n. 8. His own solution is that the glory was not in the temple itself, but in that kings brought presents to it. Ib. 10.

[2] Abarbanel, Quæst. iv. in Hag. f. רעז. He says that "the interpreters, all of them, explained it of the second house," p. רעח 2. Abarbanel subjoins a criticism, which R. Asariah, *Imre-Binach*, c. 54, saw to be mistaken, that ראשון and אחרון could not be said of two things (of which אחד and שני are, he says, used) against which R. Asariah quotes Jer. l. 17; Gen. xxxiii. 2; add Exod. iv. 8; Deut. xxiv. 3, 4; Ruth iii. 10; Isa. ix. 1.

have said of the beauty of the house of Herod is in relation to the house which Zerubbabel built. How much more, since Scripture saith not, ' Great shall be the *beauty* or the *wealth* of this latter house above the first,' but the *glory:* and the glory is not the wealth or the beauty, or the largeness of the dimensions of the building, as they said in their interpretations; for the ' glory ' is in truth spoken of the glory of God, which filled the tabernacle, after it was set up, and of the glory of God which filled the house of God, which Solomon built, when he brought the ark into the holy of holies, which is the Divine cloud and the Light supreme, which came down thither in the eyes of all the people, and it is said, ' And it was when the priests came out of the holy place, the cloud filled the house of God, and the priests could not stand to minister because of the cloud, for the glory of God filled the house of God.' And this glory was not in the second house. And how shall it be said, if so, ' Great shall be the glory of this later house above the first ' ? " The poor unconverted Jew did not know the answer to his question : " Through the Presence of God, in the substance of our flesh ; through *the Son given to us*, Whose *name* should be *Mighty God.*" The glory of this temple was in Him Who *was made Flesh and dwelt among us, and we beheld His glory, the glory as of the Only Begotten of the Father, full of grace and truth.*[1] " There Christ, the Son of God, was, as a Child, offered to God : there He sat in the midst of the Doctors ; there He taught and revealed things, hidden from the foundation of the world. The glory of the temple of Solomon was, that in it the majesty of God appeared, veiling itself in a cloud : in this, that same Majesty showed itself, in very deed united with the Flesh, visible to sight : so that Jesus Himself said, *He that hath seen Me hath seen the Father.*[2] This it was which

[1] S. John i. 14.   [2] Ib. xiv. 9.

Malachi[1] sang with joy : *The Lord Whom ye seek shall suddenly come to His temple, even the Messenger of the covenant, whom ye delight in.*"[2]

And in this place I will give peace. Temporal peace they had now, nor was there any prospect of its being disturbed. They were quiet subjects of the Persian empire, which included also all their former enemies, greater or less. Alexander subdued all the bordering countries which did not yield, but spared themselves. Temporal peace then was nothing to be then given them; for they had it. In later times they had it not. The temple itself was profaned by Antiochus Epiphanes. " Her sanctuary was laid waste like a wilderness. As had been her glory, so was her dishonour increased."[3] Again by Pompey,[4] by Crassus,[5] the Parthians,[6] before it was destroyed by Titus and the Romans. Jews saw this and, knowing nothing of the peace in Jesus, argued from the absence of outward peace, that the prophecy was not fulfilled under the second temple. " What Scripture says, ' and in this place I will give peace,' is opposed to their interpretation. For all the days of the duration of the second house were *in strait of times* and not in peace, as was written in Daniel, *and threescore and two weeks : the street shall be built again and the fosse, and in strait of time,* and, as I said, in the time of Herod there was no peace whatever, for the sword did not depart from his house to the day of his death ; and after his death the hatred among the Jews increased, and the Gentiles straitened them, until they were destroyed from the face of the earth."[7]

---

[1] Mal. iii. 1.   [2] Lap.   [3] 1 Macc. i. 39, 40.
[4] Jos. Ant. xiv. 4, 4 ; B. J. i. 7.
[5] Ant. xiv. 7, 1 ; B. J. i. 8, 8.   [6] Ant. xiv. 13, 3, 4.
[7] " Abraham B. Dior in his book of the Cabbala, p. 43," in R. Isaac Chizz. Em. l.c. p. 287. R. Isaac makes as if he had answered the explanation as to Jesus by quoting S. Matt. x. 34, l.c. pp. 292, 293.

But spiritual peace is, throughout prophecy, part of the promise of the Gospel. Christ Himself was to be *the Prince of peace;* [1] *of the increase of His government and of His peace* there was to be *no end;* in His days *the mountains were to bring peace to the people; there should be abundance of peace, so long as the moon endureth;* [2] *the work of righteousness* was to be *peace;* [3] *the chastisement of our peace* [that which obtained it] *was upon Him;* [4] *great* should be *the peace of her children;* [5] in the Gospel God would give *peace,* true *peace,* to the *far off and the near;* [6] He would extend *peace to her like a river:* [7] the good news of the Gospel was *the publishing of peace.* [8] The Gospel is described as *a covenant of peace;* [9] the promised king *shall speak peace to the Heathen;* [10] He Himself should be *our peace.* [11] And when He was born, the angels proclaimed *on earth peace, goodwill towards men:* [12] *The Dayspring from on high visited us, to guide our feet into the way of peace.* [13] He Himself says, *My peace I leave with you.* [14] He spake, that *in Me ye might have peace.* [15] S. Peter sums up *the word which God sent unto the children of Israel,* as *preaching peace by Jesus Christ:* [16] *the kingdom of God is joy and peace;* [17] Christ *is our peace; made peace; preaches peace.* [18] *God calleth us to peace,* [19] in the Gospel; *being justified by faith, we have peace with God through Jesus Christ our Lord;* [20] *the fruit of the Spirit is love, joy, peace.* [21] Spiritual peace being thus prominent in the Gospel and in prophecy, as the gift of God, it were unnatural to explain *the peace* which God promised here to give, as other than He promised elsewhere; peace in Him Who is *our peace, Jesus Christ.*

[1] Isa. ix. 6. 7. [2] Ps. lxxii. 3, 7. [3] Isa. xxxii. 17.
[4] Ib. liii. 5. [5] Ib. liv. 13. [6] Ib. lvii. 19.
[7] Ib. lxvi. 12. [8] Ib. lii. 7. [9] Ezek. xxxiv. 25.
[10] Zech. ix. 10. [11] Micah. v. 5. [12] S. Luke ii. 14.
[13] Ib. i. 79. [14] S. John xiv. 27. [15] Ib. xvi. 33.
[16] Acts x. 36. [17] Rom. xiv. 17. [18] Eph. ii. 14, 15, 17.
[19] 1 Cor. vii. 15. [20] Rom. v. 1. [21] Gal. v. 22.

10 ¶ In the four and twentieth *day* of the ninth *month*, in the second year of Darius, came the word of the LORD by Haggai the prophet saying,

11 Thus saith the LORD of hosts ; ᵃ Ask now the priests *concerning* the law saying,

12 If one bear holy flesh in the skirt of his garment, and with his skirt do touch bread, or pottage, or wine, or oil, or any meat, shall it be holy ?　And the priests answered and said, No.

13 Then said Haggai, If *one that is* ᵇ unclean by a dead body touch any of these, shall it be unclean ? And the priests answered and said, It shall be unclean.

ᵃ Lev. x. 10, 11 ; Deut. xxxiii. 10 ; Mal. ii. 7.
ᵇ Num. xix. 11.

"Peace and tranquillity of mind is above all glory of the house ; because peace passeth all understanding. This is peace above peace, which shall be given after the third shaking of heaven, sea, earth, dry land, when He shall destroy all powers and principalities [in the day of judgment].—And so shall there be peace throughout, that, no bodily passions or hindrances of unbelieving mind resisting, Christ shall be all in all, exhibiting the hearts of all subdued to the Father."[1]

11–14. *Ask now the priests concerning the law.* The priests answer rightly, that, by the law, insulated unholiness spread further than insulated holiness. The flesh of the sacrifice hallowed whatever it should touch,[2] but not further ; but the human being, who was defiled by touching a dead body,

[1] S. Ambr. l.c., n. 14 ; Opp. ii. 913.　　　[2] Lev. vi. 27.

14 Then answered Haggai, and said, ᵃ So *is* this people, and so *is* this nation before me, saith the LORD ; and so *is* every work of their hands ; and that which they offer there *is* unclean.

15 And now, I pray you, ᵇ consider from this day and upward, from before a stone was laid upon a stone in the temple of the LORD :

ᵃ Titus i. 15.   ᵇ Hag. i. 5.

defiled all he might touch.[1] Haggai does not apply the first part, viz. that the worship on the altar which they reared, while they neglected the building of the temple, did not hallow. The possession of a holy thing does not counterbalance disobedience. Contrariwise, one defilement defiled the whole man and all which he touched, according to that, *Whosoever shall keep the whole law and yet offend in one point, he is guilty of all.*[2]

In the application, the two melt into one ; for the holy thing, viz. the altar which they raised out of fear on their return, so far from hallowing the land or people by the sacrifices offered thereon, was itself defiled. *This people* and *this nation* (not " My people "), since they in act disowned Him. *Whatever they offer there*, i.e. on that altar, instead of the temple which God commanded, is unclean, offending Him Who gave all.

15. *And now, I pray you.* Observe his tenderness, in drawing their attention to it.[3] *Consider from this day and upwards.* He bids them look backward, *from before a stone was laid upon a stone*, i.e. from the last moment of their neglect in building the house of God ; *from since those* days *were*, or *from* the time backwards *when those things were*

[1] Num. xix. 22.   [2] S. James ii. 10.
[3] As expressed by נָא, here and 18.

16 Since those *days* were, [a] when *one* came to an heap of twenty *measures*, there were *but* ten : when *one* came to the press-fat for to draw out fifty *vessels* out of the press, there were *but* twenty.

17 [b] I smote you with blasting and mildew and with hail [c] in all the labours of your hands ; [d] yet ye *turned* not to me, saith the LORD.

[a] Hag. i. 6, 9 ; Zech. viii. 10.
[b] Deut. xxviii. 22 ; 1 Kings viii. 37 ; Hag. i. 9 ; Amos iv. 9.
[c] Hag. i. 11.   [d] Jer. v. 3 ; Amos iv. 6, 8, 9, 10, 11.

(resuming, in the word, *from-their-being*,[1] the date which he had just given, viz. the beginning of their resuming the building backwards, during all those years of neglect) *one come to a heap of twenty* measures. The precise measure is not mentioned :[2] the force of the appeal lay in the pro-portion : *the heap* of corn which, usually, would yield *twenty* (whether bushels[3] or *seahs*[4] or any other measure, for the heap itself being of no defined size, neither could the quantity expected from it be defined) *there were ten* only : *one came to the press-vat to draw out fifty* vessels out of the *press,* or perhaps *fifty poorah,* i.e. the ordinary quantity drawn out at one time from the press,[5] *there were,* or *it had become, twenty,* two-fifths only of what they looked for and ordinarily obtained. The dried grapes yielded so little.

17. *I smote you with blasting and mildew,* two diseases of corn, which Moses had foretold [6] as chastisements on dis-

[1] מהיותם.

[2] Ruth iii. 17 ; Neh. xiii. 15 ; 2 Chron. xxxi. 6–9.

[3] Vulg.   [4] LXX.

[5] פורה only occurs besides, Isa. lxiii. 3 ; where it is the winefat itself. The LXX render it μετρηταί ; Jon. נרבין (which they use for נבל 1 Sam. x. 3; xxv. 18; Jer. xiii. 12), Vulg. *lagenas.*   [6] Deut. xxviii. 22.

18 Consider now from this day and upward, from the four and twentieth day of the ninth *month, even*

---

obedience and God's infliction, of which Amos had spoken in these self-same words.[1] Haggai adds *the hail*, as destructive of the vines.[2] *Yet [And] ye* turned *you not to Me*, lit. *there were none—you* (accusative [3]), i.e. who turned you unto Me. The words are elliptical, but express the entire absence of conversion, of any who turned to God.

18. *From the day that the foundation of the Lord's house.* Zechariah, in a passage corresponding to this, uses the same words,[4] *the day that the foundation of the house of the Lord of*

---

[1] Amos iv. 9.   [2] Ps. lxxviii. 47.

[3] אתכם marking the acc., אין אתכם is not for אינכם, which itself, according to the common Hebrew construction, would require a participle, to express action on their part. See instances in Fürst, Conc. p. 45; v. איננּי, Exod. v. 10; Deut. i. 42; Isa. i. 15; Jer. xiv. 12 (*bis*); xxxvii. 14; אינְך, Gen. xx. 7; xliii. 5; Exod. viii. 17; Judges xii. 3; 1 Sam. xix. 11; 2 Sam. xix. 8; 1 Kings xxi. 5; Neh. ii. 2; Eccles. xi. 5, 6; Jer. vii. 17; אינכם, Deut. i. 32; iv. 12; 2 Kings xii. 8; Ezra xx. 39; Mal. ii. 2, 9; איננּו, Deut. xxi. 18, 20; Judges iii. 25; 1 Sam. xi. 7; 2 Chron. xviii. 7; Esther v. 13; Eccles. v. 11; viii. 7, 13, 16; ix. 2; Jer. xxxviii. 4; xliv. 16; אין, 2 Kings xvii. 26, 34 (*bis*); Eccles. iv. 17; ix. 5; Neh. xiii. 24; Jer. xxxii. 33; Ezek. iii. 7. ואינכם אלי would have signified, "and ye were not [well disposed] towards Me," as in Hosea iii. 3; Jer. xv. 1; 2 Kings vi. 11 (Ewald's instances, Lehrb. n. 217 c); Gen. xxxi. 5; not (as required here) "ye turned not unto Me," as in Amos iv. 6, 8, 9, 10, 11. Böttcher (Lehrbuch, n. 516. d.) compares *bene te* (which implies a verb), *en illum* (where *en* is a verb). These, however, are exclamations, not parts of sentences. He thinks that אי is joined, (1) with a nom., and then an acc. after ו, 1 Sam. xxvi. 16; that יש has an acc., Gen. xxiii. 8; 2 Kings x. 15; and הלא, Zech. vii. 7.

[4] Zech. viii. 9.

from ª the day that the foundation of the LORD's temple was laid, consider *it*.

19 ᵇ Is the seed yet in the barn ? yea, as yet the vine, and the fig tree, and the pomegranate, and the

ª Zech. viii. 9.　　　　　　　　ᵇ Ib. viii. 12.

---

hosts was laid, that the temple might be built, not of the first foundation, but of the work as resumed in obedience to the words by *the mouth of the prophets,* Haggai and himself, which, Ezra also says, was *in the second year of Darius.*[1] But that work was resumed, not now at the time of this prophecy, but these months before, on the 24th of the sixth month. Since then the word translated here, *from,*[2] is in no case used of the present time, Haggai gives two dates, the resumption of the work, as marked in these words and the actual present. He would then say, that even in these last months, since they had begun the work, there were as yet no signs for the better. There was yet no

[1] Ezra iv. 24 ; v. 1.

[2] Such use of לְמִן would be inconsistent with any force of לְ. It is used of a *terminus à quo,* distant from the present, and is equivalent to " up to and from." So Judges xix. 30, " No such deed was seen or done from the day that the children of Israel came up," i.e. looking back to that time and from it. So 2 Sam. vii. 6, " Since the time that I brought up the children of Israel out of Egypt," lit., " up to from the day." Add Exod. ix. 18 ; Deut. iv. 32 ; ix. 7 ; 2 Sam. vii. 11 ; xix. 24 ; Isa. vii. 17 ; Jer. vii. 7, 25 ; xxv. 5 ; xxxii. 31 ; 1 Chron. xvii. 10 ; Mal. iii. 7. But there is no ground for thinking that Haggai used the word in any sense, in which it had not been used before him. The only construction consistent with the use of לְמִן elsewhere is, that the *terminus ad quem,* elsewhere expressed by וְעַד, having been expressed by the present מִיּוֹם, the distant *terminus à quo* is, as elsewhere, expressed by לְמִן.

olive tree, hath not brought forth : from this day will I bless *you.*

20 ¶ And again the word of the LORD came unto Haggai in the four and twentieth *day* of the month, saying,

---

seed in the barn, the harvest having been blighted and the fruit-trees stripped by the hail before the close of the sixth month, when they resumed the work. Yet though there were as yet no signs of change, no earnest that the promise should be fulfilled, God pledges His word, *from this day I will bless you.*

Thenceforth, from their obedience, God would give them those fruits of the earth, which in His Providence had been, during their negligence, withheld. *God,* said St. Paul and Barnabas, *left not Himself without witness, in that He did good, and gave us rain from heaven and fruitful seasons, filling our hearts with food and gladness.*[1]

All the Old and New Testament, the Law, the Prophets and the Psalms, the Apostles and our Lord Himself, bear witness to the Providence of God, Who makes His natural laws serve to the moral discipline of His creature, man. The physical theory, which presupposes that God so fixed the laws of His creation, as to leave no room for Himself to vary them, would, if ever so true, only come to this, that Almighty God knowing absolutely (as He must know) the actions of His creatures (in what way soever this is reconcilable with our free agency, of which we are conscious), framed the laws of His physical creation, so that plenty or famine, healthiness of our cattle or of the fruits of the earth or their sickness, should coincide with the good or evil conduct of man, with his prayers or his neglect of prayer. The reward or chastisement alike come to man,

[1] Acts xiv. 17.

21 Speak to Zerubbabel, ᵃ governor of Judah, saying, ᵇ I will shake the heavens and the earth ;

ᵃ Hag. i. 14.   ᵇ Vers. 6, 7 ; Heb. xii. 26.

whether they be the result of God's Will, acting apart from
any system which He has created, or in it and through it.
It is alike His Providential agency, whether He have
established any such system, with all its minute variations,
or whether those variations are the immediate result of His
sovereign Will. If He had instituted any physical system,
so that the rain, hail, and its proportions, size, destructive-
ness, should come in a regulated irregularity, as fixed in all
eternity as the revolutions of the heavenly bodies or the
courses of the comets, then we come only to a more intri-
cate perfection of His creation, that in all eternity He
framed those laws in an exact conformity to the perfectly
foreseen actions of men good and evil, and to their prayers
also: that He, knowing certainly whether the creature,
which He has framed to have its bliss in depending on Him,
would or would not cry unto Him, framed those physical
laws in conformity therewith ; so that the supply of what
is necessary for our wants or its withholding shall be in all
time inworked into the system of our probation. Only, not
to keep God out of His own world, we must remember that
other truth, that, whether God act in any such system or
no, He *upholdeth all things by the word of His power* ¹ by an
ever-present working ; so that it is He Who at each moment
doth what is done, doth and maintains in existence all
which He has created, in the exact order and variations of
their being. *Fire and hail, snow and vapour, stormy wind
fulfilling His word,*² are as immediate results of His Divine
Agency, in whatever way it pleaseth Him to act, and are
the expression of His Will.

21. *I will shake.* Haggai closes by resuming the words

¹ Heb. i. 3.   ² Ps. cxlviii. 8.

22 And ^a I will overthrow the throne of kingdoms,
and I will destroy the strength of the kingdoms of
the heathen ; ^b I will overthrow the chariots, and

^a Dan. ii. 44 ; Matt. xxiv. 7.
^b Micah v. 10 ; Zech. iv. 6 ; ix. 10.

---

of a former prophecy to Zerubbabel and Joshua, which
ended in the coming of Christ.   Even thus it is plain, that
the prophecy does not belong personally to Zerubbabel, but
to him and his descendants, chiefly to Christ.   There was in
Zerubbabel's time no shaking of the heaven or of nations.
Darius had indeed to put down an unusual number of
rebellions in the first few years after his accession; but,
although he magnified himself on occasion of their sup-
pression, they were only so many distinct and unconcerted
revolts, each under its own head.   All were far away in
the distant East, in Babylonia, Susiana, Media, Armenia,
Assyria, Hyrcania, Parthia, Sagartia, Margiana, Arachosia.¹
The Persian *empire*, spread " probably over 2,000,000 square
miles, or more than half of modern Europe," ² was not
threatened ; no foreign enemy assailed it ; one impostor
only claimed the throne of Darius.   This would, if successful,
have been, like his own accession, a change of dynasty,
affecting nothing externally.   But neither were lasting,
some were very trifling.   Two decisive battles subdued
Babylonia : of Media the brief summary is given ; " the
Medes revolted from Darius, and having revolted were
brought back into subjection, defeated in battle." ³   The
Susianians slew their own pretender, on the approach of the
troops of Darius.   We have indeed mostly the account only
of the victor.   But these are only self-glorying records of
victories, accomplished in succession, within a few years.

¹ Rawlinson, Five Empires, iv. pp. 407–415, chiefly from
Behistun Inscription.
² Id. Ib. p. 2.   ³ Herod. i. 130.

those that ride in them; and the horses and their
riders shall come down, every one by the sword of
his brother.

Sometimes the satrap of the province put the revolt down
at once. At most two battles ended in the crucifixion of
the rebel. The Jews, if they heard of them, knew them to
be of no account. For the destroyer of the Persian empire
was to come from the West;[1] the fourth sovereign was to
stir up all against the realm of Grecia,[2] and Darius was but
the third. In the same second year of Darius, in which
Haggai gave this prophecy, the whole earth was exhibited
to Zechariah as *sitting still and at rest.*[3]

The overthrow prophesied is also universal. It is not
one throne only, as of Persia, but *the throne,* i.e. the sovereigns, *of kingdoms;* not a change of dynasty, but a destruction of their *strength;* not of a few powers only, but *the
kingdoms of the heathen;* and that, in detail; that, in which
their chief strength lay, the chariots and horsemen and their
riders, and this, man by man, *every one by the sword of his
brother.* This mutual destruction is a feature of the judgments at the end of the world against Gog and Magog;[4]
and of the yet unfulfilled prophecies of Zechariah.[5] Its
stretching out so far does not hinder its partial fulfilment
in earlier times. Zerubbabel stood, at the return from the
captivity, as the representative of the house of David and
heir of the promises to him, though in an inferior temporal
condition; thereby the rather showing that the main im-
port of the prophecy was not temporal. As then Ezekiel
prophesied, *I will set up One Shepherd over them, and He shall
feed them, My servant David;*[6] *And David My servant* shall

[1] Dan. viii. 5.   [2] Ib. xi. 2.
[3] Zech. i. 11.   [4] Ezek. xxxviii. 21.
[5] Zech. xiv. 17.   [6] Ezek. xxxiv. 23.

23 In that day, saith the LORD of hosts, will I take

be *king over them ; and My servant David shall be their prince
for ever ;* [1] and Jeremiah, *They shall serve the Lord their God
and David their king, whom I will raise up unto them ;* [2] and
Hosea, that *after many days shall the children of Israel return
and seek the Lord their God, and David their king,* [3] meaning by
David, the great descendant of David, in whom the promises
centred, so in his degree, the promise to Zerubbabel reaches
on through his descendants to Christ ; that, amid all the
overthrow of empires, God would protect his sons' sons
until Christ should come, the King of kings and Lord of
lords, Whose *kingdom shall never be destroyed, but it shall
break in pieces and consume all those kingdoms, and shall stand
fast for ever.* [4]

23. *I will make thee as a signet.* God reverses to Zerubbabel the sentence on Jeconiah for his impiety. To Jeconiah
He had said, *though he were the signet upon My right hand, yet
would I pluck thee thence ; and I will give thee into the hand of
them that seek thy life.* [5] The signet was very precious to
its owner, never parted with, or only to those to whom
authority was delegated (as by Pharaoh to Joseph, [6] or by
Ahasuerus to Haman [7] and then to Mordecai [8]) ; through it
his will was expressed. Hence the spouse in the Canticles
says, *Set me, as a seal upon thy heart, as a seal upon thy arm.* [9]
The signet also was an ornament to him who wore it. *God
is glorified in His saints ;* [10] by Zerubbabel in the building of
His house. He gave him estimation with Cyrus, who entrusted him with the return of his people, and made him
(who would have been the successor to the throne of Judah,

[1] Ezek. xxxvii. 24, 25.
[2] Jer. xxx. 9.
[3] Hosea iii. 5.
[4] Dan. ii. 44.
[5] Jer. xxii. 24.
[6] Gen. xli. 42.
[7] Esther iii. 10.
[8] Ib. viii. 2.
[9] Cant. viii. 6.
[10] 2 Thess. i. 10.

S

thee, O Zerubbabel, my servant, the son of Shealtiel,

---

had the throne been re-established) his governor over the
restored people.   God promises to him and his descendants
protection amid all shaking of empires.   " He was a type of
Christ in bringing back the people from Babylon, as Christ
delivered us from sin, death, and hell : he built the temple,
as Christ built the Church ; he protected his people against
the Samaritans who would hinder the building, as Christ
protects His Church : he was dear and joined to God, as
Christ was united to Him, and hypostatically united and
joined His Humanity to the Word.   The true Zerubbabel
then, i.e. Christ, the son and antitype of Zerubbabel, is the
signet in the hand of the Father, both passively and actively,
whereby God impresses His own Majesty, thoughts, and
words, and His own Image, on men, angels, and all
creatures." [1]   " The Son is the Image of God the Father,
having His entire and exact likeness, and in His own beauty
beaming forth the nature of the Father.   In Him too God
seals us also to His own likeness, since, being conformed
to Christ, we gain the image of God." [2]   " Christ, as the
Apostle says, is *the Image of the invisible God, the brightness of
His Glory and the express Image of His Person*,[3] Who, as the
Word and Seal and express Image, seals it on others.   Christ
is here called a *signet*, as Man, not as God.   For it was His
Manhood which He took of the flesh and race of Zerubbabel.
He is then, in His Manhood, the signet of God : (1) as being
hypostatically united with the Son of God ; (2) because the
Word impressed on His Humanity the likeness of Himself,
His knowledge, virtue, holiness, thoughts, words, acts, and
conversation ; (3) because the Man Christ was the seal, i.e.
the most evident sign and witness of the attributes of God,
His power, justice, wisdom, and especially His exceeding love

[1] Lap.   [2] S. Cyr.   [3] Heb. i. 3.

for man. For, that God might show this, He willed that
His Son should be Incarnate. Christ thus Incarnate is as a
seal, in which we see expressed and depicted the love, power,
justice, wisdom, &c., of God; (4) because Christ as a seal,
attested and certified to us the will of God, His doctrine,
law, commands, i.e. those which He promulgated and taught
in the Gospel. *No one*, S. John saith, *hath seen God at any
time: the Only-Begotten Son, Who is the Image of the Father,
He hath declared Him.*[1] Hence God gave to Christ the
power of working miracles, that He might confirm His
words as by a seal, and demonstrate that they were revealed
and enjoined to Him by God, as it is in S. John, [2] *Him hath
God the Father sealed.*"[3] "Christ is also the seal of God,
because by His impress, i.e. the faith, grace, virtue, and conversation from Him, and by the impress in Baptism and the
other Sacraments, He *willed to conform us to the Image of
His Son,*[4] that, *as we have borne the image of the earthly* Adam,
we may also bear the image of the Heavenly.[5] Then, Christ,
like a seal, seals and guards His faithful against all temptations and enemies. The seal of Christ is the Cross, according to that of Ezekiel, [6] *Seal a mark upon the foreheads of the
men who sigh*, and in the Revelation, *I saw another Angel
having the seal of the living God.*[7] For the Cross guardeth us
against the temptations of the flesh, the world, and the
devil, and makes us followers, soldiers, and martyrs of Christ
crucified. Whence the Apostle says, [8] *I bear in my body the
marks of the Lord Jesus.*"

"This is said without doubt of the Messiah, the expected," says even a Jewish controversialist,[9] "who shall
be of the seed of Zerubbabel; and therefore this promise

[1] S. John i. 18. [2] Ib. vi. 27.
[3] Lap. [4] Rom. viii. 29.
[5] 1 Cor. xv. 49. [6] תו Ezek. ix. 4.
[7] Rev. vii. 2. [8] Gal. vi. 17.
[9] R. Isaac Chiz. Em. l.c., pp. 289, 290.

saith the LORD, [a] and will make thee as a signet: for [b] I have chosen thee, saith the LORD of hosts.

[a] Cant. viii. 6 ; Jer. xxii. 24.   [b] Isa. xlii. 1 ; and xliii. 10.

---

was not fulfilled at all in himself : for at the time of this prophecy he had aforetime been governor of Judah, and afterwards he did not rise to any higher dignity than what he was up to that day : and in like way we find that God said to Abraham our father in the covenant between the pieces, *I am the Lord who brought thee out of Ur of the Chaldees to give thee this land to inherit it*,[1] and beyond doubt this covenant was confirmed of God to the seed of Abraham, as He Himself explained it there afterwards, when He said, *In that day God made a covenant with Abraham, saying, To thy seed have I given this land*, &c., and many like these."

Abarbanel had laid down the right principles, though of necessity misapplied. " [2] Zerubbabel did not reign in Jerusalem and did not rule in it, neither he nor any man of his seed ; but forthwith after the building of the house, he returned to Babylon and died there in his captivity, and how saith he, ' In that day I will take thee ? ' For after the fall of the kingdom of Persia Zerubbabel is not known for any greatness, and his name is not mentioned in the world. Where, then, will be the meaning of ' And I will place thee as a signet, for thee have I chosen ? ' For the signet is as the seal-ring which a man putteth on his hand, it departeth not from it, night or day. And when was this fulfilled in Zerubbabel ? But the true meaning, in my opinion, is, that God showed Zerubbabel that this very second house would not abide ; for after him should come another captivity, and of this he says, ' I shake the heaven, &c.,' and afterwards, after a long time, will God take His vengeance

[1] Gen. xv. 7, 18.   [2] p. רעט.

of these nations 'which have devoured Jacob and laid waste his dwelling-place;' and so He says 'I will overthrow the thrones, &c.,' and He showeth him further that the king who shall rule over Israel at the time of the redemption is the Messiah of the seed of Zerubbabel and of the house of David; and God saw good to show him all this to comfort him and to speak to his heart ; and it is as if he said to him, 'It is true that thou shalt not reign in the time of the second temple, nor any of thy seed, but in that day when God shall overthrow the throne of the kingdoms of the nations, when He gathereth His people Israel and redeemeth them, then shalt thou reign over My people ; for of thy seed shall he be who ruleth from Israel at that time for ever, and therefore he saith, 'I will take thee, O Zerubbabel, &c.,' for because the Messiah was to be of his seed he saith, that he will take him ; and this is as he says, 'And David My servant shall be a prince to them for ever;'[1] for the very Messiah, he shall be David, he shall be Zerubbabel, because he shall be a scion going forth out of their hewn trunk."[2]

For I have chosen thee. God's forecoming love is the ground of all the acceptableness of His creatures. *We love Him, because He first loved us.*[3] Zerubbabel was a devoted servant of God. God acknowledges his faithfulness. Only, the beginning of all was with God. God speaks of the nearness to Himself which He had given him. But in two words[4] He cuts off all possible boastfulness of His creature. Zerubbabel was all this, not of himself, but *because God had chosen* him. Even the Sacred Manhood of our Lord (it is acknowledged as a theological Truth) was not chosen for any foreseen merits, but for the great love, with which God the Father chose It, and God the Son willed to be in such

---

[1] Ezek. xxxvii. 24.   [2] Isa. xi. 1.
[3] 1 S. John iii. 19.   [4] ‏כי בחרתיך‎.

wise incarnate, and God the Holy Ghost willed that that Holy Thing should be conceived of Him. So God says of Him, *Behold My Servant whom I uphold, Mine elect in whom My soul delighteth;*[1] and God bare witness to Him, *This is My Beloved Son in Whom I am well pleased.*[2]

[1] Isa. xlii. 1.   [2] S. Matt. iii. 17 ; xvii. 5.

Printed by BALLANTYNE, HANSON & CO.
Edinburgh & London

23
58
62
77   2:1
81   2:3
83
84
86
100
142
152
175
181
188
202
199
200
212
230
242
252